Achieving QTS
Teaching Design and Technology
at Key Stages 1 and 2

D0120906

Teaching Design and Technology
at Key Stages 1 and 2

Gill Hope

Learning Matters

First published in 2006 by Learning Matters Ltd.

British Library Cataloguing in Publication Data
A CIP record for this book is available from the British Library

ISBN-10: 1 84445 056 2
ISBN-13: 978 1 84445 056 5

Cover design by Topics – The Creative Partnership
Project management by Deer Park Productions, Tavistock
Typeset by PDQ Typesetting, Newcastle under Lyme
Printed and bound in Great Britain by Bell & Bain Ltd, Glasgow

Learning Matters Ltd
33 Southernhay East
Exeter EX1 1NX
Tel: 01392 215560
Email: info@learningmatters.co.uk
www.learningmatters.co.uk

CONTENTS

Achieving the TDA Standards in teaching design and technology at Key Stages 1 and 2 – how this book can help

The aim of this book is to support primary teacher trainees and newly qualified teachers to deliver creative and effective design and technology lessons in the primary classroom. It is especially intended for those who have had only an introductory course in the subject during their Initial Teacher Education (ITE) course. The book is organised into clear chapters in which the subject matter is set out in a way that can be accessed quickly whilst providing a depth of understanding beyond the 'survival in the classroom' level. It is the author's belief that to do something well, especially something as complex as teaching, you need to know *why* to do it as well as *how* to do it.

The intention of this book is to support all students to become effective teachers of design and technology. The target audience of this book, therefore, is all students who want to help themselves to achieve the Training and Development Agency's Standards in design and technology and want to be sure of teaching the subject well and that they will be effective in the classroom.

There will be references throughout to:

- *National Curriculum for England and Wales* **(readers in Scotland should refer to the National Curriculum for Scotland and Welsh readers are advised to acquaint themselves with Curriculum Cymru; the differences between the national curricula for design and technology are not sufficient to hinder the content of this book's applicability across the United Kingdom);**

- *Excellence and Enjoyment: a strategy for primary schools (2003);*

- *Guidance for Foundation and Primary Phases Initial Teacher Training and Continuing Professional Development in Design and Technology* **(2005), DATA (the Design and Technology Association).**

Note on the DATA Guidance Booklet

The brief of the working party for the DATA booklet (which included the author of this book) was to apply the QTS standards to the teaching of design and technology and to provide guidance for student teachers, mentors, ITE educators and teachers. The working party identified three levels of competence in teaching design and technology in the primary classroom, according to the level of professional development and/or teaching input during Initial Teacher Education. These were called Tiers rather than Levels, to avoid confusion with the use of the word 'Level' in National Curriculum documents. Tier 1 contains the competences necessary to teach design and technology satisfactorily. Tier 2 builds on Tier 1 and applies to those choosing to become design and technology specialists and Tier 3 is for subject leaders. This book covers the competences identified under Tier 1 of the DATA publication.

How to use this book

The format of the book is designed to be accessible but also to make you think. You will find clear guidance on how to teach effective design and technology lessons and on the learning that you can expect from your pupils. However, the aim of the book is also to help you to become a reflective practitioner, as it is the author's belief that unless you are a *reflective* practitioner, you are unlikely to be an *effective* one.

In each chapter, therefore, there are *reflective activities* and *practical tasks*.

* **Reflective activities are those in which you are asked to think about the points that have been made, for example, thinking about how you would define design and technology education.**

* **Practical tasks are for you to do on your own away from the book, for example, reading the relevant section of the National Curriculum before reading the rest of the chapter.**

It is strongly recommended that you keep notes on your responses to these activities, even when they do not specifically suggest that you write, draw, make or collect something. In that way you will build up your own portfolio of your developing understanding of good design and technology education, which will enable you to become a more effective and reflective practitioner in the primary classroom.

Reference and resources

Government documentation

DfEE (1999) *The National Curriculum*. London: Department for Education and Employment.

TDA (2002) *Qualifying to Teach – Professional Standards for Qualified Teacher Status and Requirements for Initial Teacher Training*. The Training and Development Agency (TDA) Standards for Qualified Teacher Status (QTS).

DfEE (2003) *Excellence and Enjoyment: a strategy for primary schools.* London: Department for Education and Employment).

Government websites
The National Curriculum for Design and Technology can be found at:
 www.ncaction.org.uk/subjects/design/index.htm

DATA (the Design and Technology Association)
Wellesbourne House, Walton Road, Wellesbourne, Warwickshire CV35 9JB.
 www.data.org.uk
DATA (2005) *Guidance for foundation and primary phases initial teacher training and continuing professional development in design and technology.* Wellesbourne: DATA (the Design and Technology Association).

1 DESIGNED TECHNOLOGY AND EDUCATION

This first chapter will address those first questions about design and technology as a primary school subject through defining the subject area, its way of seeing the world and its specific contribution to children's learning and examining the way in which humanity has shaped the environment through designing technological solutions to perceived needs and wants of its members.

So, this chapter will:

* *consider the nature of design and technology;*
* *reflect on the difference between technology and science;*
* *become aware of some of the history of technology;*
* *start to understand the key issues in teaching design and technology.*

Defining design and technology

Ask anyone in the street the question 'What is design and technology?' and, if they left school fewer than 10 years ago, they will probably tell you it was something they did at school, or if they are older than that, they will look blank. Try shortening it to 'DandT' and the proportion of blank stares goes up. Try asking someone from another country, preferably a long way from your own … A young woman newly arrived in the UK from East Asia said, 'I have never heard of putting the word "design" with "technology". What does that mean?'

Practical task

What is your reaction to the question 'What is design and technology?' Don't skip through to try to find the answer further down the chapter! Fold a piece of paper in half and head one side 'Design' and the other side 'Technology' and then list all the things you associate with each word under each heading – both processes (e.g. investigating) and products (e.g. wheel).

Now look at your two lists. Could you begin to combine them to make a first go at a definition of design and technology? Try to write a short paragraph rather than a sentence.

This is not an easy task. The experts at an international conference recently came up with a long list and an even longer discussion.

Does it matter how we define the subject? Surely everyone has a pretty good idea of what design and technology in school is from what they see children doing, just like we do with history or geography. But that's the problem. Many people can say in a sentence what history and geography are, but for design and technology it is not quite so simple. Most people's simple response to 'What is design and technology?' is 'making things', which is partly true. Steve Kierl, from South Australia, said that 'ours is essentially a *doing* field' (Kierl, 2000; original emphasis). But it is possible to make without designing and design without making. And if teachers are going to get it right in school, they need to have thought about these issues first.

Frequently Asked Questions about design and technology

FAQ 1: *What is design?*
FAQ 2: *What is the difference between the 'design' in art and design, and 'design' in design and technology?*
FAQ 3: *Isn't technology just applied science?*
FAQ 4: *What is technology?*
FAQ 5: *So, what is design and technology education?*

Reflective task

Before reading on – what are your responses to these FAQs?

FAQ 1: What is design?

Design is a creative response to a perceived need, want or opportunity, regardless of context.

FAQ 2: What is the difference between the 'design' in art and design, and 'design' in design and technology?

As a cognitive skill, not a lot. If there is any difference, then it is probably in the hair-splitting category. The cognitive process of design is basically the same, whether art, literature, mathematics, science, music or technology. It is the context and outcomes that are different. Nearly everything that humans make or use has been designed by somebody. We cannot escape to a non-technological Shangri-la because the most basic human needs (food, shelter, etc.) are dependent on the creatively designed technological solutions of our earliest ancestors. Humans inhabit a creatively designed life-space in a way that no other creature on the planet does. One that incorporates objects fashioned by species members to be visually, auditorally and intellectually satisfying, to be functional in supporting the desires of other species members (who may never meet the creator of the object – sometimes even designer and manufacturer do not meet), and which lead constantly to the invention and development of other objects (or tools to create other objects) that are considered to better fulfil the intended function.

However, even if the mental process is the same regardless of subject matter, the outcomes are very different and there is great variation in the knowledge, skills and understandings needed to perform well as a creative problem-solver in each field of human endeavour. Humans have a vast amount of knowledge about the world and how to manipulate its resources, together with a diverse array of shared cultural worlds of imagination and abstract thought that have been created across the world and across the ages. Yet all of these stem from the human capacity to imagine alternatives, to image new solutions, to analyse, synthesise, innovate, re-use, develop ideas, to *design*.

The relationship between art and design and design and technology is discussed further in Chapter 8.

FAQ 3: Isn't technology just applied science?

In most people's minds technology is something modern and dependent on science for its answers to manufacturing problems. But this is only part of the truth. Before science became seen as the major source of knowledge, technology already existed. In fact, science is a very new way of seeing the world in comparison to the practical problem-solving of technological thinking.

There was a series of white goods advertisements in the late 1980s (around the time that the first National Curriculum for design and technology was being introduced into schools) with the caption 'the appliance of science'. Unfortunately, at about the same time, a definition of technology was in circulation which went along the lines of, 'Technology is the application of scientific and other knowledge to practical tasks by organisations that involve people and machines.' This may define modern Western industrial activity but technology is much older than the Industrial Revolution and was carried out in people's homes for millennia with very little knowledge of science. Stonehenge was constructed with the latest technology of its time. So were the pyramids, the Mayan temples, the Great Wall of China. Go back far enough and it was religion or magic that was invoked in the smelting shops of the ancient world, not the appliance of the god of science.

The invention of the wheel, for example, led to the development of:

- **innovative ways of transporting goods and armies;**
- **making pots;**
- **spinning thread for clothes;**
- **grinding grain;**
- **lifting water to irrigate or drain the soil;**

and all without a true understanding of science as we would recognise it.

Buchanan (1995) said that design is concerned with the *particular*, a solution for this specific problem, whereas science is concerned with the *general* and with universal principles.

Reflective task

Look at each of the following pairs of questions:

Science	Technology
What makes plants grow?	*How can I increase the yield of my tomatoes?*
Does all light travel in straight lines?	*Would lasers be useful for delicate surgery?*
Is the universe expanding?	*How can we launch a space probe?*
Can a non-green organism be a plant?	*How can I make lighter, tastier bread/better beer?*
How does the evolution of the cotton plant illustrate the symbiosis between humans and plants?	*How can the cotton plant be bred to have longer fibres that are easier to spin into thread?*

1. **Which prompted the other, the science or the technology question?**
2. **What kinds of questions are the technology questions?**
3. **What is the relationship between the science and the technology question in each pair?**
4. **Does knowing the answer to the scientific question help to answer the technology question?**

Think of another five question pairs of your own – and consider questions 1–4 in relation to these.

Scientific answers are concerned with establishing rules and understandings that can be applied across as many different fields as possible, in order to create a complete understanding of the physical universe. Technological solutions may have wide application but usually originate in a specific practical problem or perception of potential. Scientific understandings and principles may be used, but so too may a whole range of other human skills, knowledge and opportunities. The relationship between science, and design and technology in the primary school is discussed in Chapter 8.

Many design theorists, including Buchanan, reject the notion that technology is science-based. Design problems have been called 'wicked' or 'fuzzy' because they cannot be clearly defined. What is wanted is something that will work better *in this particular situation* than what exists already, and the parameters of what that is may be very woolly. Such problems are called 'indeterminate', as the parameters might be different in each instance or occurrence of the problem. Buchanan says, *There is no science of the particular.* Furthermore, many solutions are equally right in the world of design, although some may be better than others. The choice of best solutions may be in response to such whims as personal preference and fashion. Middleton (2000) devised a diagram to represent this process.

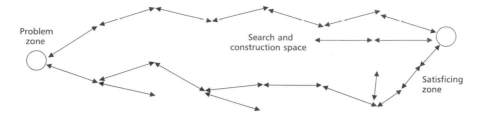

Middleton's representation of the relationship between problem and solution

FAQ 4: What is technology?

Technology began when the first fully human primates looked at the choppers they had produced according to the pattern handed down for generations (several million years) and thought about improving them. Before then, choppers had been produced to a standard pattern much as birds of each species produce fairly standard nests. Museum store-rooms have boxes and boxes of these choppers. Suddenly, between 100,000 and 50,000 years ago, a creative explosion occurred. Stone tools were made to make other tools – in bone, wood or antler. And these tools had parts, held together with twine made of the guts of animals that had been slaughtered. Suddenly, the bodies of other animals were seen as having tool potential rather than just food potential. A whole new way of seeing the world, physical and animal, had been born. That creative leap was the birth of technology. It was also the birth of design.

The Greek word *techne*, from which the English word 'technology' derives, implied skill, knowledge and practical capability. It also involved getting the hands dirty and working for a living. Archimedes must have known as much *techne* as he did science, but Greek philosophers wanted the science without the *techne* to avoid getting their hands dirty. Thus came the division between the two in Western society that only came together again in the Age of Enlightenment in the eighteenth century, when groups of industrialists and scientists in England and Germany started meeting together to discuss how the new scientific discoveries could help solve practical industrial problems. These people became the fathers of the Industrial Revolution and the founders of modern science.

In England the earliest groupings (called Lunar Societies because they met at the full moon so they could see their way home afterwards) included:

- **Isaac Watts (father of James, of steam engine fame)**
- **Erasmus Darwin (father of Charles)**
- **Joseph Dalton (chemist)**
- **Josiah Wedgwood (ceramicist).**

Not quite part of this inner circle, but also benefiting and exchanging ideas were:

the Darby family of Coalbrookedale (the first blast furnace and the first iron bridge at Ironbridge);
the Earl of Bridgewater (who built the first canal to transport coke and iron);
the Stephensons (locomotives and railways);
the Brunels (tunnels, railways, bridges and ships).

All these people were part of the creative ferment of their time. Then there was the textile industry, needing power to drive the mills. Again inventive geniuses such as Arkwright transformed the age-old cottage industry practices of spinning and weaving and harnessed the new technology to push themselves and Britain into the forefront of manufacturing production.

The rapid changes of the Industrial Revolution also brought a shift in the relationship between people and the landscape. The growth of towns and cities reached a peak in the mid-nineteenth century when, for the first time, more people lived in urban surroundings than in the countryside. This transformed the countryside from being a network of largely self-supporting communities to being feeder zones for the towns (quite literally). The idea that environmental degradation began with the advent of the Industrial Revolution is, however, not true. Humans have always been rather poor at preserving their environment: evidence the number of 'cities in the sand' that ate themselves out beyond the capability of the surrounding landscape to support them. The scale and nature of the degradation that large industrial manufacturing capacity can inflict on its environment is, however, unprecedented. That humans should, as a species, be concerned is unique. Other species do not have the reflective capacity to analyse their impact on their environments. Humans also, unfortunately, have the capacity to destroy theirs too, and on a global scale. The challenge for the future of human technological innovation is to counteract human impact. This must become a major focus of design and technology education for the future.

All this starts to raise the social and ethical issues involved in value-laden judgements about 'advanced technologies' and a Western-centric world-view, which denigrates simpler systems that are less harmful to the planet. There are power and dominance issues here too. The West conquered the rest by having bigger guns – is this the appliance of science?

Reflective task

Think about the relationship between technology and machines:

- *Is a spinning wheel a machine?*
- *Is spinning a craft or is it technology?*
- *Does it become technology when it is done by a machine and craft when done by hand?*
- *What were the machines of textile technology before nineteenth century industrialisation?*
- *Does the definition of a machine depend on place and time?*
- *If someone has a machine to do a task do they have 'technology' and if some other group do the job by hand are they crafts-people?*
- *If someone else has a machine for something the first group do by hand, are they the crafts-people?*

If a teacher were to borrow a spinning wheel and

- **talked about how some people do this as a hobby (and find someone to demonstrate),**
- **provided opportunities for children to explore the way fibres are twisted together,**
- **taught children how to make cording from wool, which could then be used in simple products,**
- **related the activities to the clothing the children are wearing,**
- **talked about the long search to find a way to automate the process to speed production using the power of water and steam, supported by photographs or visits to textile mills,**

they would enhance the children's understanding or sense of wonder at the creativity and ingenuity of past ages as well as providing opportunities for practical work that would increase children's understanding of how clothing products are made.

Teachers must beware of presenting the history of technology as a male domain. Basket-weaving woman roamed the African savannas alongside Stone Age man (how else did they carry all those carefully worked stone tools about?). Although not a suitable occupation for young ladies, there were rather a lot of women crawling through tunnels and climbing up and down ladders with baskets of coal on their backs to fuel all those machines that got the Industrial Revolution off to a good start. But even young ladies got involved in designing. The Pre-Raphaelite wives and daughters were employed to create Morris and Tiffany designs and ran industrial workshops as well as teaching classes in technical subjects such as ceramics and specialist weaving methods.

Design and technology education, by including cookery under food technology and sewing under textile technology, has done much to reclaim as *technology* those creative skills that were taken for granted as part of women's everyday lives from the advent of the Industrial Revolution. The alliance between technology and innovation has always meant that traditional and everyday skills tend to be downgraded as non-technological. Since women's domestic lives were largely untouched by industrial innovations until the advent of washing machines and vacuum cleaners, their activities were not seen as being technological or contributing to 'progress' and, therefore, not important. Ironically enough, nowadays, when it is possible for the average person to acquire, store, prepare and present food with almost minimal skill in the technology of food production, 'food technology' as innovative practice (irradiation, GM crops, etc.) has become the focus of much technological attention and innovation. Meanwhile, the old skills of *home* food technology (salting, drying, bottling, the making of beer, bread and wine) have largely been lost.

FAQ 5 So, what is design and technology education?

Design and technology has been accused of being an ill-conceived marriage of disparates, artificially created to satisfy political whim in the late 1980s and to bring together under one subject heading all the vocational subjects of the secondary school curriculum, i.e. the previously unrelated subjects of woodwork, metalwork, business studies and home economics. The politics were largely played out in the forum of secondary education and the curriculum was scaled down for smaller hands and minds without very much research into its suitability.

Could this, then, have created a programme of worthwhile learning activities for small children? Paradoxically, yes.

In spite of all the problems that surrounded the introduction of the design and technology National Curriculum and the revisions to get it right, it has at its heart a belief in the importance of hands-on problem-solving activity that allows children to grapple with ideas and produce creative solutions – which they don't have to write down! Plus, the criterion of success is not *the* right answer but *a right answer that works*.

Design and technology has the capacity to:

- **challenge the most able;**
- **provide opportunities for the less academic to achieve real success;**
- **encourage teamwork and co-operation;**
- **accept diverse responses and answers to the same problem;**
- **foster creativity and innovation.**

It is imperative that teachers have a clear understanding of what design and technology *is* (and also what design and technology *is not*) in order to teach the subject well.

Design and technology is not just making models. Good design and technology is *not*:

- **any activity that culminates in a class-set of almost identical products, because the children will not have engaged in autonomous and creative problem-solving;**
- **any activity for which the children cannot identify a clear purpose, otherwise they are following instructions and not designing their own solution;**
- **any activity in which children 'design' ideas onto paper in one lesson and then make something different next lesson once they see what and how much of the materials they get – especially if they are then expected to compare their 'design' with their 'finished product' when they write their 'evaluation' in which they write about what they could do better next time.**

Unfortunately, these basic misconceptions about the nature of design and technology still lurk in schools, due to poor conceptions of what design and technology teaching and learning really involved when the subject was first introduced into primary schools, along with lack of teacher time to personally research it properly, coupled with continuing low levels of provision of In-service Training (the 'basics' having priority).

What do I need to know in order to teach design and technology effectively at Key Stage 1 and Key Stage 2?

Answering that question is the aim of this book!

1. You need to understand what design and technology is about. The groundwork for this has already been laid, but that discussion will continue throughout the book.

2. You need to know the requirements of the National Curriculum (the subject of Chapter 2) and what that means in relation to recent government initiatives (Chapter 3).

3. You need to know how children progress in design and technology and how you can aid that progression of skills, knowledge and understanding (Chapter 4).

4. You will need to be able to plan effective lessons (Chapter 5) and know how to assess children's progress (Chapter 6) in the major content areas of the subject (Chapter 7).

5. Then you need to be able to look across the boundaries into cross-curricular thinking with other subject areas (Chapter 8) and to relate this to a global perspective and think about the important issues for education for the future (Chapter 9).

At this point, that probably seems a lot to take on board. So let's start quite simply with something manageable.

Practical task

Have another look at the list you made under the two headings 'Design' and 'Technology' and add to it any new thoughts you have as a result of reading this chapter. This will form the starting point of your design and technology scrap-book.

Begin a collection of pictures and short articles which relate to specific areas of design and technology that might prove useful in the classroom. Sunday supplements and adverts in magazines are a good source. Plastic pockets keep them flat and easily accessible.

Suggestions:

*   *vehicles: lorries, tractors, trains, cars, etc.;*
*   *clothing: fashion shots (how do they define feminity/masculinity?); children's clothes, washing and care;*
*   *food: kitchen appliances as well as promotion of specific food products;*
*   *homes: lifestyle images, furniture, lighting.*

Some definitions of design and technology

Kimbell et al. (1991):

> *From the earliest work in this field, there has been general agreement on certain basic tenets of design and technology. It is an active study, involving the purposeful pursuit of a task to some form of resolution that results in improvement (for someone) in the made world.* (p17)

Ritchie (2001):

> *From the earliest times human beings have endeavoured to control the world around them in order to survive and to enhance the quality of their existence ... They have done this by imagining new possibilities, putting their ideas into action and evaluating the outcome to decide whether the need has been met or further action is necessary.* (p1)

Kimbell and Perry (2001):

> *a distinctive model of teaching and learning ...*

> *The subject matter of design and technology is our made world ... uniquely design and technology empowers us to change the made world ... It is about the future; about what might or should be ...* (original emphasis)

> *Design is not just about change, it is about improvement and the concept of improvement is essentially value-laden.* (p3)

Harrison (2001):

> *Capability in engineering and in engineering design depends on the creative use of both scientific/articulate and the intuitive/tacit forms of knowledge. Universal education for a technological society must cultivate both forms of knowledge and understanding more systematically than at present.* (p8)

Reflective task

What are the buzz-words in each of these definitions?

Put together your own 50-word definition of design and technology education that incorporates:

- *your own developing ideas on design and technology education as you have read this chapter;*
- *your new thoughts sparked by reading these definitions.*

Designed technology and education:
a summary of key points

In this chapter some of the big theoretical issues that underlie design and technology education have been introduced and the subject area of design and technology has been defined through:

— *considering the nature of design within design and technology;*

— *thinking about the role of technology in the history of human society;*

— *examining the relationship between technology and science;*

— *beginning to consider what good design and technology teaching might look like.*

You are now ready to look at the requirements of the National Curriculum for design and technology, the subject of Chapter 2.

References

Buchanan, R (1995) Wicked problems in design thinking, in Margolin, V and Buchanan, R (eds) *The idea of design.* Cambridge, MA: MIT Press.

Harrison, G (2001) *The continuum of design education for engineering.* London: Engineering Council.

Kierl, S. (2000) An episode in technology curriculum refinement: it's only another design brief, in Roberts, P and Norman, E W L (eds) *Conference Proceedings International Design and Technology Education Research Conference (IDATER2000).* Loughborough University: Department of Design and Technology.

Kimbell, R and Perry, D (2001) *Design and technology in a knowledge economy.* London: Engineering Council.

Kimbell, R, Stables, K, Wheeler, T, Wosniak, A and Kelly, V. (1991) *The assessment of performance in design and technology.* London: Schools Examinations and Assessment Council.

Middleton, H (2000) *Design and technology: what is the problem?* in *Conference proceedings*, Design and Technology International Millennium Conference, London.

Ritchie, R (2001) *Primary design and technology.* London: David Fulton Publishers.

2 REQUIREMENTS OF THE NATIONAL CURRICULUM FOR DESIGN AND TECHNOLOGY

This chapter provides an overview and introductory explanation of the requirements of the National Curriculum for Key Stages 1 and 2. Later chapters (especially Chapter 5) will help you to plan suitable activities for children that conform to the National Curriculum's expectations.

After an introductory practical task to familiarise you with the requirements, this chapter will introduce you to:

- *the expectations of teachers and learners of design and technology;*
- *the Knowledge, Skills and Understanding to be taught within design and technology;*
- *the Breadth of Study for design and technology.*

Practical task

Look at the pages about design and technology in the National Curriculum (1999).

Read the 'mission statement' on page 90, 'The importance of design and technology' and make a list of learning outcomes that are expected to result from a child's experience of education.

Now look at pages 93–6. These list the requirements for Key Stage 1 and Key Stage 2. These can also be found on www.ncaction.org.uk/subjects/design/index.htm.

For the next part of the task you will need either to photocopy these pages or download and print them from this National Curriculum website. Lay them out side by side and highlight/underline in different colours the points of

> *similarity,*
> *difference, and*
> *progression.*

Expectations of teachers and learners of design and technology

The distinguishing nature of design and technology as a subject is crystallised in the 'mission statement' on page 90 of the 1999 National Curriculum:

> prepares pupils to participate in tomorrow's rapidly changing technologies. They learn to think and intervene creatively to improve quality of life. The subject calls for pupils to become creative and autonomous problem-solvers, as individuals and members of a

team. They must look for needs, wants and opportunities and respond to them by developing a range of ideas and making products and systems. They combine practical skills with an understanding of aesthetics, social and environmental issues, function and industrial practices. As they do so, they reflect on and evaluate present and past, its uses and effects. Through design and technology, all pupils can become discriminating and informed users of products, and become innovators. (DfEE/QCA 1999, p90)

The aim of design and technology as a subject is clearly set out in the first sentence of this mission statement: the preparation of participators in the technology of the future. In 1970 Alvin Toffler warned of the danger of education *cranking out Industrial Man – people tooled for survival in a system that will be dead before they are* (p 361) *without any understanding of what skills Johnny will require to live in the hurricane's eye of change.* (p 371)

Reflective task

Was Toffler right?

What changes in technology have occurred since 1970 that a 16-year-old leaving school in that year would have been unprepared for?

What knowledge, skills and understanding would still be relevant?

What knowledge, skills and understanding should design and technology education aim to equip children with today, given that the pace of change in the next 30 years might be even faster or moved into unimagined areas?

Think of the projected challenges to human life over the next 30 years – how can education help to equip children to surmount these?

The design and technology mission statement says that children are to become autonomous, creative problem-solvers, aiming to improve the quality of life. While they are still children, their ideas are not to be judged according to adult standards. Children can have wonderful ideas that they may not be able to put into practice. They may only be able to make a model of their ideas in simple materials that does not function as a 'real' one would. This does not matter. The child's imagination is actively engaged in devising solutions and their model is a representation of those ideas, to be applauded and encouraged. This theme is developed in the section on Design Capability in Chapter 3.

Identifying needs, wants and opportunities is a skill that grows across the primary years. Young children can only imagine that others will like what they like. By the end of Key Stage 2, children should be able to design solutions to problems that do not affect them directly. They will have learnt to take on the perspective of others. The inclusion of the word 'opportunities' is interesting. Earlier versions of the National Curriculum had only the needs and wants. But not all designed objects are strictly needed and wanting often comes after the object is produced (how else do the fashion shops keep people buying new clothes every season?). This is one of the themes developed in Chapter 4.

Understanding of technological activity beyond school, within wider society, is also important. This kind of understanding can be linked with history, geography, RE and science. For example, studying the Victorians should also include the impact of the Industrial Revolution: railways, factories and the growth of towns, and also the rapid growth of scientific understanding. The 'heroes of science and technology' (Watt, Stephenson, Brunel, Faraday, Davy and Maxwell), as well as Florence Nightingale and David Livingstone, should be included when studying the Victorians. How to fit design and technology into a cross-curricular way of working is covered in Chapter 8.

The last sentence of the mission statement enshrines both the present and the future, users and producers, evaluators of what already exists and creators of the future. The choice of the final word, innovators, encapsulates the needs of society for its future citizens. Whatever their futures, this generation of children needs to grow into innovators, whether thinking of global problems of pollution and the effects of global warming, or whether thinking of ways to house, feed and clothe a family. It is the most basic intellectual skill that distinguishes humans from other species, and the one which is most needed in order to live happy and fulfilled lives. The final chapter of the book (Chapter 9) considers design and technology for global citizens of the future.

The 1991 National Curriculum split the range of activities in which children engage while designing and making into separate, numbered Attainment Targets. This proved confusing for non-specialists, who took this to mean that these were an ordered list of aspects to be included in every project, thus perpetrating a linear view of design and technology (see Chapter 3), that was unintended by the curriculum writers. The current National Curriculum, therefore, has one Attainment Target which fully includes the Knowledge, Skills and Understanding that children should acquire within the Breadth of Study for design and technology.

The Knowledge, Skills and Understanding to be taught within design and technology

Knowledge, Skills and Understanding for both Key Stage 1 and Key Stage 2, is sub-divided into:

1. developing, planning and communicating ideas;
2. working with tools, equipment, materials and components to make quality products;
3. evaluating processes and products;
4. knowledge and understanding of materials and components.

Many lessons will include elements of all four of these strands of capability but, con-versely, there is no requirement that any particular project or term's work should include all of them. Some aspects, such as Key Stage 1: 1d 'Plan by suggesting what to do next as their ideas develop', will occur naturally, provided children are being given sufficient autonomy in their work to make the product their own creative solution to the task in hand. Teachers will encourage children to develop their reflective and analytical skills by asking skilfully worded questions about the progress of the product.

Unfortunately, some schemes of work and books of suggested topics, and, therefore, teachers who rely on them, seem to work to a linear view of designing (lesson 1 = draw plans on paper, lessons 2–4 = make 'the design', lesson 5 = draw/write evaluation of the final product). This formulaic way of working is a very poor model of how designers (and design processes) work and will not enhance children's design capability. Its rigidity does not reflect the iterative nature of design as an ongoing, constantly evolving resolution to a problem that is newly perceived at every stage of the solution process (see Chapter 3).

There is no implied order between the four major sections of Knowledge, Skills and Understanding. Developing ideas and explaining them clearly (Key Stage 2: 1b) may come at any point in the project. Indeed it might come after 3A (reflecting on progress). An implied order can be read into the four points under 'Developing, planning and communicating ideas', but these are all skills that are needed throughout the duration of a project. There is no implication that these plans and ideas need to be recorded in writing or drawing. A list (1b) or a planned sequence of actions (1c) can be communicated verbally. It can be recorded on large scrap paper shared between a group of children brainstorming ideas together. It can, of course, be neatly presented in a 'design folder' on pre-printed 'design sheets' but there is no guarantee that these represent more dynamically creative thinking – in fact the opposite is likely to be the case.

Developing, planning and communicating ideas

This is *not* 'Lesson 1: Draw your ideas'.

It is difficult to comprehend the rationale behind using the school photocopier to produce 30 sheets of paper with a pretty border and the words 'My Design' on it. These sheets immediately inhibit the kind of rough scribbling that real design development entails. What happens when this neatly bordered frame is filled with ideas that have been considered and rejected? Can the child have the courage to change the title to 'Not My Design' or to ask for another sheet? If given blank paper, children feel less inhibited, can cross out, score through, scribble over their developing ideas, and then they are genuinely working towards a creative solution. They may well, at the end of the generating and planning process, ask for a fresh piece of paper on which to make a fair copy of their final idea – for their own satisfaction and to clarify the final idea in their heads. Or they may have used the paper to think through all the possibilities that they *do not* want to make and have come to a really clear image in their heads of what they will make and want to move straight into making it – no more forward planning or recording on paper needed.

Or they may not be using paper to develop, plan and communicate their design ideas at all. They may be:

- **talking, discussing, role-playing, singing, rapping;**
- **using construction kits;**
- **writing – making a list of resources, jotting down ideas, conducting a survey, writing a specification;**
- **using ICT – taking photographs or video footage, perhaps even CAD-CAM;**
- **using paper, card, wood, or other consumable or recyclable resources.**

Working with tools, equipment, materials and components to make quality products

The range of tools that primary school children have available to them should be appropriate to their physical capabilities. The size of the child's hand in comparison to the size of the tool is a good guide as to safety and suitability. If a particular tool is not manufactured in a size small enough for a child's hand, then this is a good guide that the tool in mind is unsuitable for the child at that stage of their development.

Safe working practices should be uppermost in teachers' minds whenever practical activities are planned. However, children can use potentially hazardous equipment given adequate supervision and preparation. Chapter 5 provides more detailed guidance in the section on Health and Safety.

The difference between materials and components is basically that materials require cutting and shaping, whereas components are items that do not. Of course, some materials are components, components are made from materials (sometimes several) and components may be cut and shaped for a particular purpose within a project (e.g. to fit into a hole).

Examples of materials	Examples of components
Sheet materials – paper, card, board, plastic sheeting, bubble wrap, fabric Structural materials – lolly sticks, pipe cleaners, wood, art straws, whithies Joining materials – thread, wool, glue, Blu-tak Recyclable materials – cartons, pots, tubes	Pieces of construction kits Ready-made cams, pulleys, cogs and gears Card, plastic and wooden wheels Beads, sequins, buttons, zips Joiners – paper clips, treasury tags Recyclables – bottle tops, corks, CDs

The production of a quality product is an important aim within education. Teachers need to have high expectations of children's products but at the same time to value products that represent a high level of thought and imagination that perhaps do not look too good by adult standards. Whether or not the result of activity can be classed as quality product depends on the design brief set to the children. It is usually accepted that it would be unfair to mark a child's piece of creative writing harshly for its spelling if the learning outcome had stated that the focus of the lesson was on generating ideas, so also in design and technology. Outcomes from a lesson focusing on group problem-solving with temporary materials and fixings would be unfairly assessed by criteria of aesthetic appeal.

Evaluating processes and products

Evaluation is not a skill to be tacked on the end of a project – the 'write up' or 'what I could do better next time.' It is an ongoing part of every aspect of a design project. From the first vague formulation of ideas, rejecting one in favour of another, evaluation is taking place. This is why the Key Stage 2 wording stresses the ongoing nature of evaluation within a design project and includes the evaluation of existing products for their social, economic and environmental implications.

Johnsey (1995) coined the mnemonic MEM-cycles (make–evaluate–make) to indicate the process he observed young children employing as they were engaged in design activity. They were interacting directly with the construction materials, having ideas, trying, estimating, comparing outcomes with ideas in their heads, changing, adapting in the light of success or otherwise of the developing artefact. He considered prolonged MEM-cycles to be evaluate–analyse–improve cycles and all these processes occurred as the children were engaged directly in making their products. For the children, this evaluative process was such a natural method of operation that they were not aware that this was what they were doing.

Knowledge and understanding of materials and components

This is not just a repetition of 'working with tools, equipment, materials and components' The implication is that, as a result of planning, experimenting, evaluating, learning, children have gained new knowledge and understanding that they will be able to take on into the next lesson or the next project. The teacher's role is to assess what the children have learnt in order to move them on further. The context for the gaining of such knowledge and understanding may be within any of the three aspects that the National Curriculum identifies under Breadth of Study for design and technology, which is the topic of the next section of this chapter.

Breadth of Study

The aim of the Breadth of Study statements is to specify the learning contexts envisioned by the writers of the National Curriculum within which children will be taught the Knowledge, Skills and Understandings.

For design and technology, these are:

- **investigating and evaluating familiar products;**
- **focused practical tasks;**
- **design and make assignments.**

Although listed as (a), (b) and (c) in the National Curriculum, there is no intention that these three elements should be taught in this order within any one project, nor is the time balance between the three elements specified. Different projects can, therefore, major more strongly on one of the aspects, although it is likely that most time will be spent designing and making.

All activities must lead towards children having opportunities to be innovative problem-solvers who can respond to the needs and wants of potential users of the quality product that they have planned to make. Focused practical tasks provide the knowledge, skills and understanding to be able to achieve these goals. Looking at existing products develops children's evaluative skills and acts as a starting point for their own creative ideas. However, the aim of both of these kinds of activities is to enable children to successfully undertake design and make assignments. It is imperative that there be sufficient design choices and opportunities within the design brief for children to become autonomous problem-solvers within the activity. Obviously children's ability to develop their design ideas increases with age, as does development in every subject in the curriculum. It is important not to limit children's opportunities for imaginative problem-solving through applying to their work inappropriate standards based on perceptions of adult design work.

Investigating and disassembling familiar products

You will see this as 'IDEAs' (Investigating and Disassembling Existing Artefacts) in guidance on how to teach (including government publications), which can be confusing since investigating and disassembling products may or may not spark new *ideas* in children's heads. You also need to be aware that the word 'disassembling' does not necessarily mean physically take apart. It is a technical term used in design schools meaning to analyse a product and work out what it is made from, how it was made, what it might be used for and so on. Therefore, you do not need to provide 30 clocks for your class to take apart and then not be able to put back together again.

It is unreasonable to ask children to design something from their mind's eye if they do not know what real products of the kind you have in mind are like, or if they have never really thought about the component parts of, say, a clock or a backpack. Investigating and evaluating existing products is also important for children to develop a critical understanding of the world of product development and marketing. This will be at a simple level with younger children but older Key Stage 2 children can begin to consider such issues as environmental impact of production, social implications, the way products are packaged and marketed, in order to develop their awareness as informed consumers. Some of this work will be especially appropriate, even with younger children, with regard to food products and those such as toys and games that are aimed especially at children as consumers.

Examples of products can be used to stimulate design ideas. Seeing a range of ideas that have already been made can spark children's imaginations and bring to mind other examples that they have seen. It is difficult to visualise a solution to a design problem through verbal descriptions alone, and the evaluation of existing products can help to focus children's minds on possible solutions and alert them to less well thought-out or less appropriate ones. These should not be too close a match to the kind of products that the teacher has in mind for the children to make. Otherwise there is little design thinking involved and the children are simply following a shown pattern. For example, if the class mascot needs a new chair, then it is better to show the one that has fallen apart is the wrong size or shape, or has no desirable gadgets like automatically opening sunshade, milk-shake dispenser or whatever. The aim of evaluating existing products is to stimulate children's own design ideas and the teacher needs to choose carefully the kind of product and the way in which they are presented in order to enhance the children's design capabilities.

Practical task

Find/think of something (other than food) that you have bought for less than £10 in the last month.

- **Why did you choose this product?**
- **Has the product given you customer satisfaction? Why (not)?**
- **Would you buy another of the same type? In same/ different circumstances/ occasion?**
- **Were there other similar products that you rejected?**
- **Did cost feature in your decision?**
- **Would the same choice criteria apply if it were a £100 item? £1000?**
- **If you were to design a product for the same purpose, how would you want to change/adapt it?**
- **How could you use/adapt this activity for Year 2? Year 6?**

A collection of products relating to a topic can act as a valuable resource for evaluative discussion and inspiration for children's own design work. For specific topics that you teach regularly (e.g. making slippers, bags, hats, etc.) collect as wide a range of examples as possible, especially unusual ones, to stimulate children's imaginations. This will yield a far higher standard of work from the children than just showing them a couple of conventional examples. Begin with the line 'Here are the slippers I wear when I get home' and produce the most ridiculous pair you have collected. All right, it's not true – you bought them from a car boot sale – but does it matter? Good teaching is closely allied to good acting and all children think good teachers are mad anyway.

Product collections can serve many design functions, including:

- **clarifying the task and focusing children's attention on what you want them to design and make;**
- **enabling evaluative discussion, looking for advantages and disadvantages and seeing both sides of a situation, and suggesting improvements and alternatives;**
- **widening children's horizons to solutions with which they are not familiar (historical, geographical, cultural);**

- unpicking assumptions about existing products (e.g. gender stereotypes implied through colour, shape, advertising imagery);
- finding out how things work (or why they don't).

Suggested product collections are:

- **Anything to do with food is easy to collect – dried beans or pasta to sort, feel and examine; things to stir with (throwaway plastic stirrers for disposable polystyrene cups through to huge ladles borrowed from canteen kitchens); egg whisks (birch twigs through to electric hand whisks); plus the obvious food collections to taste and compare – breads, fruit, teas, for example, and the food of any country being studied in geography or modern foreign language (MFL) lessons.**

- **Packaging – Easter egg boxes, Christmas paraphernalia, unusually shaped cartons and boxes, ones that can be opened out to see the net design, ones with good/bad fitting lids, packing such as bubble wrap and polystyrene (parents always want to donate polystyrene bits – send them back in brightly decorated boxes holding festival gifts safely).**

- **Fabrics and fibres – collect a range of fabric samples illustrating different fibres (wool, cotton, silk, etc.), techniques (weaving, knitting, felting) and decoration (printing, top stitching, etc.). Raw fibres such as cotton bolls and fleece wool can make useful additions. Look out for unusual clothes too, especially old ones with lace or net. For Foundation Stage children, collect a set of warm weather, hot weather and rainy day clothes.**

- **Toys – depending on the focus, can be old/new, girl/boy, specific topic (teddies, robots). Your own toys from childhood are a source of fascination to all children (see Pandy's suitcase example below).**

The lists above might suggest that you need a great range of products for every topic and your heart sinks at the thought of storage. However, here is an example from my own experience of a great deal developing from not much (see Hope, (2005)).

EXAMPLE: PANDY'S SUITCASE
Pandy was the author's comfort toy from earliest childhood. He is a poor tatty thing with barely any fur, wearing such a disgracefully stained shirt that he has finally been retired from active service. He arrived in school to support a 'toys of yesterday' event and never left. Children never tired (although colleagues certainly did) of the tale of him being left on the train and Dad the hero leaping back on to rescue him. This prompted the idea of asking children to design him a suitcase for his sunglasses and other holiday essentials. As a variation, the children would be shown a little kit bag (it was in the cabin on a cruise holiday, containing soaps, etc.) and asked what Pandy needed to put inside. This theme developed further through the arrival of Renauld the Reindeer from Norway who came to collect his kit bag and wore a woolly jumper and plastic dungarees and hat (What is the weather like in Norway? And would the things Pandy had put inside the bag be suitable there?).

This encourages design thinking skills at Key Stage 1:

- **needs of another;**
- **suitability for purpose (his sunglasses and rainmac must fit inside);**
- **size and scale (must fit over paw but not drag on ground);**
- **properties of materials;**
- **reality** *vs.* **fantasy,**

This last point is an important one in relation to young children's thinking. Key Stage 1 children have no difficulty entering into the fantasy of the situation: Pandy going on holiday, needing a suitcase, Renauld arriving and examining the content of his kit bag. But in their minds, anything could substitute for anything and they can pretend that anything can have any properties they chose it to have. They will draw bags onto card, cut them out and declare that Pandy could put his things inside this cut-out picture. They will be totally confused at the suggestion that it needs an inside and that they need to cut out two sides to make one. By the transition to Key Stage 2, children generally have an understanding of the rules of the game in school and can balance the elements of fantasy and reality embedded in the task.

Fantasy	Reality
Pandy is going on holiday	The children will be making something
Pandy needs a travel bag for his clothes, etc.	The product has to be able to have things put inside it
Pandy can walk around carrying a bag	The product must have a handle that will fit over Pandy's paw but not scrape the ground
Travel bags can be made with the materials provided by the teacher	The children have a choice of coloured card or felt with which to make the bag
Travel bags can be held together with PVA glue	The lesson will last 1 hour so there is no time for sewing
Realistic travel bags are made by young children in school for soft toys to go on holiday	The work is going on the wall as part of the 'Holidays' display

A sub-plot to this particular use of an existing product is couched in the words of the introductory sentence to the above example: *Pandy was the author's comfort toy from earliest childhood.* As well as the physical aspects of products that can be analysed by children:

- **What is it made from?**
- **What does it do?**
- **How does it work?**

there are also the functional, purposive and social aspects:

- **Who does/did this belong to?**

- **What is/was it used for?**

- **How did the owner feel towards it?**

- **How did it affect the owner's feelings towards other people/similar products?**

There was, you see, also the story of the nasty cousins who threw Pandy up so high he hit his head on the ceiling …

Products can have associations of memories and emotions:

- **Well-crafted products elicit a warm sense of appreciation for their crafts-manship or ingenuity (hand-made lace, clocks, astronomical instruments).**

- **Large products that enclose or move through space can inspire feelings of awe, danger, fear or excitement (Great Hall in the British Museum, Stonehenge, cranes, fairground rides).**

- **The unusual or unexpected can prompt pleasure or pain in their surprise (Jack-in-the-box, cuckoo clock, dungeon).**

Key Stage 1 children will respond appropriately to such emotional stimuli and begin to attach words to their feelings. As children move through Key Stage 2 they will be able to articulate not just how they feel now, but how they would have felt at a younger age in response to products and artefacts. Articulating these reactions enables them to incorporate into their own work specific features or decorative effects for different users and purposes.

Focused practical tasks

'Focused practical tasks' are frequently abbreviated to FPTs. For the sake of clarity and to aid understanding of the underlying principle behind these tasks, it has been decided that in this book the full term 'focused practical tasks' will be used. The scheme of work promoted by the Nuffield Foundation (www.primarydandt.org.uk/home/) has slightly different terminology. They use 'Small Steps – Big Task', which is a useful, child-friendly way of explaining to children how focused practical tasks relate to the design and make assignment.

The aim of focused practical tasks is to provide children with the knowledge, skills and understanding necessary to complete a design and make assignment. A scheme of work that focuses only on developing children's skills without being firmly linked to design opportunities will not have satisfied the National Curriculum requirements for designing and making innovative products. The principle underlying focused practical tasks is of learning the techniques required for the successful completion of the design and make assignment. The idea works on the principle that 'practice makes perfect' and that it is unrealistic to expect children to learn new skills and techniques and also produce a quality product at the same time.

Except where older children have sufficient design capability and experience to decide for themselves what skills and techniques they need to practise in order to complete a design task, the teacher will have to be proactive in planning activities that will provide children with sufficient knowledge, skill and understanding to be able to successfully design and make a quality product. Such tasks need to enable children to practise and develop skills whilst undertaking personally meaningful activities. Planning a succession of activities that each lead to a small-scale but satisfying outcome is one way to overcome this dilemma.

EXAMPLES

- **Electrical circuitry – put together the circuit on the desk first to ensure understanding before attempting to fit it into the product.**

- **Paper engineering – make a range of levers from scrap card and split pins.**

- **Sewing – practise some stitches on Binca with a blunt needle before working with sharp needles on material with no guiding holes.**

- **Structures – build in rolled newspaper to discover how to make a stable structure before using wood.**

- **Sawing wood – make a picture frame before trying to design an off-road vehicle.**

- **Pneumatics or hydraulics – have a fun and messy session with syringes, balloons, elastic bands and tubing before deciding what they will move or control.**

As can be seen from the list above, the focused practical task might be a quick practice task (putting together the circuit or making the card levers) or it may last a whole lesson and produce a product in its own right (the picture frame). The pneumatics example raises a particularly important point about focused practical tasks. They are ideal opportunities for children to start to develop their design ideas. They are actively engaged in experimenting with the tools, materials and techniques that they will need for their design and make assignment and can begin to have ideas and modify them in the light of experience. They will be evaluating the suitability of their ideas against the reality of the materials and their own capability in working with them. As they talk and discuss and share and compare ideas, so they will begin to build a clear picture of what is realistically possible. Their design ideas will reflect their greater confidence in using the materials and techniques.

EXAMPLE: YEAR 2 – MAKING PUPPETS
The children are to make finger puppets from felt.

They need to practise:

- **making a suitable-sized template (on scrap paper, drawing round and cutting out two fingers and gluing together to see if fingers fit inside);**

- **fringing the felt to make hair (using scrap paper);**

- **sewing (on spare felt).**

While they are doing these activities, they are beginning to:

- **gain confidence – 'I can sew!'**

- **realise design faults – 'My finger won't go in here!'**

- start to get ideas for their finished product – 'I'm having mine green with orange hair and red eyes. Can I stick sequins on to be his beady eyes – no – have you got real beads and will I be able to sew those on?'

Practical task

Think about and debate the following:

Suggest suitable focused practical tasks in preparation for:

- *designing a desk tidy from card and recycled materials;*
- *designing a festival greetings card that must incorporate movement;*
- *designing a space rocket from recycled materials.*

What role could construction kits have as focused practical tasks?

What activities could be described as focused practical tasks in food technology?

Construction kits can be a very useful way of modelling ideas as they can be taken apart and re-used over and over again without worrying about wastage of materials. So as focused practical tasks they can be used to decide on the size, shape and form of a product that will then be made from other materials. For example:

- Year 1 – making a space rocket for Mouse to visit the Cheesy Moon.
- Year 4 – making a bridge that spans a gap between two tables that will then be made from card strips.
- Year 6 – making a crane that really works before cutting up expensive consumables such as square section wood.

(See Chapter 3 for a discussion of the role of construction kits throughout the primary years.)

Design and make assignments

Once children have acquired the appropriate skills for a project, through focused practical tasks, then they are in a position to making their own design choices. This will develop children's autonomy through enabling ownership of the task and make real design choices. The role of evaluation and self-assessment is also important and this subject is developed further in Chapter 6. 'Design and make assignments' are frequently abbreviated to DMAs, but, as with focused practical tasks' it was decided that this book would not use abbreviations, to ensure clarity and enable understanding.

For planning any design and make assignment, the teacher needs to analyse the knowledge, skills and understandings required for the children to complete the activity and ensure that practice opportunities are provided before asking the children to work on the final product. In preparation for making a cross stitch place mat, for example, the children can be provided with a short strip of Binca on which to master the technique. Chapter 7 contains examples of focused practical tasks linked to other subject areas of the design and technology curriculum.

Design and make assignments do not have to last across several lessons. Neither do they need to result in a usable product. They might include making a model or drawing of a product, or a discussion about a product, or even an ICT presentation about a product. Design and make assignments are the real meat of the curriculum and it is here that activities stand or fall.

Practical activities that provide no opportunities for genuinely creative and innovative design work do not satisfy the National Curriculum criteria for designing and making. To claim that such activities are, therefore, 'focused practical tasks' instead fails to appreciate that these need to contribute towards the knowledge, skills and under-standing required for a specific, relevant design and make assignment. Teachers should be especially aware of this in relation to cross-curricular work, where there is a strong temptation to call any practical work with card and scissors 'design and tech-nology', regardless of whether there are any genuine opportunities to design innovative products. A row of shadoofs made from dowel and string, for example, is a practical activity in a history topic. It is not designing and making.

Encouraging children to talk and discuss their design ideas is essential, both with each other and with adults. must not just become an activity which occupies children's hands and they are left to follow their own whims and ideas once the making of the artefact begins. Teachers need to circulate and discuss the children's developing ideas in order to refocus them on the design outcome and task criteria.

- **Is the size right?**
- **Is it strong enough?**
- **How will it work?**
- **Will it stand up on its own?**
- **What colour will it be?**

And teachers can make suggestions. Teachers are not interfering or inhibiting a child's creativity if they suggest a better way to do something. For reasons associated with the idea that creativity unfolds from within and that young children are naturally (more) creative than adults (highly disputable!), teachers seem reluctant to sit down with a child and collaboratively re-design what they are trying to make so that it works. Teachers sometimes seem to operate from two different poles – either giving the children a template or ready-to-cut photocopy so everyone makes the same thing or they let them get on with it completely on their own, with no guarantee that any child in the class will have any measure of success. The former is recognised as having zero creativity and design choice but what about the other? How creatively successful at solving a design problem can a child be if they are lacking information vital to the success of the project? Surely this is the essence of successful teaching, which Bruner (1966) calls 'scaffolding' and Vygotsky (1978) calls the 'zone of proximal development'. The child needs some help from a more skilled practitioner and is ready to learn a new skill or concept.

Design solution from a child's perspective (1): Rain hats

Case study

Year 3, Greenway School, October:

Some children are happy to pretend that the yellow paper is waterproof and choose this on the basis of colour rather than material property. Their teacher, Mr McC., expected them all to have chosen the black plastic bin bag and pretend it was a nice colour.

Making one thing stand for another is a basic design skill. The children are just choosing a different part of the problem to model than that which the teacher had in mind. As children move through their primary school years, so they learn which aspects of the problem are expected to be imaginatively modelled and which are expected to be treated literally. It is all part of learning the rules of the game.

A lot of paper and card is used in primary schools as a substitute for materials that are inappropriate for children's use. For example:

- **making a mirror for Sleeping Beauty (out of card, collage materials and silver paper);**
- **making a throne for Henry VIII out of corrugated card (rolled and sheet);**
- **making a bridge, shelter for aliens, crane or gantry, etc. out of rolled newspaper.**

Many primary school 'products' would be described as 'mock ups' in the real world of adult design. The status of these as models, in the technical design sense, is as temporary externalisations of on-going thought. In these, yellow paper could substitute for a waterproof material, because everyone would be aware of the rules of the game. Architects' models (for example, that of a new supermarket and entertainment complex) are displayed, celebrated and become the centre-piece of the promotional reception, with no criticism of the yellow paper masquerading as waterproof tiling!

It follows, therefore, that it is important to be specific about which part of the problem is to be considered important enough for a specific solution to be found. If a greetings card is for a specific person (Mum on Mother's Day) and children have been asked to list Mum's favourite activities as a starting point for designing the card, then it is reasonable to query why a child has abandoned all apparent reference to the list. There might be a valid reason (flowers to cheer her up, perhaps). Respect children's design choices and ask sensitively why the design criteria have been abandoned.

Design solution from a child's perspective (2): Bridge building

Case study

Year 1, Greenway School, February

Since The Three Billy Goats Gruff was the story of the week, their teacher, Mrs A., would like to find out whether her class could solve a specific construction problem. Given a card 'river', could they build a bridge to cross it using wooden bricks, none of which was long enough on its own. She was intrigued that many of the children seemed to be building a bridge that was upside down, with the piers standing on top of the roadway, for which they just laid slabs across the 'river'. Glancing across at the group busy making model bridges from recycled packets and cartons, her eyes focused on a particularly realistic representation of the nearest bridge to their homes, which had two concrete piers for raising and lowering the bridge for passing shipping.

The children's experience and concept of 'bridge', therefore, was not based on a sideways view of the structure, as shown in picture books, but of the real and frequent occurrence of sitting in the traffic jam looking at this superstructure. What was below their line of vision from their back seat in the family car was of no concern or focus of attention. All eyes would be on the raising and lowering carriageway and all minds would be focused on how long would they sit here today.

Mrs A. may have wondered to herself whether her time would have been better spent asking them to rewrite The Billy Goats Gruff with the Troll in the Control House that some of them had even included in their model.

Outline of project for Year 6: cloaks

Possible contexts linking to other areas of the curriculum

History and geography: Africa, Aztecs, the Middle Ages and Knights of the Round Table

RE and cross-cultural studies: festivals, faith stories

Fiction texts: traditional tales, magic and mystery genres

Music, dance and theatre: could become the goal and overriding context of the whole cycle of activity

Focused practical tasks

- **printing**
- **appliqué**
- **batik**
- **tie-dying**
- **fabric paint**
- **sun paint (if sunny!)**

This looks like a recipe for disaster. You could not possibly have all this happening at once, and if you did one per week that would take the whole term, so think creatively about time and classroom management. Have just one activity set up in a corner on a day when you are not constantly in and out of the room, or you may prefer to spread this across several afternoons. What the rest of the class are doing requires careful planning. It must be something they can get on with while your attention is focused on the group. Allow about half an hour for each group to have their turn of each focused practical task. They will need to do several pieces for each activity as at least one will probably be chosen to appear on their finished product.

If you do all six focused practical tasks and you have five groups in the class, it will take 15 hours for everyone to have a turn at everything, not allowing for 'swap-over' time. Therefore it could all be done across the afternoons of 4 school weeks (assuming that PE and other fixed timetable events occur some afternoons).

Once everyone has tried all the focused practical tasks you can move on to a whole class lesson.

Investigating existing products – cloaks

- **Examine and handle real cloaks (these can be hired from fancy dress shops).**
- **Look at a range of pictures from books and the internet showing cloaks from around the world.**
- **Cut one seam of large old skirts so children can try them on and practise moving in them.**
- **Immediately after wearing a cloak and swirling around in it, children draw quick sketches to record their observations and sensations. They can take turns to model the cloak as they each draw. Focus children's attention on catching the movement and feel of the cloak – this is sketching to record sensation of movement and colour. Use wax crayon or pastels on large sheets of paper.**

Now the class are ready for their design and make assignment.

Design and make assignment

You will need to decide whether each child is making their own cloak or whether this will be a group project.

- Each child/group needs an old skirt as a base for the cloak, to be decorated with pieces from the focused practical tasks. Children can be asked to bring these from home. The skirts need to be full (at least half circle) and quite long, preferably close to ground length from a child's shoulders.

- The amount of space needed to transfer the design to the cloak will require considerable floor or table space to be available for each group, so some careful planning is needed. Consider having one group working at a time.

- The children will make small-scale design sketches of their ideas for their cloak (cutting their paper into the same shape as their cloth will help them to more easily imagine the finished cloak and plan their design).

- They could plan to cut their focused practical task squares into interesting shapes and baste these to the skirt, or attach tassels, cord, etc. to it, or even decorate the skirt directly using the less messy techniques.

- They will need to transfer their final design to the skirt with chalk and make a detailed annotated plan to record their final design.

- At least 3 hours will be needed for children to work on the decoration of their cloak.

Opportunity for celebration

This kind of project cries out for the products to be used in other creative contexts. The children will have built a narrative into their cloak and created a character who would wear it, even if no context has been provided by the teacher.

- Use the cloaks in a drama lesson but leave it undirected – allow the children a set time in which to create a two-minute drama involving the cloak and its wearer.

- Alternatively, stage a fashion parade, either amongst themselves or in front of an audience. The children can choose appropriate music and design the catwalk show for each cloak.

Practical task

Questions to ask when observing or planning lessons, starting from the Breadth of Study statements in the National Curriculum (or glance back up at the textiles example scheme of work above and consider the way you would develop this into a more formalised scheme of work).

Investigating existing artefacts:

- *When are products analysed (e.g. first lesson)?*
- *How is the analysis used to help children to develop their own design ideas?*

Focused practical tasks:

- *Where are these placed within the scheme of work?*

- *Do all children do them, because it is anticipated they will all need them, or are they practice opportunities tailored to individual needs?*

- *Is there a product to the focused practical task or just a 'sample piece'?*

- *Do the children discuss (or record) their design ideas while making the focused practical tasks?*

Design and make assignments

- *What emphasis is given to discussion, recording (words, drawings) and mock-ups (including focused practical tasks) in developing design ideas?*

- *Do children work individually or in groups?*

- *If templates are used, are they adult- or child-manufactured – what impact does this have on the finished product?*

- *Where does evaluation feature – is it a separate formal activity at the end of the series of lessons, are children's reflections recorded along the way, or is it implicit in the process?*

One last question (that you will be able to answer much more readily after reading the next chapter) is: What model of the design process appears to underlie the scheme of work being followed?

Requirements of the National Curriculum for design and technology:
a summary of key points

This chapter has examined the requirements of the National Curriculum for design and technology in terms of:

- *its expectations of teachers and learners of design and technology as set out in the 'mission statement' on page 90 of the National Curriculum (1999);*

- *the Knowledge, Skills and Understanding to be taught within;*

- *the Breadth of Study for –*
  investigating and evaluating familiar products;
  focused practical tasks;
  design and make assignments.

This chapter has also provided some examples both of each aspect of the curriculum and also of how they might fit together into a project with potential for cross-curricular learning.

References

Bruner, J (1966) *Towards a theory of instruction*. Cambridge MA: Harvard University Press.

Hope, G (2005) Making a bag, *5 TO 7 educator*, 4 (8): National Curriculum Section, D&T.

Johnsey, R (1995) The place of process skills in *Lessons from research into the way primary children design and make*. *Conference Proceedings,* International Design and Technology Education Research Conference (IDATER95). Loughborough University: Department of Design and Technology.

Toffler, A (1970) *Future shock*. London: The Bodley Head.

Vygotsky, L, (1978) *Mind in society: the development of higher psychological processes*. Cambridge, MA: Harvard University Press.

3 FRAMEWORK FOR TEACHING AND LEARNING DESIGN AND TECHNOLOGY

This chapter will place the teaching and learning in design and technology within the context of recent government initiatives (the National Strategy for Primary Schools and the re-emphasis on creativity in teaching and learning) and also look at the core skills within design and technology as a subject area, in preparation for following chapters that go more deeply into specific teaching and learning issues such as progression (Chapter 4), planning (Chapter 5), assessment (Chapter 6) and subject content (Chapter 7).

Therefore, this chapter covers:

- *Excellence and Enjoyment in design and technology*
- *Creative teaching and creative learning within design and technology*
- *Design capability.*

Excellence and Enjoyment in design and technology

The National Strategy for Primary Schools, *Excellence and Enjoyment*, (DfEE, 2003) sets out principles that should underlie good teaching for effective learning, and build on the successes that schools have achieved over recent years. This document has been hailed in many quarters as supporting a far greater freedom in teaching and an opportunity for schools to develop creative subjects and creative approaches to teaching and learning that they had felt constrained to abandon or avoid during the years of somewhat tighter government control of both subject content and method of delivery. The government intention is to enable schools to develop more innovative and creative approaches to teaching without sacrificing high standards of learning. This is the message of the Executive Summary that fronts the document. It is absolutely vital that teachers take this opportunity to do so.

How does this document relate specifically to design and technology?

The principles of learning and teaching on page 29 of *Excellence and Enjoyment* should underpin all lessons, regardless of subject (and so should be an integral part of good design and technology education. *Excellence and Enjoyment* is a document of general principles rather than specific subject advice and so these principles will now be examined to see how they apply to teaching design and technology.

Practical task

Read the executive summary of Excellence and Enjoyment *and pinpoint statements that impact on teaching and learning in design and technology.*

Ownership of innovation

The first page of the Executive Summary speaks of schools 'taking ownership of the curriculum', becoming more autonomous and developing innovative approaches to their work. This means in practice that there is no longer pressure to adopt a particular way of working or scheme of work in the delivery of the designand technology curriculum. This is reinforced in Section 1.4 (p9) of the main document, which stresses that outstanding schools are those in which the curriculum changes and improves over time, which implies, conversely, that those schools that are repeating the same topics, year on year, are not only less dynamic, but that they are becoming left behind in the race for excellence. This implies that schemes of work should be overhauled regularly. A three-year life-span for any topic is probably more than sufficient. The first year it will be exciting and fresh and teachers will learn alongside the children. The second year, it will be delivered with confidence and all the resources will be in place. By year three, it will be have become routine, the enthusiasm is still there (this is a successful project after all, hopefully) but the excitement has gone. The teacher would want to move on and develop something new. Beyond the third year of delivery, the resources will have gained their accustomed place in the cupboard, ready for recycling with each successive class. It would have been better to have planned something new.

Section 1.14 (p12) challenges schools to 'Take a fresh look at their curriculum, their timetable and the organisation of the school day and week, and think actively about how they would like to develop and enrich the experience they offer their children.'

Practical task

Read Excellence and Enjoyment, *pages 16–17 'Existing and planned freedoms', and note down how these points affect teaching design and technology.*

Reflect on the practice you have observed in schools.

How far do you think those schools and teachers have embraced these freedoms?

If they have not yet done so, what, do you think, is holding them back?

Read paragraphs 2.5–2.7 on page 16. Why do you think these misconceptions exist?

Schools are increasingly taking a cross-curricular or topic-based approach to the foundation subjects. Chapter 8, Crossing Curricular Boundaries, discusses ways in which design and technology can enhance and be enhanced by combination with other areas of the curriculum.

The materials prepared by the QCA, *Creativity: Find it, promote it*, contain guidance for each subject, as well as discussing general principles.

> Promoting creativity is a powerful way of engaging pupils with their learning. (Excellence and Enjoyment, *p31*)

Reflective task

How can creativity be promoted within design and technology?

Compare your responses to the 'Creative teaching, creative learning' section later in this chapter.

High standards for all

An equally strong emphasis in the Executive Summary statement, however, is that standards of achievement must not fall as a result of greater curriculum flexibility, and the responsibility for this is placed firmly in the court of schools and teachers.

This is linked in the Executive Summary to a focus on the individual child (and to target-setting arrangements being school- rather than LEA-driven). This is not, however, a step back from a common curriculum for all and, despite the rhetoric about innovation and creativity, the Annex to the document (pp77–9) stresses the support available from existing government-funded and promoted schemes. It would be difficult for the government to suggest that its previous documents had been too restrictive or that they did not contain good advice and structure for teaching. The time has come, however, to move on and for schools to become places of innovation and excellence in their own right.

Design and technology as a subject has an important role in this process. Children explore materials, apply techniques and skills to new situations and solve problems in a way that is meaningful to themselves and in response to those set by the teacher. There is scope for both individual and group projects. Teachers need to promote good design strategies and inspire children to aim to produce high quality products that satisfy the criteria of the task. Evaluation by children of their own and each other's work can help to promote a culture in which new opportunities for excellence can be sought.

See also: Chapter 5, Planning: Differentiation and Inclusion, and Chapter 6, Assessment, Evaluation and Celebration of Learning in Design and Technology, both of which stress the importance of ensuring that all children achieve their potential, regardless of age or gender or family, religious and cultural background or capability.

Although *Excellence and Enjoyment* does not promote a return to the child-centred educational philosophy of the pre-National Curriculum days, there is a measure of recognition that some of the principles that underlay those previous ways of working had lasting value. Entwistle (1970) provided a valuable critique of the issues and principles underlying child-centred education and in his conclusion stresses the importance of children *possessing* the learning which they have been taught:

> *Learning should have* meaning *for the child:*
>
> *To enable the child to grasp the meaning of what he is attempting to learn.*
>
> *The learner needs to possess what he knows.*
>
> *The learner should know how to do something with what he knows.*
>
> *What he knows ought ... to be transferable to novel situations.*
>
> *Learning should be related to the child's own experiences – weaknesses as well as strengths.*
>
> (1970, 203–4)

Excellence and Enjoyment identifies difficulties experienced by some children at transfer between Foundation Stage and Key Stage 1: 4.14–18. This may be related to the more formal, curriculum-centred way of working within Key Stage 1, which may not be appropriate to all children. Design and technology can provide learning opportunities that are more akin to the child-initiated learning that children will have enjoyed in their Foundation Stage settings.

Not alone – support is at hand

Excellence and Enjoyment recognises and promotes the role of support networks in enabling schools and teachers to achieve high standards in teaching and learning. Use the support of expertise available within schools:

Talk to the design and technology co-ordinator.

- **How does the school decide what topics to teach in design and technology?**
- **Does the topic I am planning to teach fit into the whole school plan?**
- **Will the approach I am considering build on the children's prior learning?**
- **What outcomes for future learning are expected from design and technology within this year/term?**
- **How should I assess/record my assessments of pupil learning?**
- **Are there display spaces/boards around school so other classes can see good work?**

Do not be shy to ask this last question. Expect that children will produce work that will be good enough to show others. If you do not, then you are automatically lowering your expectations of pupil attainment.

Talk to colleagues.

- **Have you tried this activity/something similar?**
- **How did you organise the children (whole class, independent or supported groups)?**

- **How did you organise access to resources and tools (on tables at start, at side, by your desk)?**
- **Did you have support from another adult (TA, LSA, parent volunteer)?**
- **Where/how did you store work-in-progress/display finished work?**

Talk to colleagues from other schools – and ask all the questions in both lists above.

Links with secondary schools and technology colleges may provide:

- **support for primary teachers through**
  - **expertise in unfamiliar processes;**
  - **technical support for introduction of new processes;**
  - **advice on unfamiliar equipment and processes;**
- **opportunities for primary children to**
  - **work collaboratively with secondary school pupils;**
  - **use facilities housed in secondary school specialist workshops;**
  - **access expertise of secondary school teachers.**

When engaging in partnerships with secondary colleagues, ensure that it is a two-way process, a collaboration amongst equals. Secondary colleagues will gain from your understanding of:

- **juggling the whole curriculum and its innovations, not just one subject;**
- **cross-curricular working as well as subject-specific knowledge;**
- **how younger children learn.**

Do not be overawed by the large and high-tech equipment in their workshops. You come to the discussion with a secure knowledge about what is appropriate for the children you teach. You are the judge of the benefits to your pupils of their contribution. At the same time, be open to new ideas and to be stretched and challenged by their way of thinking about design and technology.

First establish your common ground.

- **What do you each believe to be the value of design and technology to your pupils?**
- **How do you each understand the process of design, in relation to the age of pupils that you teach?**
- **How do you plan schemes of work, what constraints are there?**
- **How do you assess pupils' learning?**

This establishes the status of all parties as professionals seeking to collaborate. From this secure position, you can then begin to explore some ways of working together, to the mutual benefit of yourselves as teachers and to the benefit of the pupils of both schools.

Reflective task

What about teaching assistants or design and technology technicians:

- **How could they benefit from exchange visits between key stages?**
- **How would this benefit: schools, individual classes, learners?**

Continuing professional development in design and technology

DATA (the Design and Technology Association) the UK design and technology professional association, exists to promote design and technology across all educational stages, from Foundation Stage to Higher Education. They provide support and advice for all teachers and student teachers through a range of publications (journals, magazines, books and loose-leaf format support files) as well as through national conferences. Contact details can be found in the references at the end of the Introduction chapter of this book. Their website **www.data.org.uk** has a list of current publications as well as information on all things realting to design and technology.

If you are interested in becoming a subject leader in design and technology after you have achieved QTS, then DATA can provide details of design and technology Subject Leadership courses that are available at universities across the country. You can opt to gain M-level credits from these courses, if you wish to, by completing extra assessed components.

Creative teaching, creative learning

This section of the chapter explores:

- **the nature of creativity;**
- **creativity within the design and technology curriculum.**

Case study

Two parallel mixed Foundation Stage/Year 1 classes

In Blue Class
The teacher shows the children two cards. One has a large red Santa and the other a large snowman, both cut from paper and stuck onto the front of the cards. The teacher says : Now, my Year 1 children, you are going to make the Santa card. What colour are Santa's clothes? Look, Simon, what colour? Red! Not green or blue ... but red! *(appropriate audience reaction).* Now, my new children, my Reception children, all you have to do is colour snowman's nose and scarf and hat! Can you do that for me? *(Chorus of Yes, led by Year 1 children who know the rules of the game.)* Then Mrs Smith will cut them out for you and stick them on a

card like this and you can try to write your name inside. Don't worry if you can't, we will do it for you. *(Mrs Smith wonders if she is to cut out the Year 1 Santas)* No, no, I'll do that later. They can stick them on, or we will, tomorrow.

Next door, in Red Class:
Teacher: What am I doing? *Child:* Playing with a piece of card! *Teacher:* Am I? What am I doing with it? *Several children:* Folding it. *One child:* Over and over! *Teacher:* Is it, or is it backwards and forwards? *Many children chorus:* Backwards and forwards! *Teacher:* That's right. Shall I do another one? *(Lots of yes's, a couple of no's)* Well, I will because I want you all to watch closely because this is something you can use on your Christmas card you are going to make today! *The children watch intently as the teacher folds up another strip of card.* Now, we have some little pieces of card just like this on your tables, ready for you to fold up just like this. You will need two really good ones, one for Santa and one for Snowman. *(The teacher holds up a small picture of each on thin card).* Do you need to colour Snowman? *(Some no's, 'Cause he's white' – and 'His hat and scarf' from a boy at the side)* Yes, well done, Darinderjit – his hat and his scarf! I wonder what colour they will be? *(children call out out colours but teacher indicates quiet with finger)* They could be striped or spotty *(Child: Or zig-zag)* or rainbow or sky blue pink polka dots with yellow elephants!

Reflective task

If you were a pupil of the Infant School, which class would you like to be in?

Which teacher would make you feel confident in your own ability to design and make a Christmas card?

In which class do the children feel most ownership of the task?

How does teacher talk influence the way the children perceive the task?

How does the organisation of resources reflect this?

What skills will the children in each class be taking forward into their next design and technology project?

How do these differences in the two classes relate to issues of creative teaching and creative learning?

There are multiple views on what creativity *is*, with definitions proffered from such standpoints as psychodynamics, humanism, cognitivism, social constructivism and more. Away from the debate of an inner quality, ethereal (perhaps ephemeral?), designing technology equates to producing something tangible, viewable, open to comment and appraisal. Design and technology educators are interested in the process (how to foster it) but also look to the product: what will they produce (by end of the term). A significant contribution to the understanding of creative learning is Anna Craft's (2001) distinction between everyday 'little c' creativity and the 'big C' creativity of Picasso or Einstein.

There is general agreement that technology is rapidly changing the world in which we live and that teachers need to prepare children to survive and flourish in this ever-changing environment:

Pupils who are creative will be prepared for a rapidly changing world, where they may have to adapt to several careers in a lifetime. (**www.ncaction.org.uk/creativity/ index.htm**)

Design and technology prepares pupils to participate in tomorrow's rapidly changing technologies. (The National Curriculum, 1999, p90)

In our view, all people are capable of creative achievement in some area of activity, provided the conditions are right and they have acquired the relevant knowledge and skills. Moreover, a democratic society should provide opportunities for everyone to succeed according to their own strengths and abilities. (NACCCE, 1999, p28)

By providing rich and varied contexts for pupils to acquire, develop and apply a broad range of knowledge, understanding and skills, the curriculum should enable pupils to think creatively and critically, to solve problems and to make a difference for the better. It should give them the opportunity to become creative, innovative, enterprising and capable of leadership to equip them for their future lives as workers and citizens. It should enable pupils to respond positively to opportunities, challenges and responsibilities, to manage risk and to cope with change and adversity. (The National Curriculum, 1999, pp11–12)

(Compare this last quotation to the design and technology mission statement on page 90 of the National Curriculum (quoted in full in Chapter 2). Similar?)

Wittgenstein (1969) referred to the construction of meanings within separate domains of human endeavour as 'language games', each with their own rules and internal logic from which phenomena are viewed or 'seen as'. Liddament (1991) applied Wittgenstein's concept of language games to designing. In design terms, Wittgenstein's 'seeing as' is the ability to juggle conflicts inherent in the problem-space and find a creative solution that satisfies both user and situational constraints. Successful problem-solving depends on the ability to set up, reason and imagine within a clearly defined mind-space. It is the ability to image fantasy onto reality, what *might be* onto what *is*, and to accept and reason within the fantasy/reality interface inherent in the design task. It has a family resemblance to a game of football in which players with flair can exploit the game potential whilst remaining within the constraints of the game's rules.

If the end-game of design and technology education is to equip young people to be personally creative within a technological society, and indeed to contribute to that society, then, at the end of the day, the aim is to produce the technological innovators of the future. With apologies to Anna Craft, these could be called 'Big I' innovations (Hope, 2004a). The development of creativity can be viewed as a continuum from its earliest beginnings in infancy to its full flowering in adult genius; between the two are the influences that will foster or inhibit that development, one of which is education.

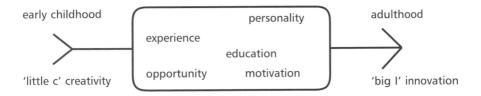

The development of creativity

Creativity is, almost by definition, a non-linear process and so this continuum must not be interpreted as representing anything like a 'from here to there' straight line. A map of the development of even one strand or train of thought would probably look more like this:

The QCA website **ncaction.org.uk/creativity/index.htm** suggests three characteristics of creative action, which are explained as:

1 *Imagination and purpose*: Creative people are purposeful as well as imaginative. Their imaginative activity is directed at achieving an objective (although this objective may change over time).
2 *Originality*: What do we mean by originality? What might we mean by originality when we are talking about pupils' learning? Original in relation to their previous work? Other pupils' work? Work that has gained public recognition?
3 *Value*: Imaginative activity can only be creative if it is of value in relation to its purpose.

Reflective task

How are these three characteristics reflected in the work that children do in design and technology?

Is imagination always purposeful? Do the kinds of activities that we set up in design and technology promote a particular kind of imagination activity and ignore/suppress others?

Discuss with colleagues the questions that the QCA list under 'originality'.

How far do you (and your colleagues) agree with the QCA's definition of the value of creative activity?

If part of the aim in design and technology education is to produce the innovators of the future, 'big I' and not just 'little c', then knowing how to foster such talents is vital. Without creativity and innovation, society stagnates, yet other converses to creativity (often associated with 'Big I' innovations) are anarchy and destruction. The beginnings of truly innovative movements are frequently highly anarchic within themselves, if not destructive of what has gone before. Are teachers brave enough to foster ground-breaking talent?

The juxtaposition of creativity, culture and citizenship as the sub-title of Howe, Davies and Ritchie's (2001) book **Primary design and technology for the future**, strongly links the discussion over creativity with the political agenda. Children are to learn about roles and responsibilities, not their right to protest, take to the streets or lobby Parliament about injustice or object to new technologies, any more than they are to be prepared to up-turn the current social paradigm with ground-breaking innovations – the 'Big I' stuff of dreams and visions of a non-consumerist brave new world or a twenty-first century return to flower-power, free love or a new way of interacting with the environment that does not enhance the country's economic standing on the world stage. Citizens are to be 'useful' and their products to be 'useful'; they are not to turn the status quo upside down.

Reflective task

How does this relate to the claims of **All our Futures** *(NACCCE, 1999, one of the four quotations above) about the opportunities that a democratic society should provide?*

Why do Howe, Davies and Ritchie relate education and politics in this way?

How does design and technology education relate to citizenship education? Think of specific issues relating to new technologies that have hit the headlines because of public protest.

Might it be that the kind of creativity fostering that appears to be on offer within the educational framework in the UK is 'little c creativity', to go hand in hand with 'little c citizenship'?

How does this relate to '[Design and technology] calls for pupils to become creative and autonomous problem-solvers, as individuals and members of a team' ?

A challenge from Toffler

It is no longer sufficient for Johnny to understand the past. It is not even enough for him to understand the present, for the here-and-now environment will soon vanish. Johnny must learn to anticipate the directions and rate of change. He must, to put it technically, learn to make repeated, probabilistic, increasingly long-term assumptions about the future. And so must Johnny's teachers. (Toffler, 1970 p364)

Design capability

This section discusses the nature of the process of designing. This is sometimes referred to as 'the design process' which, unfortunately, can suggest an unintended emphasis on the word 'the', as if there were one, universally agreed process called designing, which, if followed, will ensure success. This is far from the case, and many experts in the field have attempted to analyse this complex process and created diagrams to convey their thinking.

Representing ideas, making models and products

The unpicking of this topic began in Chapter 2, when discussing design and make assignments, and it was noted that, in designing, the word 'model' has a broader meaning than that used in ordinary speech. It means any representation of an idea so this can be an image inside someone's head, a drawing, a discussion which clarifies the idea, a computer-generated image, or a physical representation of a real object (the ordinary use of the word). This last differs from a product in that it is something that does not fully function in the way the real object would. For example, if children make a water wheel out of paper and card, they have made a model. If they make a biscuit or a greetings card, they have made a product. 'Modelling', then, is creating any representation of a product in the head (cognitive) or concrete (on paper or computer screen, from any materials or in any scale other than those appropriate to the real product). The boundaries between models and products can be rather fuzzy, especially taken from the child's perspective, since children are more than happy to believe they have made a 'real torch' from an empty snack tube and some simple circuitry and indeed they have, except that it is not what is bought in the shops. Just to add confusion, the word 'artefact' is often used to denote anything that has been made, whether model or final product.

The next section of this chapter, then, examines:

- **the relationship between cognitive and concrete modelling;**
- **the way in which children design artefacts and imagine future products;**
- **talking, writing and drawing to develop design ideas.**

Practical task

To develop your awareness of the nature of cognitive modelling:

Imagine you are on the beach, sitting on a lounger, on a hot Mediterranean coastline. The sky is blue, the sand is soft and pale gold, the blue sea is lapping against the shore. You reach out your hand for a cooling drink and suck it through the straw.

- *What flavour is it?*
- *What sounds can you hear as you lie there?*

Imagination uses all the senses, including the ability to sense temperature.

Imagine sitting at start of a large tube – a flume ride at a swimming pool. Imagine sliding down it, around the twists and turns, and finally into the splash pool. Imagination can include movement. It also involves memory. If you have no experience of flume rides, this activity would be impossible.

Finally, imagine a favourite chair, turn it around in your mind. See it from the side, then the back, the other side, look at it from on top, far above, be a small creature and crawl underneath it. Small children find this kind of manipulation of objects difficult. They need experience of fiddling with things, disassembling artefacts and products, and making things from construction kits.

What is happening inside a person's head is called *cognitive modelling*. And what they are making with their hands is called *concrete modelling*. As design ideas develop, there is an interaction between the two.

Kimbell et al. (1991) considered the process of designing as a constant interaction between the head and the hands, leading towards the creation of a final product.

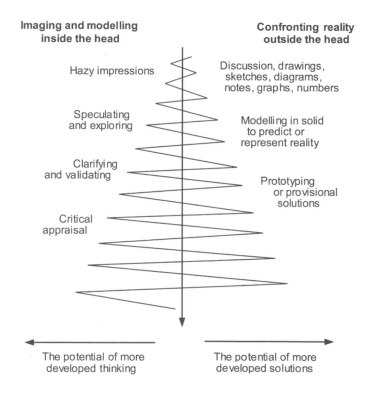

The interactive design process

Practical task

You are making a greeting card for a friend. Think through the processes you will go through. Which are in the head and which through the hands?

Draw and complete the zig-zag diagram:

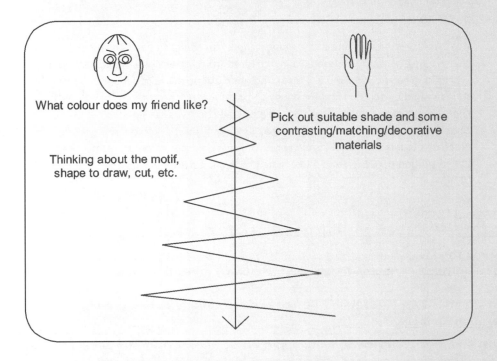

What colour does my friend like?

Pick out suitable shade and some contrasting/matching/decorative materials

Thinking about the motif, shape to draw, cut, etc.

Even in such a simple activity as making a card, you have used both cognitive and concrete modelling interactively, and at times would be doing them simultaneously. Needless to say, people are usually unaware of the process, as it is so natural to the way that all humans solve practical problems.

Eileen Duckworth wrote a book entitled *The having of wonderful ideas* (Duckworth, 1987), and that phrase sums up so much of children's design activity. It is so easy, as an adult, to dismiss their ideas as implausible, unrealistic, to say that they will not work – without appreciating the wonder of the fact that little heads that are still coping with learning their place in the world and their society can yet imagine such wonderful ideas.

One of the examples that Kay Stables uses (Stables, 1992) is of a child who designed a playground sweeper and rubbish collector. The child had devised how this complicated machine would work and explained it to an adult in great detail. Then, at the end of the conversation, the child said, *But it's only pretend, you know.*

Reflective task

Does it matter that the models children make will not really work?

What would you have said in reply to the child?

Kay has little time for those who want to apply an adult's understanding of 'reality' to the thinking of young children. Young children have little problem understanding the world of make-believe, and are less concerned about the hard-facts reality that is so much valued by adults. They are happy to pretend that they have to hand is whatever their imagination decides it will be. Are not all children's toys *pretend*, even 'realistic' ones? How well could you cook Sunday lunch in a plastic microwave, even one with electronic 'controls'? (Think again about the 'waterproof' yellow tissue paper example in the section on design and make assignments in Chapter 2.)

Case study

A day in the life ...
... of a university primary design and technology education tutor

Context: *Year 2 BA (QTS) Year 2 Design and technology option group, Friday afternoon, October.*

Focus: *textiles/cross-cultural; initial input on beadwork from sub-Saharan Africa followed practical workshop using range of 'found objects' that could be used as beads with the question 'How could you do this in school?' to think about while working.*

Carole: *Would you do this like this with children? Would you have it as open-ended as this?*

Tutor: *Yes*

Carole: *In school, at least, in the one I was in last year on placement, they had to design what they were going to make first. Would you just let them get on with it like this?*

Holly [nodding in agreement]: *Yes, same in mine. That's what schools usually do, I think.*

Tutor: *That's based on a very poor model of designing. Adults don't do it. 'I don't know any adult designer that works in such a peculiar way.' That's a quote from Ken Baynes, more or less.*

It is a poor model for several reasons:

- **'Design' in the context in which Carole has used it meant 'draw'. It was not long before the words 'in their books' entered the conversation.**

- **This implies a linear model of the design process (designing → making → evaluating) as separate activities occurring, in all likelihood, in different lessons.**

- **This is not only *not* how adult designers work, but neither does it represent how adults make *anything* (stand in any DIY superstore and count how many customers are walking around with a design drawing in their hands rather than in their heads). So why should children be asked to do it?**

- **It reflects easy management of the activity rather than a good learning environment.**

So why is does it occur in schools?

- **GCSE portfolios demand this kind of separation of process skills to make assessment easier.**

- **The original National Curriculum Orders for design and technology presented the design process skills in a numbered list, which implied that they would occur sequentially in every project.**

- **Primary teachers had not been consulted on the content of the document and were presented with a 'new' subject written in jargon they did not understand and did not have the time, expertise or energy to question.**

- **Primary teachers have had very little on-going professional development in design and technology education, because of the focus on 'basics' and so a folk-design and technology has developed based on the management (linear) model which appears easy to understand and implement.**

Models of design processes

The earliest attempts to analyse how design as a process worked saw it as a linear process, and diagrams like this were produced:

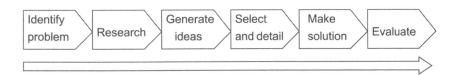

This was quickly criticised as not representing anything close to the reality of how real designers work. What it represents is how large-scale organisations (car manufacturers, for example) manage their research and development departments. It is a model of design *management*, not of design *process*.

Imagine RMH Motors identifying a problem – they are losing ground against the opposition. They research what RJH are doing better (sexier styling, classier advertising) and brainstorm ideas for their counter-attack. They chose their new livery, go into production and employ a team of market researchers to assess the consumer response ...

In 1986, Richard Kimbell produced this much more realistic model of how *designing* occurs:

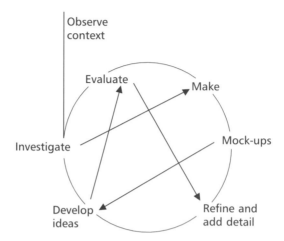

It conveys a sense of the way in which different aspects of the design process inter-relate.

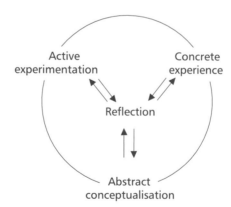

Maggie Rogers and Dominic Clare (1994) placed reflection at the centre of the process of design activity which they saw as a spiral, with reflection as a central spine:

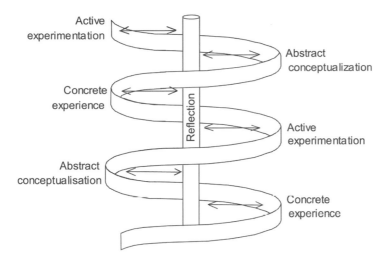

Rogers and Clare's design-process model

In a sense, this is Kimbell's diagram rolling along.

The author's own attempt to explain designing to children resulted in a diagram which appears to be a simplified version of these ideas (Hope, 2000a, 2000b; see next section, Drawing for Designing).

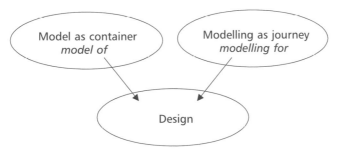

A simplified design process diagram

This was originally conceived as a way of explaining the way drawing can be used for designing and the original diagram appears in the following section in the discussion of drawing. The diagram here is a generalisation of that drawing diagram to all forms of modelling (see Hope, 2004b) 'Modelling' as a technical term in design theory means the representation of a design idea – whether in your head (cognitive modelling) or in writing, drawing, temporary or permanent materials (concrete modelling).

- A *model of* something contains design ideas. It is a *container*, a product (noun) that exists, either in the head of the designer or in the real world.

- Taking ideas on a *journey* through *modelling for* a future project or product is a process (verb) that may happen inside the designer's head, on paper or through interaction with materials, tools and components.

- **The combination of** *container* **and** *journey,* **the** *model of* **and** *modelling for,* **is** *design* **(as either/both noun and verb:** *a design/designing***).**

This kind of indeterminate thinking also underlies Middleton's 'satisficing zone' in his problem-solving diagram that was discussed in Chapter I (see page 8).

Reflective task

How do these attempts to capture the process of designing reflect your own experience as an adult designer?

How do they capture the intuitive designing of young children?

Which most reflects the schemes of work/practice you observe in schools?

If you have chosen differently for your answers to these questions, why do you think this might be?

Is there a difference between what people do naturally, and what children should be taught to do?

Drawing for designing

If you watch a group of people (adults or children) deciding what they will make in response to a design problem, you will see them using their hands as they talk, to try to make more explicit what they are talking about – both to themselves and to the others in the group. Some adults will automatically reach for pencil and paper and sketch what they mean so that the rest of the group can understand what they are talking about and this is a very important design skill that children need to learn. Unfortunately, teachers often formalise this so that all children have to draw their ideas before they are allowed to start making anything. This can be counter-productive, as the children will see the drawing merely as a 'permission ticket' that they have to complete before being allowed to get on with the real business of designing. Drawing is a powerful means of modelling ideas. It is not, however, an essential part of every design and technology project, nor is it always the best way to start.

Bridget Egan (1999) identified the need for children to understand the purpose of the drawing as a means of clarifying and progressing design ideas.

Drawing can be used in design and technology lessons for:

- **recording observations of existing products;**
- **clarifying the design problem;**
- **generating possibilities;**
- **developing design ideas;**
- **working out how parts might fit together;**
- **planning decorative finishes;**
- **finalising a possible design proposal;**
- **communicating design ideas to others.**

Practical task

To highlight the importance of close observation of structures and mechanisms:

You are planning a topic on playgrounds. Jot down specific activities to develop children's ability to draw for design and technology, observing and recording how parts:

- *fit together, and*
- *move in relation to each other*

on a range of playground equipment (swings, slides, roundabouts, see-saws, etc.).

(Children will see the shape of the whole structure but not see the way these interact.)

Research conducted by the author (Hope, 2000a, 2000b) showed that in Key Stage I children can use drawing to clarify for themselves the nature of the task – but will be less able to use drawing as a means of developing their design ideas. By the beginning of Key Stage 2, children will be able to understand that design is like a journey and that drawings can contain ideas that form part of that journey. A key feature in enabling children to make this leap of understanding is to make explicit to them that the purpose of the design drawing is to develop ideas.

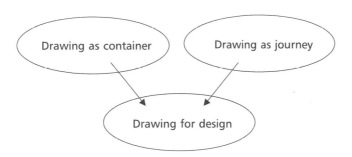

The purpose of drawing

Journey's end is the finished product. Drawing can support thinking and help to clarify ideas as they develop. Real design drawings are scruffy affairs. They have crossings out, false starts, words written on them at angles. Real design drawings get covered in glue and thrown in the bin at the end of the lesson. Pictures that go on the wall labelled 'Our Designs' have rarely acted as a means to develop design thinking. They convey no sense of the dynamism of the interaction of creative thought with hand and eye and someone else's bright idea. Of the list of eight uses of drawing in design and technology above, their only function is in communicating design ideas to others. There is nothing wrong with this, as long as this is not thought of as using drawing to support designing.

Progression in using drawing for designing

In Foundation Stage, children will have been encouraged to use a combination of drawing and writing to record their story ideas as part of their emergent literacy. They move comfortably between drawing and using letters, single words and letter-like symbols to represent and place-mark their ideas. This flexibility needs nurturing as this is not just the foundations for writing, but also for developing design ideas on paper.

Building on this capability, teachers can ask Year 1 children to make a narrative drawing from which they will go and make a product. For example, they can be asked to draw Teddy sitting on a new chair and to think really carefully about the kind of chair he would like as they are going to make a model of it later. Developing their observational drawing ability is also important and this can be part of the work of investigating familiar products. Observational drawing involves careful looking and understanding how parts of products fit together and even if children find it difficult to record the relationships between parts of the object, the processes of analysis and synthesis are important design skills that need to be developed.

By Year 2 most children will be able to draw an object that they wish to make without needing the supporting framework of the narrative context. Encouraging children to discuss the drawings will clarify their thinking and focus their minds on the task in hand. It will also aid the development of empathy and understanding of user needs as they share their perspectives with each other and realize that others have different ideas to their own. The children will swap and share ideas freely, just like adults. Be aware, however, that doing a drawing before making does not always function in a young child's mind as a means of clarifying design ideas. Unless the children are taught the purpose of the drawing, it is a more likely to function as a kind of passport to getting their hands on the real stuff, especially if there is glitter, feathers or fur fabric available! Children rarely value these design drawings and will throw them in the bin if they are on loose paper. However, if they are in books, children will spend more time improving their drawing because they want it to be their best work to show the teacher, rather than using drawing to develop design thinking. Any evaluation happening here is of the drawing not of the design idea. This might be happening in the child's head as a parallel process while neatly redrawing their first idea. They might, alternatively, draw several totally different ideas and reject them all once they get to collect the materials. This is the acid test of whether the child has been using the drawing as a genuine design tool or not. If the majority of your class are making something that has little resemblance to their drawings, then you need to teach them the *purpose of the drawing*: to develop design ideas. And model it. Show children how to use drawing to support design thinking. They will not guess. Design drawings do not feature in books to which children have access.

Practical task

Use drawing and writing to design a mechanical salt cellar that delivers exactly the right amount of salt on your chips.

When you have finished, answer the following questions:

1 *How many false starts did you have?*
2 *How many drawings did you cross out or erase parts of?*
3 *Did you record one good idea and develop it, or record several ideas as quick sketches to help decide which was viable?*
4 *What parts of your design did you record in writing? Drawing?*
5 *How much of the designing happened in your head without drawing or writing anything?*
6 *Did you use drawing, writing, both or neither to clarify the task and how the product would work?*
7 *Can you detect a design journey within your drawing/writing as you developed your ideas?*
8 *Have you ended up with a working drawing that would communicate your ideas to someone else, or does it place-mark your ideas for your own benefit?*
9 *What would you expect a child to produce on paper in response to this task?*
10 *Are teachers' assumptions/expectations of children's use of drawing in design and technology sometimes somewhat unrealistic?*

By the time they move into Key Stage 2, children have a greater fluidity in their understanding of the possible functions of drawings within a design task. This is paralleled in their art work by a greater facility in adopting different genres for different purposes. They can produce a range of quick sketches of several possible ideas or develop a single 'good idea' some way towards resolution. They can evaluate the feasibility of their designs by looking at the materials that the teacher has provided and put a tick by the drawings that could be made with those materials, choose which design to make, collect the materials and make it. They can also start from the materials on offer and draw something that can be made with them, but are unlikely to record more than one idea. Children of this age can label their drawings to indicate parts and materials, so as the year progresses, they can learn to write a list of the materials they will need next to their drawings of their design ideas, so that by Year 4 they can predict whether or not a good idea can be made easily and adapt their plans according to the resources available. Although much younger children do this too, by Year 4 children are sufficiently meta-cognitively aware to give account of their reasons for doing so.

Year 5s should be able to think of several possibilities, discuss some, draw some, and identify parts and techniques that might need some practice before making the final piece. They can think about how they would make the product and start to incorporate this into a plan that includes a simple working diagram. They can redraw small detailed parts larger, draw the product from different viewpoints, jot down how they will make certain parts. They can discuss and share their ideas about fastenings, hinges and so on with friends and discuss the viability of the options. They can use other resources, such as catalogues, to inform discussion, and create a final working drawing of a product that they would like to make.

By the time children are entering Year 6, they have the ability to work in a range of materials, and can become realistic about what is possible in the materials provided and have a sense of what can be achieved within the time available. They are increasingly aware of the need to communicate clearly to others. They can be asked to swap their final drawing with a friend (it is easier to evaluate someone else's than your own). Ask them to discuss each other's drawings, focusing on:

- **Does it convey a sense of the object to be made or does it rely on shared meanings?**
- **Is it clear enough for someone else to make the product?**
- **Does it specify techniques, tools and equipment as well as materials?**
- **Is there sufficient level of detail, but not inappropriately over-detailed?**
- **Are the materials suitable, would they be available in the primary classroom?**
- **Could it be made within a suitable timeframe, using the techniques specified?**

These are important things to teach children about planning their products from Year 4 on. Up to this age children can use drawing to generate ideas and support their thinking about what they would like to make, but do not see the need to make it clear enough for someone else to read, or even for themselves to follow next lesson.

Finally, do not insist that children stick rigidly to their plans or criticise their drawings if they are unrealistic by adult standards. Remember that for the stage of development that they are at, children are often being asked to plan to make a complex object to be made in unfamiliar materials with untried techniques.

Practical task

What about writing?

Create an annotated list of ways in which writing can be used to support the development of design ideas.

This topic is developed under 'Literacy Links' in Chapter 8.

Other applications of the container/journey metaphor:
This chapter has included two different applications of the author's container/ journey diagram – one for modelling and one for drawing. They depend on the use of words that are both products (nouns) and processes (verbs). What other product/process words can be fitted into this pattern and what would be the third, combination word, if one exists?

Construction kits

Construction kits are a common feature of Foundation Stage and Year 1 classrooms, usually as child-initiated activity and not supported by adult guidance or even supervision, except to re-enforce safety rules. Through the use of construction kits, children learn:

- **fine hand–eye co-ordination and motor control of fingers;**
- **the basic structures of vehicles, houses and other familiar objects;**
- **to abstract from these objects their basic topological features;**
- **to work within restrictions of size, shape and joining mechanism;**
- **control over these restrictions, leading to a search for creative solutions;**
- **a sense of achievement through creating something unique that achieves a desired purpose.**

Children have greatest access to a range of construction kits in their earliest years of schooling. For historical and cultural reasons, related to the definitions and divisions of 'work' and 'play' inherent in classrooms, opportunities for developing children's design learning through construction kits are missed. They form part of the staple of child-initiated activity. Teachers rarely get involved in guiding the activities or teaching skills through the use of the kits and thus, in the children's minds, these are their free-time activities and they become quite resistant to teacher involvement in their play.

The advantage of construction kits as a design medium is that:

- **they enable children to engage in three-dimensional modelling of design ideas;**
- **being temporary and non-consumable, ideas can be readily changed and adapted;**
- **parts are rigid, ready-made and fit together accurately, with no need to wait for glue to dry;**
- **the resulting products can be used/played with/experimented on;**
- **they can be combined with other products (see below).**

The disadvantages are that:

- **the pieces are not interchangeable between sets (and even sometimes between different ranges from the same manufacturer);**
- **losing key pieces can limit the possibilities of the whole set;**
- **the pieces are set lengths with set fixing techniques, which limits the applicability of the kit to specific kinds of projects (e.g. vehicles);**
- **children and teachers frequently view them as toys rather than design media.**

EXAMPLE

The following represents an attempt by an ITE tutor to extend students' appreciation of the potential of construction kits in the primary classroom. The students are working in groups of four.

Stage 1:
One construction kit placed on each table and students invited to explore what they can do with the kit they have been given.

Result:
Enthusiastic individual making, some discussion and showing each other what they have made.

First reactions to tutor-led feedback time to identify skills used:
Finding out what the pieces do and how they fit together. Thinking what I could make with it/what it looked like it could be made into.
Remembering what my children use this kit for/what I have observed children in nursery do with it.

Pushed a little further:
Imagination, ideas, trying things out.
Designing? Yes, suppose so, for younger children anyway (this comment can be allowed to pass at this stage.)

Stage 2: Everyone has been working individually although parallel to each other. That is what young children do. Now the students are to move to a different construction kit and make one product between them as a group.

Feedback time:
Identified skills such as team-work, negotiation, discussion, compromise, communication skills, transfer of skills and ideas from one kit to another, realisation that different kits have different possibilities and limitations, leading to re-evaluation of knowledge and application of skills.

With children:
At what age could you insist that a group product resulted from the activity? After some discussion, the students agreed this could be done across Key Stages 1 and 2, depending on the topic and the parameters.

Stage 3: Introduction of parameters:
The students are to make something that can move upwards. At what age could you limit parameters in this way and expect children to have come up with a solution that satisfied the criteria? Again, Key Stage 1 was suggested, but there was some uncertainty whether this was appropriate or whether children this young should still be free-playing with construction kits. The tutor suggested that this should not be considered as an either/or but that both free-play and teacher-initiated tasks were appropriate in Key Stage 1. The students agreed with this. One asked: what sort of things would you ask Year 1 to make? Bridges to span two tables, houses or vehicles for range of story characters, which leads on to …

Stage 4: Passengers: A selection of teddies and dolls. Each group of students is to choose one toy. They are to use the construction kit to send that toy into space (launcher to be included).

Reflective questions:
How did the addition of a passenger change the task?
How could you use the limitation of parameters/inclusion of other products to extend the use of construction kits in purposeful design activities in Key Stage 2? See Chapter 7 sections on 'Structures, Moving Things' and 'Mechanisms and Control' and think about contexts for using construction kits with older children.

Framework for teaching and learning design and technology:

a summary of key points

In this chapter you have been introduced to the framework within which teaching and learning in design and technology is placed in relation to:

____ *the principles outlined in The National Primary Strategy* **Excellence and Enjoyment,** *and government expectations of the way teaching and learning is to be developing;*

____ *the perspectives of design theorists and the QCA materials* **Creativity: find it, promote it** *to the promotion of both* **creative teaching** *and* **creative learning;**

____ *the cognitive processes that underlie* **design capability** *and which will be part of all work in design and technology lessons.*

References

Craft, A (2001) 'Little c' creativity in Craft, A, Jeffrey, B and Leibling, M *Creativity in education.* London: Continuum.

DfEE (2003) *Excellence and enjoyment: a strategy for primary schools.* London: DfEE (Department for Education and Employment).

Duckworth, E (1987) 'The having of wonderful ideas' and other essays on teaching and learning. New York: Teachers College Press.

Egan, BA (1999) Children talking about designing: a comparison of Year 1 and Year 6 children's perceptions of the purpose/uses of drawing as part of the design process, in Juster, NP (ed) *The continuum of design education.* Proceedings of the 21st SEED Annual Conference and 6th Annual Conference on Product Design Education, pp111–17.

Entwistle, H (1970) *Child-centred Education.* London: Methuen.

Hope, G (2000a) Beyond 'draw one and make it', in Kimbell, R (ed) *Proceedings,* Design and Technology International Millennium Conference 2000. Warwickshire: The Design & Technology Association.

Hope, G (2000b) Beyond their capability? Drawing, designing and the young child. Journal of Design and Technology Education, 5 (2) pp106–114.

Hope, G (2004a) 'Little c' creativity and 'Big I' innovation within the context of design and technology education, in Norman, E W L, Spendlove, D, Grover, P and Mitchel, A, *Creativity and Innovation: DATA International Research Conference 2004*; Wellesbourne, Warwickshire: DATA (Design & Technology Association).

Hope, G (2004b) *Teaching design and technology 3–11*. London: Continuum.

Howe, A, Davies, D and Ritchie, R (2001) *Primary design and technology for the future: creativity, culture and citizenship*. London: David Fulton Publishers.

Kimbell, R (1986) *Craft, design and technology*. Buckingham: The Open University Press.

Kimbell, R, Stables, K, Wheeler, T, Wosniak, A, and Kelly, V (1991) *The assessment of performance in design and technology*. London: Schools Examinations and Assessment Council.

Liddament, T (1991) Design talk, in *Design & Technology Teaching*, 23(2) pp100–10. Stoke-on-Trent: Trentham Books.

NACCCE (National Advisory Committee on Creative and Cultural Education) (1999) *All our futures: creativity, culture and education*. Sudbury, Suffolk: Department for Education and Employment.

Rogers, M and Clare, D (1994) The Process Diary: developing capability within National Curriculum design and technology – some initial findings, in *Conference proceedings*, International Design and Technology Education Research Conference (IDATER94). Loughborough University: Department of Design and Technology.

Stables, K (1992) The role of fantasy in contexualising and resourcing design and technological activity, in *Conference proceedings*, International Design and Technology Education Research Conference (IDATER92). Loughborough University: Department of Design and Technology.

Toffler, A (1970) *Future shock*. London: The Bodley Head.

Wittgenstein, L (1969) *Philosophical Investigations: The Blue Book; The Brown Book*. Oxford: Basil Blackwell.

4 PROGRESSION IN DESIGN AND TECHNOLOGY LEARNING

Children's developing autonomy and increasing sophistication in approaches to designing is the key content of this chapter, alongside the specific expectations for Key Stages 1 and 2. As well as detailing the essential knowledge, skills and understanding that children should be able to grasp at various stages in their primary school career (as indicated in Chapter 2), this chapter will give guidance to enable teachers to ensure progression of learning opportunities.

In this chapter you will learn about:

* *aspects of child development that relate to design and technology;*

* *learning design and technology within the Foundation Stage;*

* *the development of evaluating, making and designing skills in Key Stages 1 and 2;*

* *expectations at Key Stage 3.*

Cognitive and physical development

This chapter begins from a typical and familiar scenario: four children at home engage sequentially in what Bateson and Martin call *pointless fun* (2000, p196).

Case study

Late afternoon in a suburban household

Tommy, the baby, picks up a discarded plastic drinks bottle and bangs it on the floor, it rolls away. His mother rolls it back and baby squeals with delight, pushes it back towards smiling Mummy, then wants it rolled back to roll again. It is left in the middle of the floor.

Jenny, the pre-schooler, picks up the bottle and bangs it on the floor and the arm of the sofa. She then goes around banging everything, saying 'Bang bang! Bang, bang!' She starts to sing 'Bob the Builder', throws the bottle onto the sofa and goes to the rack by the television and searches through the videos.

Hayleigh, just home from second day in her new Year 1 class, picks up the bottle and opens it to see if there is any drink inside. Empties out what there is and starts rummaging in the larder cupboard. Mum says 'What are you doing?' 'Making a rain stick like Mrs Hughes. We have to be stop what we're doing, sit down if we're standing up, not a word and listen to what she says. Have you got some dried beans I could have?' Mum suggests something that won't get soggy would be better and they find some plastic beads and on goes the music and she's dancing.

Big brother Alex comes in from football, kicks the bottle across the floor: 'Goal!' as it hits the wall. Later he's playing with his pool cue, crawling around the floor, chasing a ball, hitting out from under the sofa or wherever it hides. At low level, from the other end of the room, he spies the bottle. He quickly gets a pair of scissors and cuts the end off: goal.

Each of the children in the example above has responded to a found object in a different and increasingly sophisticated way.

Tommy, the baby, is discovering properties of rounded objects and is practising making them roll across the floor in a predetermined direction. He is also experiencing two of the most important drivers in play, curiosity and creativity: pleasure and response from others.

These skills in relation to sensing the environment are summarised in Geoffrey Harrison's book *The continuum for design education for engineering* (2001) as:

- **discovering they can rearrange it;**
- **problem-solving by trial and error;**
- **making things happen;**
- **recognising diversity in materials;**
- **meeting problems;**
- **thinking about thinking.**

Jenny, the pre-schooler, is at the stage of metaphorical transfer. She already knows that the neck end of the bottle fits nicely in the hand and the other end makes a pleasurable thump on a range of hard surfaces. *Bob the Builder* is her favourite video right now, since Nanna bought it for her last Friday. Playing with her impromptu prop has sparked off her memory of the song and the video, and using language to establish connection between areas of experience (Wells, 1986, p111). She can competently find the right video, put it in the player and press the play button.

Harrison's summary of the Foundation Stage child is:

- **riding a bicycle as a complex but entirely intuitive control operation;**
- **just beginning to make sense of a technological world;**
- **gaining confidence;**
- **familiarity with materials, which are seen as a resource to be used;**
- **the 'back of the envelope' and the pencil as aids to thinking;**
- **beginning to learn the skills of learning.**

Hayleigh, new to Year 1, is making sense of her new world in a more formal classroom setting. The new rules and events of the day fill her mind. She has, in Wells' words, 'already acquired a considerable degree of competence as a purposeful actor and as effective communicator' (Wells, 1986, p68) and is making the transition from one stage of her life to the next.

Seeing the bottle and its potential helps Hayleigh to role-play one of these new aspects and by making it into something that Mrs Hughes uses helps this assimilation process. But something else is going on too: in her last class, she made musical instruments and put dried beans in empty yoghurt-based drink bottles. She is unconcerned about the fact that beans will go soggy in this wet and sticky bottle. (She knows the effect of water on beans but she's into fantasy play and the property of the beans can be pretended too.) As an adult, Mum wants the product to work properly, incongruously since her daughter's interest will be transitory and both bottle and beans would be in the bin by bedtime. Hayleigh has made imaginative connections between past experiences of making things out of bottles and her new experience in Mrs Hughes' class. She uses the bottle as part of a dancing game before abandoning it because she has got Mrs. Hughes and her rainstick out of her system now and can go and relax into another game.

Harrison's 6-year-old:

- **can successfully design and make functional models;**
- **designing and decision-making are almost entirely intuitive;**
- **is becoming more aware of engineering surroundings and as part of the environment;**
- **is beginning to develop concepts such as rigidity, stability, precision;**
- **shows curiosity;**
- **realises that if they are going to make something, they are going to have to think.**

Alex also brings his immediate out-of-home experience to his perception of the bottle but he has an invented game of his own he wants to play – pool football, which combines the concepts of table football, pinball and pool, only it is played on the floor and the furniture provides the obstacles around and under which to chase the ball. Although it is quite a fun game, it needs a target. As he spies the plastic bottle, he remembers his initial response to it, and realises its potential. Two things happen in Alex's head – he is metacognitively able to recall, deconstruct, analyse and evaluate his previous mental process, and he is able to see potential in the bottle as a deconstructed object. All three of his younger siblings have used the bottle as a complete entity. Alex is able to see the application of an abstract part of the object and has the manual skill to fashion it into something that will serve his purpose. Bruner calls this skill the ability to build 'possible castles' from what people see around them (Bruner, 1986, p44), the skill of adults to create mental worlds of mathematics, scientific theory, poetry and art.

Alex is using the bottle for the topological properties of only part of the whole form and knows enough about the material properties of plastic bottles to know that it will sustain his cutting and shaping. He is not yet mature enough, however, to perceive that whichever of his younger siblings had filled it with beads might have prior rights to the bottle and that he should care about his appropriation of it. If trouble comes, he can say sorry, make a better one, or it will be their bedtime and by tomorrow they will forget. After all, there is a backlog of similar appropriation of his things that can be invoked should Mum get involved.

Harrison's list of a child's developing engineering capability through the upper primary years is impressively long:

- **growth of technical language developing because it is essential;**
- **engineering in support of science – making something work before understanding why it works;**
- **science in support of engineering – experimental methods;**
- **active learning links with the engineering environment;**
- **engineering – a special kind of understanding;**
- **tacit technological concepts of energy sources, power transmission and efficiency;**
- **developing an intuitive understanding of vectors;**
- **strategies for problem-solving and design becoming more explicit – technology transfer;**
- **learning strategies for problem-solving – combining understanding with strategies for thinking;**
- **teamwork more effective;**
- **knows computers can provide a resource for understanding and thinking;**
- **safety awareness;**
- **judging and evaluating their own work;**
- **tacit understanding: the seeds of technological concepts are sown, germination will come through a more structured learning experience in Key Stage 3.**

Each child in the suburban family, Tommy, Jenny, Hayleigh and Alex, has learnt and extended their design skills, developed their interaction with the made environment and placed their activity within their developing social world. The skills, knowledge and understandings that have been displayed by each child in their interaction with this empty plastic bottle could be analysed on many fronts. It would be a false move to try to correlate these with aspects of design and technology lessons, but underlying skills relating to designing, making and exploiting the potential of found or recycled objects are, of course, exactly those which teachers encourage and want children to develop through learning design and technology in school.

Janet Moyles, in *Just playing* (1989, ch 5), links play with creativity and problem-solving with science, technology and art, as well seeing the importance of language development and symbolic systems (e.g. painting and model making) as essential for cognitive growth. She quotes Pluckrose (1984) as claiming that the ability to select materials and understand which one will give the desired result underlies aesthetics and then goes on to say:

> *Science and technology can easily intermingle with art for young children but what must be emphasised is that the processes of design, choice, shared meanings, interpretation … were far more important than … what transpired eventually to be a*

successful [product]. This is where problem-solving and creativity meet but equally diverge. (1989, p80)

Reflective task

Why is this last, insightful, sentence important for learning within design and technology in school?

How does Moyles' position, as demonstrated in the whole quotation, fit with adult (teachers') desire for a finished 'quality product' at the end of the lesson?

In the following tables, the four children's interactions with the bottle have been analysed and tabulated under six headings:

1 Evaluation of the object, seeing its potential
2 Modelling skills
3 Use of material properties
4 Processes and techniques
5 Developing autonomy
6 Metacognition and self-awareness.

All of these skills form part of the National Curriculum requirements for teaching and learning design and technology. The word 'designing' has not been included in the list because all of these skills are just aspects of that overarching capability.

Evaluation of the object, seeing its potential			
Baby	**Pre-schooler**	**Key Stage 1**	**Mid-Key Stage 2**
Can be handled, used to make noise, has potential for game with adult	Its metaphorical similarities with ideas from different contexts can be exploited	Can be adapted and combined with other objects to use for a different purpose	Can be altered to become a component for a different situation or purpose.

Modelling skills			
Baby	**Pre-schooler**	**Key Stage 1**	**Mid-Key Stage 2**
Learning and internalising the physical properties of found objects	Can make one object stand for another for which physical similarities are perceived	Can see how an object can be adapted or combined with other objects to make an object with a different purpose	Can deconstruct an object into its material and topological properties in order to see their potential as materials or components of another object with a different purpose

Use of material properties			
Baby	**Pre-schooler**	**Key Stage I**	**Mid-Key Stage 2**
Learning, sorting and classifying the material properties of objects found in the environment	Exploiting knowledge of materials and objects in extending the boundaries of the object's potential into fantasy realms	Willing to exploit, ignore or ascribe other material properties to an object to fit it to its intended purpose	Accurate knowledge and understanding of the object's material properties is important for it to perform its new function satisfactorily

Process and techniques			
Baby	**Pre-schooler**	**Key Stage I**	**Mid-Key Stage 2**
Developing hand–eye co-ordination, gross and fine motor skills	Combining gross motor skills in the manipulation of objects	Developing fine motor skills and accurate hand–eye co-ordination to manipulate small objects	Using ability to cut and shape materials to change objects from one form to another

Developing autonomy			
Baby	**Pre-schooler**	**Key Stage I**	**Mid-Key Stage 2**
Looks to others (e.g. mother) for support and confirmation of learning experience	Developing own internal world based on experiences and observations	Combining objects and experiences that are separated in time and context to serve a present inner need or purpose	Combining range of aspects of outer social worlds and inner imaginary constructs to create new autonomous activity

Metacognition and self-awareness			
Baby	**Pre-schooler**	**Key Stage I**	**Mid-Key Stage 2**
Aware of self and own body in space as actor on objects and of initiator of noise, movement and social interaction	Developing ability to place self in variety of roles for which found objects can serve as play props	Able to reflect on own role in experiences and adapt found objects into role play props to experiment with possibilities and solutions to problems and dilemmas	Can analyse own previous thinking and relate this to potential in new situations and possibilities presented by material and topological properties of found objects

Reflective task

How does this relate to design and technology?

Summarise holistically the skills that each child is developing, e.g. the baby can grasp objects, explore their physical properties and perceive their potential for games with adults. He is learning the physical properties of a range of objects and ...

In their response to the bottle, each child was using a range of both cognitive and physical skills, the combination of which is the essence of design capability (see Kimbell et al.'s diagram in Chapter 3). Beginning with Jenny, the pre-schooler, who represents Foundation Stage children, the design capability skills that each child displays can be unpicked under two headings: cognitive and physical skills.

Cognitive skills

Jenny sees the metaphorical similarities between the noise she makes with the bottle and Bob the Builder's hammering. The ability to combine apparently disparate concepts, ideas and objects and to apply them in new situations is the essence of human creativity and, hence, of design capability. Jenny has already surpassed the intellectual capability of all non-human primates in that she can extend the boundaries of the object's potential into the realm of story, imagination and fantasy that is forming part of her internal world and frame of reference. Her experience of role play areas in pre-school will build on that ability, and extend it to encompass the need to negotiate with others within the play space, forming the foundational skills for teamwork. The ability to see potential of objects and ideas in other, apparently unconnected, contexts will be used by her teachers when they supply recycled materials for designing and making. She moves seamlessly into and out of the role of 'being' Bob the Builder. This will form the basis of her developing empathy with others that will inform her ability to design something for someone else. She will gain experience of that in her pre-school setting when she makes festival cards and gifts.

Hayleigh already knows that recycled materials can be adapted and combined with other objects for a different purpose because she has experience of doing this already at pre-school. Her willingness to ascribe other material properties to an object to fit it to its intended purpose had been encouraged when it was made clear to her that she was expected to choose the corrugated card for the Little Pig's 'wooden' house. Moyles reports a group of 7-year-olds struggling to make a realistic raincoat for a doll, that developed from the desire to make the doll look pretty to grappling with the functional aspects, including how to keep the doll's legs and feet dry (Moyles, 1989, p79). Hayleigh has not yet reached the stage of needing to satisfy the requirements of realism. So she was confused as to why she could not choose the pink sticky paper for Teddy's umbrella and why Miss Cunningham ('our new helper') gave her a funny look when she said 'because my brelly's pink' and just handed her the piece of crumpled yellow plastic bag. This comment, incidentally, illustrated Hayleigh's skill in combining objects and experiences that are separated in time and context to serve a present inner need or purpose as well as demonstrating her ability to abstract salient features of one object and apply it to a new context. As she experiments with the possibilities presented by the multiple properties of found objects and materials, she will be able to fine tune her adaptations of them to create appropriate solutions to design problems and opportunities.

Alex has become a quite sophisticated user of found objects and has no qualms about adapting the bottle for his present purpose. He can mentally deconstruct the bottle into its material and topological properties and demonstrates his knowledge and understanding of its properties in order to adapt it to its new function.

He has had much experience at school of making cardboard boxes, card tubes and plastic cartons into a whole range of products to which metaphorical labels have been applied, based on their similarity with objects in the real world – whether the 'racer' from a milk carton and coffee jar lids or the 'fun fair ride' based on a cheese box and a CD ROM. Working with his friends to combine aspects of the outer social world with that of the imagination enables the construction of a shared designed world that inhabits that middle ground between fantasy and reality with socially agreed rules about which properties of the product need to be real and which can be ascribed.

By the end of Key Stage 2, Alex's desire for 'reality' will all but overpower his willingness to ascribe imaginary properties to objects and materials as his metaphorical capabilities move into the purely conceptual realm. His ability to mentally manipulate ideas, form and properties of objects will depend largely on the richness of experience he has had with real objects and materials during his childhood years. In other words, his capability as a designer, whether this be related to technology, commerce, home-making, or any other field of human endeavour, will depend on those early experiences of playing with found objects.

Physical skills

Returning to Jenny, the pre-schooler, who is combining gross motor skills in the manipulation of objects, she can grasp, turn, lift, twist the bottle in relation to herself and the furniture. She is aware of her own body in space and can move the bottle as an extension of her own hand. This is a base skill for using a paintbrush, pencil, needle or saw. Her awareness of herself in space gives her a sense of physical proportion and an intuitive sense of scale, although she will freely disregard this in her playing and toys will be given roles and play-props used as if they had correct scale with respect to each other. Her fine motor skills are developing; she can locate and press the correct button on the video player. She has already an expectation of being able to control and use technology for her own purposes.

Hayleigh's fine motor skills include the ability to remove the twist-cap from the bottle as a matter of course. Her fingers have gained in strength as they have grown: her bones have hardened and her muscles and tendons can accurately move them into a wide range of positions, including the use of scissors and pencils, fitting together ever smaller pieces of construction kits, threading beads and buttons onto needle and thread. This process will not, however be complete for many years, and throughout her schooling she will continue to develop her ability to co-ordinate her hand movements to the focus of her eyes. This co-ordination develops in conjunction with her ability to accurately distinguish and name small objects by sight alone. She no longer needs to handle objects in order to appreciate their physical properties as she has sufficient experience to see whether something is hard, squashy or will fit inside another, although accurate estimates of the behaviour of liquids may still give problems. Thus she can choose quickly the object or materials to suit her purpose, although, as discussed above, she may not use the physical property of a material as the basis for her choice.

Alex has considerable strength and flexibility in his hands. He also knows to a fair degree of accuracy how much pressure needs to be applied in order to cut and shape particular materials. His control of his hand muscles enables him to control the scissors to accurately cut the plastic bottle into the correct shape for his purposes. This enables a far better finish on his design work. No longer need he be content with approximation to size and contour, as he can cut and shape using a range of tools. He is unlikely to be content with his progress. In fact, he is more likely to be growing in frustration at his inability to produce artefacts to the level of precision that he desires. This may lead to a general dissatisfaction with all design activities, as he is unable to accept an approximation of his ideas.

As Alex moves into the top of Key Stage 2 he is likely to begin to see himself as either someone who enjoys making things or as someone who is not very good at it. His teacher's role in encouraging evaluative discussion about the things he has made might be crucial. Clearly identifying the parts that give dissatisfaction and initiating an honest discussion about what can reasonably be expected with the tools, equipment and materials on offer in the classroom set-up may allay his fears that what he can do is 'no good'.

Progression within the National Curriculum for design and technology

Chapter 2 outlined the structure of the National Curriculum for design and technology, indicating the Knowledge, Skills and Understanding expected at each key stage, and discussing the way in which this is to be taught through investigating existing products, focused practical tasks and design and make assignments. This section of the present chapter will examine the development of children's design capability and understanding of technology across Key Stages 1 and 2. This is summarised in the National Curriculum as Level Descriptors and can be found in the back cover section of the National Curriculum for Key Stages 1 and 2, page 25.

Practical task

Read the Level Descriptors for levels 1–6. They do not relate directly to school years. Very few Year 6 children will be working at level 6, rather, this represents the possible attainment of the highest achieving children in Year 6. Conversely, many children have already achieved level 1 on entry to Year 1 but, for many, this will be achieved within their first few months in Key Stage 1. Some, of course, will still be working within this level on transition to Key Stage 2. Depending on your experience of primary-aged children, you should be able to recognise the process skills described in the Level Descriptors. Make a note of the ages of the children that you have observed working at particular levels. As with all curriculum subjects, there will be a big range of attainment within each class.

If you have access to a Year 3 or Year 4 class, focus on level 3. Many children will achieve level 3 within these two years, some will still be working at level 2 (and a few even will still be working at level 1 in some aspects of their work) but you may well be able to identify aspects of level 4 amongst the work of the most able children.

How would knowledge of these Level Descriptors help you to move the children forward in their acquisition of design and technology skills? Make specific notes on one or two children you have observed.

Chapter 6 will return to the National Curriculum Level Descriptors in the context of assessment. Here they will be related to expectations of Knowledge, Skills and Understanding within the context of the Breadth of Study (see Chapter 2) in each key stage. This section begins with a brief introduction to the Foundation Stage in order to indicate the kinds of activities and ways of working that children will experience and that form the basis of design and technology at Key Stage I. The expectations of Key Stage I are outlined, stressing the importance of developing children's confidence and capability with simple tools, developing evaluative and reflective skills and their ability to juggle both reality and fantasy whilst developing their design ideas. Suitable topics for specifically design and technology work and cross-curricular learning are suggested and detailed examples given.

In Key Stage 2, children are more able to become involved in longer projects sustained across several lessons, and are developing perspectives beyond the immediate environment of family, home and school. Their increased capability with tools and sense of responsibility towards others enables a wider range of tools and equipment to be used. Again, suggestions for suitable topics and examples are given.

Beyond the end of the primary phase into Key Stage 3, children are quickly absorbed into a world of rigid timetables, dedicated workshops and unfamiliar equipment. How well they cope with this transition depends not only on the welcoming nature of the secondary school but on the preparation of the primary school. How do teachers enable these blossoming designers to flourish in their new world? This section gives some insights into secondary practice and offers some advice.

Foundation stage

Unlike the National Curriculum for Key Stages I and 2, the Curriculum Guidance for the Foundation Stage (CGFS) is organised into areas of learning rather than subjects. These are:

- personal, social and emotional development;
- communication, language and literacy;
- mathematical development;
- knowledge and understanding of the world;
- physical development;
- creative development.

Work that prepares children for Key Stage I design and technology will mainly come under creative development (CD) and knowledge and understanding of the world (KUW), although both these areas of learning are much wider than this. Many National Curricula (e.g. Australia) organise the whole of the primary school curriculum under broad learning headings rather than under traditional subjects as we do in the UK.

Learning through playing

The Curriculum Guidance for the Foundation Stage sets out ten Principles for Early Years Education (page II). One of these is that children should engage in activities that are planned by adults and those which they initiate themselves: *Children do not differentiate between 'play' and 'work' and neither should practitioners*. Play is essential to human creativity. Many would argue that the two activities have the same root and many overlapping characteristics. For example, the ability to imagine alternative possible outcomes or the ability to see several uses for the same object (or several objects for the same purpose) come from early play experiences. In Foundation Stage, children are given the opportunity to explore materials and use them for their own purposes in a way that does not occur within Key Stages I and 2. For example, a tray of collage materials, paper, scissors and glue might be placed in the middle of a table and the children are able to use these to make whatever they like. This child-initiated creative activity has little parallel within older classes, where it is more common for the teacher to set the task parameters and the children are asked to use the materials to solve a specific design problem. Child-initiated activity is beginning to creep upwards into Key Stage I in some schools. It needs careful planning and the skills children are acquiring need to feed into or re-enforce other learning across the curriculum. There is still prejudice against children 'just' playing in school when they should 'learning', but the issues of what counts as play and how this relates to learning, especially for very young children, is a bigger topic than can be covered within this book. Moyles' book *Just playing* (1989) is an excellent introduction to the curiosity-led explorations of young children learning through play.

Case study

Puppets

Raji, on her Final Teaching Placement in a Foundation Stage classroom

Next to the book corner, in sight of the 'Book of the Week' and its story-sack contents (which include some simple stick puppets that the children have been using for role play), Raji has placed on the table:

- *a selection of coloured paper and card, including matt, shiny and sticky-backed papers;*
- *some feathers, sequins, stars and other small stick-on items;*
- *a tub each of lolly sticks, pens, pencils and scissors;*
- *glue-sticks.*

When introducing the choices available during this learning session, Raji says:

On the table by the book corner there are some paper and things for making. Some of you might like to make your own puppets with them and so I have put some lolly sticks there too.

None of the children makes a puppet but several children spend a considerable time sticking feathers, sequins and stars onto sheets of paper. One little girl takes the stars and sticks them onto other children's work, saying Good work! A star for you! Two stars for you! *and so on.*

Reflective questions

The children appear to have completely subverted Raji's intended activity at this table.

How much to you think this matters?

What did children learn through this child-initiated activity?

What skills did they acquire?

If Raji had wanted a puppet to be each child's outcome from this activity, how could she have set up the learning situation differently?

There is, of course, room for both approaches within the Foundation Stage curriculum, and rightly so. Children need time to explore materials and techniques at their own level and acquire these skills at their own speed. However, children also need to be guided through the making of a specific product (e.g. a puppet) in order for them to learn the making processes and have a quality product at the end. This will give them the knowledge, skills and understandings on which to base their further child-initiated activities. Also more obvious in Foundation Stage is the extent to which children learn from each other as well as from the adults. Once one child discovers a new technique (or more often introduces an idea learnt at home with carers or older siblings) then this will permeate the class culture of shared expertise. For example, one child might draw a figure as a single outline rather than separate circles for head, body, etc. This will immediately be noted, copied and tried by others. Making fans, baskets, lists of party guests are also likely to sweep in waves through the cultural milieu of the Foundation Stage classroom.

The use of construction kits forms a separate section at the end of the chapter.

Key Stage I

Investigating familiar products

Most children, when they arrive in their Year I classroom, will be working just within level I, or will attain it within their first few months in Key Stage I. They can describe familiar products, although they may not know the names of all the parts. This can be a fun game, sitting in a circle and passing around a familiar toy (a range of vehicles is useful for this) and each child points to and names a different part (roof, bonnet, axle, hub). This extends children's vocabulary in a fun and non-threatening way. Team points can be given for each child who names the last part of each object.

A game that the children will know from Foundation Stage is the Feely Box. This can be made more sophisticated by asking children to describe what they have found in the box for others to guess. This develops the vocabulary of material properties (soft, smooth, rough) and words to describe function and effectiveness (*This will smooth wood and is easy to hold.*). This kind of activity is especially valuable for children with English as an additional language and the teacher may consider asking a TA to play this game with the children ahead of the practical work so that they can follow task instructions more easily.

For Year 2 children, a set of photos of familiar objects in unfamiliar close-up or from strange angles can be used for a similar circle game, although they too will enjoy Feely Bags, for which they are only allowed to feel the object through the bag and describe it to the rest of the class. This can create hilarious fun, especially if the child is unsure what the object is, but be careful that you do not choose over-sensitive children for this role.

Making skills

At entry to Key Stage I children will have experimented with a variety of simple techniques and used a range of simple and safe tools and equipment. Basic skills and understanding still need to be developed and may include:

- **which type of glue to use and how much to apply;**
- **which type of paper or card to choose for fitness for purpose (e.g. rigidity, strength, ability to be folded easily);**
- **accurate cutting (on a line, around a curve);**
- **estimation of size, including choosing appropriate size of materials (not whole sheet of card for small object);**
- **when/when not to use sticky tape rather than glue (e.g. not right across middle of almost finished product). This is especially apposite where coloured sticky tape is available.**

These and other basic skills will need constant re-enforcement within all projects for which they are relevant.

Safety reminders will need to include:

- **safe use of scissors (e.g. points in hand when moving around the room);**
- **safe playing rules for construction kits (e.g. care over small parts/large or long parts);**
- **how to avoid and deal with spillages (e.g. stand paint or glue pots in centre of table, preferably in a tray lined with newspaper).**

Health and safety issues (including scissors) are discussed in more detail in Chapter 5. It is worth noting here, however, that many things that are commonsense working with older children will need to take the form of clear instructions in Key Stage I, especially with Year I Term I.

Making holes

To make a single hole (e.g. for puppet string), Key Stage I children can be taught to use:
- one end of a standard paper double hole punch;
- a single hole punch that works like a pair of scissors;
- a large (150 mm long) nail to push through paper and thin card onto a piece of carpet tile;
- a ballpoint pen or sharp pencil pushed through card onto a ball of modelling clay.

Do NOT allow children to use one half of a pair of scissors.
A bradawl is also unsuitable for small hands – these are designed for large hands to make holes in wood.

As children progress through Key Stage I, they will become more able to make realistic suggestions about materials and techniques for achieving their purposes. They will be able to use simple tools such a scissors, needles, hole punches and staplers safely.

Designing skills

Most of the design and make assignments in Key Stage I will be of single lesson duration, although by the end of Year 2 children can sustain their sense of purpose across several lessons. Younger than this, children will be disappointed not to have completed their work and will often show little interest in finishing it later, having lost momentum. They will have forgotten their original design idea and, even if this has been recorded in drawings, these will not be sufficiently clear to act as a reliable aide memoire. Teachers need to plan schemes of work carefully so that children feel a sense of achievement at the end of each lesson. This does not need to be a completed product; it could be evaluating, experimenting, learning a new technique or designing their ideal product.

Within each scheme of work, however, it is essential to give children real design opportunities. Your planning could allow for children to make their own design choices within the framework of learning a skill, or you could embed learning how to handle an unfamiliar material or master a new technique within the making of a simple product over which children have some degree of choice. Children need to learn to plan their own activities and this can be linked to literacy learning through writing lists of materials or equipment they might need. This is part of the skill of communicating design ideas through writing. It does not have to be 100 per cent accurate, spelt correctly, written in books (scrap paper will do) or be marked by the teacher. Notice that the Level Descriptors for levels 1 and 2 say that the children will *use pictures and words to describe what they want to do.*'There is no requirement that these words should be written. Children can choose their materials and tell their teacher, TA or even a tape recorder what they are going to make with their choice of materials: *Hallo, tape recorder. I'm making a puppet with two pipe-cleaners and a little paper ball for his head ...*

Frequently, in Foundation Stage, children have been given considerable freedom in deciding for themselves what they will make and how they will proceed. It is important for children not to lose this autonomy as they progress through Key Stage 1 owing to the curriculum becoming more structured. Teachers need to maintain a balance between clearly defining the task parameters and allowing for innovative and individual responses. The child who appears 'off task' is seeing things from a different perspective to the teacher and this contribution needs valuing. Lesson plans that are too prescriptive as to learning outcomes may not give sufficient room for creative interpretations or even of design choices. Tightly defined tasks with limited scope for imaginative response are often, unfortunately, seen as easier to manage and the danger is then that the children experience a series of focused practical tasks and never really engage in genuine design and make assignments.

Case study

A bag for Mother's Day

A scheme of work developed by Kelly Punter at St Stephen's Infant School, Maidstone (see Hope, 2005).

Lesson 1: Looking at bags
A huge pile of bags of all sorts, shapes and sizes is in the middle of the circle of children. Kelly says, 'I like bags, and I bet your Mums do too. I use this bag when ... and this is my bag for ... and I bet your Mum has a special bag that she takes to parties – which one do you think is my special party bag?' ...

The children handle, explore, try out, walk about with the bags, role-playing shopping, partying ... They draw their favourite bag. When they come back together at the end of the lesson, they are shown some denim trousers that can be cut up to be made into a bag for Mum – 'trendy'.

Lesson 2: Experimenting with decorative techniques
Scrap denim and a whole range of techniques to try: fabric paint, glitter pens, sewing, appliqué, etc. At the end the children have pencils and paper to draw bags, design decorations and decide which technique they want to use.

Between lessons, Kelly has been using her sewing machine in class to sew the cut-off trouser legs into bags. This stimulates discussion about sewing and sewing machines, how they work, who uses them and so on.

Lesson 3: Transferring their design ideas onto their bags
Kelly was quite clear with the children that they needed to follow the design they had worked out at the end of the previous week, because they had chosen which techniques to use on the basis of which ones they liked best and had found easiest to do. Nearly all children made a bag that closely resembled the one they had designed.

Reflective questions

How does Kelly use the children's home experience to set the scene for the task?

How does she ensure motivation and engagement in the project?

How would you organise the focused practical task (experimenting with different techniques)? Kelly had different techniques on each table and the children circulated with their fabric. What class management strategies would you need in place to be able to do this?

How did Kelly use the sewing machine to extend the children's knowledge of control technology?

Why was Kelly insistent that the children followed their drawings? What impact would it have had on the finished products if she had allowed them to work freely? Would you have done this? Why/why not?

(There is no right or wrong answer here. It is not just a question of class and/or resource management. It is to do with how you perceive the aims and objectives of the project and how you choose to structure it. Kelly has taught this scheme of work three years running and has made changes each year. This is normal practice and part of teachers' ongoing evaluation and experimentation with teaching and learning.)

Finally, where are children given opportunities for reflection and evaluation? Note how these skills are integral to the project and enable the children to maximise their design choices. Refer to Chapter 3 for discussion of the place of evaluation in design and make assignments.

Key Stage 2

Investigating and evaluating familiar products

A social dimension has been added to the investigation of familiar products. Children are to consider how products are used and how people who use them feel about them. There is a wide range of opportunities in linking design and technology projects to other areas of the curriculum in this work (discussed in Chapter 8, Crossing Curricular Boundaries).

For example, in Food Technology in Key Stage 2:

- **Tasting (Years 3 and 4):** **A class survey to discover the favourite bread/biscuit/ scone flavour before making their own.**

- *Appearance (Years 4 and 5):* **Take photos of standard supermarket pizzas to compare to the picture on the packaging or advertising materials. How carefully are the ingredients arranged? Does this relate to price? How does this compare with a take-away or eat-in restaurant pizza?**

- *Healthy eating (Years 5 and 6):* **Use packaging to compare clarity of nutritional information before planning their own healthy snack whole school survey of blind-tasting of breakfast cereals, in conjunction with analysing the nutritional information to discover the relationship between sugar level and consumer choice at different ages (extension for gifted and talented children in Year 6).**

- *Packaging (Years 3 and 4):* **In preparation for designing an Easter Egg holder – what does it need to do? What kind of egg(s) will it hold? How can it be personalised to include favourite TV characters holding the egg or football players heading it? Note that this 'holder' will not be a standard box shape. It could have a cut out tummy, the egg could sit in a 'cup' or balance on the head of a free standing figure.**

- *Advertising:* **Links with media studies aspects of literacy hour here. Year 3 can discuss who the advertisement is aimed at – young children, their own age group, parents. Years 4 and 5 can begin to unpick the unspoken messages, e.g. 'Your children will love you more if you give in to them and buy this product.' But do not expect this discussion to make children reflect on their own choices until Year 6, and then you need to be honest about why advertising works with adults too. Making their own advertisements for food products that they make can be fun and encourage thought. The same is equally true for packaging – how will they make that pizza look?**

Designing skills

The desire for increased realism in their products enables children across Key Stage 2 to think more analytically about their own ideas and those of others. In Year 3 many children will still be using personal preferences to guide their choices but increasingly they will be able to empathise and take on board the views and wishes of others. This can be encouraged by holding class debates in which groups of children represent opposing factions in debates about changes in local amenities. This can be linked to geography, history, ICT and literacy. For example, when learning about the Victorians, children can hold a railway planning meeting, and take the roles of the railway builders, factory owners and workers, landowners and farmers and other interested parties. Exploring the history of technology in this way enables children to under-stand the reasons for differing viewpoints concerning today's technology and create a respect for a range of perspectives. This can then be applied within their own designing as they research and analyse existing problems and solutions.

It is generally assumed that across the course of Key Stage 2 children will increasingly use drawing to record and develop their design ideas. The development of design drawing across Key Stages 1 and 2 was discussed in Chapter 3. They can also use writing, three-dimensional modelling, for example using construction kits (also in Chapter 3) and ICT drawing packages. Some primary-aged children have the opportunity to visit their local secondary school to use CAD-CAM equipment, usually as part of a specific project. This should be seen as one of a range of ways to develop design ideas, rather than the goal to which primary design is heading. Much design work, even by adults, is conducted through talk. Children need to discuss their design ideas with each other.

Design discussions

- **enable children to clarify the requirements and parameters of the task;**

- **encourage creativity through exposure to a range of ideas that they compare/ contrast/place alongside their own;**

- **open up ideas for analysis and critique – the wild and wacky will either be embraced as the most creative solution to the problem or be seen not to satisfy the task criteria.**

A single large sheet of paper on which to jot down/draw ideas can encourage children's skill in drawing and writing clearly to communicate to others within their group. Asking children to present their ideas to other groups (either orally or as a poster) can further focus children's minds on clarity of communication, but this must not take precedence over using paper to develop ideas, rather than neatly record the finished design.

An important statement in the National Curriculum for design and technology for Key Stage 2 is: *3a – reflect on the progress of their work as they design and make, identifying ways in which they could improve their products.* This gives a quite specific purpose to evaluation in the process of designing. It is on-going, continuous throughout the project, in order to improve the product that they are making. There is no suggestion here of the need to write a project evaluation at the end of making.

Process diary

Key Stage 2 children can keep a process diary, which they fill in at the end of each working session. In this they can keep drawings, photographs, notes on progress, reminders and ideas they think of between lessons. The term 'process diary' was coined by Maggie Rogers and Dominic Clare. The theoretical model on which this practical idea is based was described in Chapter 3.

By completing a short entry at the conclusion of each lesson, children can keep track of their work and thoughts. This encourages children to become reflective of process and progress. It develops metacognitive skills of analysis and self-evaluation. The teacher should allow 5 minutes for this at the end of each lesson. There should be no expectation of standard format. This is the children's diary and they should be free to record by drawing or writing whatever they feel is important to record. In order to establish the routine and to guide the children on the kind of comments and reflections that will be helpful to record, some time will need to be allocated for the teacher to model this process in their first few lessons. It should be handed in to the teacher at the completion of each project, which should then lead on to teacher-led group discussions about the children's learning across the project. Refrain from marking spelling and punctuation in the diary.

Making skills

As well as the techniques that they have already experienced and skills that they have begun to develop and hone in Key Stage 1, Key Stage 2 will present children with a whole new range of tools, techniques and understandings. These might include:

- **working with wood, using saws, bench hooks or vices;**
- **using cool melt glue guns, craft knives and other more hazardous processes;**
- **batik and other more advanced printing techniques;**
- **combining electrical with mechanical control;**
- **using CAD (computer-aided design).**

Health and safety must be uppermost in the teacher's mind and the organisation and supervision of children working with unfamiliar and potentially hazardous equipment must be stated explicitly in lesson plans. However, children appreciate being allowed and trusted to use tools and equipment that they feel respects their growing maturity and will generally respond accordingly.

Do not assume that children will have remembered how to use a particular tool or techniques on the basis that they have used it before in Key Stage 1 or lower Key Stage 2. Plan a short focused practical task as a 'review' exercise, especially for those techniques that are less frequently used.

Example: Year 5 sawing wooden dowel

The children used saws for the first (and last) time making a card-backed picture frame in Year 3. In Year 5 you want them to make a frame from dowel as the base of a battery-powered vehicle. It is likely that having the ends cut square is going to be more important for the construction of the vehicle than it was for the picture frame that was glued to its card base. Sawing always excites children and so some practice will diffuse some of this hyperactivity and will enable them to then concentrate on the development of their vehicle. A box of off-cuts from previous woodwork is useful for this practice work and the challenge is to be able to cut a piece of dowel so that it can stand on its cut end. This gives purpose and incentive to the focused practical task that must be completed before being allowed to measure, mark and cut the dowel for their vehicle.

You might also want children to model ideas in an easier material first.

In Key Stage 1 it is easy to see the results of your teaching since the children are developing and maturing so rapidly. It is less easy to see progress in Key Stage 2, especially in Year 5 and 6 where maturation happens at a much slower rate. It is sometimes difficult, therefore, to see how a single lesson or even a half-term's scheme of work has contributed to children's learning and development. In the following example, *Year 4/5/6*

'The Aliens have Landed', the teacher, Sue, has been asked to come and take the children for a whole day as part of design and technology week, an annual event in a small village school where children are in mixed-age classes. Sue did not know these children very well, in fact she had only met them once before briefly, as link tutor for a student in the school. How could she make an impact on the children's design and technology learning in one day without knowing what they had done before?

Case study

The Aliens Have Landed

This is the storyline on which Sue based her planning for this activity with Years 4/5/6.

Lesson 1: 9.15–10.20
Introduce the aliens, who have landed on the top of Dungeness lighthouse, using PowerPoint to show the lighthouse and the 360° view from the viewing platform: sea, pebble foreshore and sky. The children complete folding 'helpsheets' to focus their minds on the things that the aliens will need and how they might begin to plan the building of a shelter.

Lesson 2: 10.40–12.00
Shelters: Unfortunately the aliens can only find a heap of old newspapers with which to make their shelter, but they really like the designs the children have developed. Can they be made from newspaper? Especially if one roll of sticky tape is allowed per group?

Lesson 3: 1.10–2.30
Getting comfortable – furniture and fittings: The aliens have not managed to get their spaceship started and so have settled in for the long haul. They have found some wood and recyclable materials and are beginning to make their temporary shelter into a proper home.

Reflective task

The 'helpsheet' was a single folded A4 sheet that was designed to guide the children through the initial planning stages. Given that it was the first time Sue had taught these children, what other functions did it serve?

When do you think the project moved from individual to group work?

What was Sue's underlying aim in asking children to use newspaper for the shelters?

What focused practical tasks might she have set up whilst this activity was happening, so that she was sure they had the skills for the afternoon session?

In the afternoon, Sue supervised the saws and bench vices at one end of the room and the class teacher supervised the cool-melt glue guns at the other. What skills (social, cognitive, emotional and physical) did the children need to be able to work together on their shelters with little direct intervention or support from the adults?

What new skills do you think the children learnt as a result of this day's work?

What skills that they had already were developed as a result? What progress had they made in their design and technology capability as a result of Sue's visit?

It is easy to think of progression only as small incremental steps. Progress can happen rapidly as a result of a high impact intensive day's work such as this.

Finally, how could the class teacher build on what Sue has done with the class?

Key Stage 3

As children transfer to secondary school, they meet new challenges in design and technology:

- **dedicated rooms that they visit only for design and technology;**
- **potentially more hazardous equipment and challenging materials (plastics and possibly metals, for example);**
- **teachers who teach only design and technology;**
- **other pupils whose experience of design and technology at primary school is different from their own.**

Although primary schools are required to asses children's capabilities across the foundation subjects against the Level Descriptors, this is often done in a holistic way and, unfortunately, for design and technology, not always with a great deal of accuracy. The level to which children's work and capabilities are attached may well reflect the capabilities of the school rather than the potential of the child. Thus many secondary schools have traditionally assumed that children join them with very little understanding of the nature of design and with low levels of hand skills. Co-operative ventures between secondary schools and their feeder primary schools, have had significant impact in developing upper Key Stage 2 teachers' own confidence in design and technology as well as smoothing children's path into the secondary way of working.

Primary teachers with limited knowledge of designing can hold the view that secondary schools expect children to work to a linear model of designing. This is definitely not the case. Secondary design and technology teachers are specialists who understand the variation in process and procedures within design processes and are unlikely to adhere to a linear model and would probably be aghast at the suggestion that that was what some primary teachers thought they believed in. Because of their personal expertise and capability, secondary teachers are far more confident about allowing children to make design choices within a project and more inclined to encourage personal creativity and innovation. They are also concerned for the intellectual rigour of their subject and to ensure that the children are engaged in high-level thinking as well as being able to produce quality products.

Opportunities exist within most partnerships between secondary schools and their feeder primaries for upper Key Stage 2 teachers to visit and observe the kind of work that is carried out in design and technology in Key Stage 3. This would be a good use of an NQT's release time. As well as developing their own knowledge and understanding, it will also further the development of collaborative cross-partnerships and understanding between local schools.

Bridging the gap (Barnard *et al.* 2000) is a Centre for Research in Primary Technology (CRIPT) publication whose aim is to smooth the transition between primary and secondary school. Its intended audience is teachers of Year 7 children, to help them enable children to bridge the gap between their experiences of design and technology in their primary school and their new environment. It is a useful guide for non-specialist teachers of Year 6 children and the expectations of knowledge, skills and understandings that the Year 7 teachers will have of them.

Harrison (2000) lists the engineering skills gained between ages 11 and 14 as:

- **technological concepts – stability, rigidity, nature of failure, lift and drag, turbulence;**
- **technological systems and sub-systems, mechanisms – links and levers, amplification of force and movement;**
- **engineering economics;**
- **interaction of science and technology – scientific investigations;**
- **thinking strategies – observing nature for inspiration;**
- **realisation of importance of knowledge and understanding in design decisions;**
- **importance of precision and high-quality craft work;**
- **safety in production, in use and effect on others;**
- **participation in 'big' engineering;**
- **strategies – sketching helps thinking;**
- **motivation through achievement.**

This seems a very sophisticated list. It is, of course, the foundational knowledge, skills and understanding on which a GCSE course in design and technology would build.

Progression in design and technology learning:
a summary of key points

In this chapter you have learnt about the development of children's design and technology skills in relation to:

——— *how children's cognitive and physical development relates to design and technology;*

——— *progression within the National Curriculum at Key Stages 1 and 2, relating this also to the Foundation Stage and Key Stage 3;*

——— *how to ensure progression of children's acquisition of knowledge, skills and understandings in design and technology.*

References

Barnard, J, Farrell, A, Mantell, J, and Waldon, A (2000) *Bridging the gap*. Birmingham: CRIPT. (Available from DATA.)

Bateson, P and Martin, P (2000) *Design for a life*. London: Vintage.

Bruner, J (1986) *Actual minds: possible worlds*. Cambridge, MA: Harvard University Press.

Harrison, G (2001) *The continuum for design education for engineering*. London: The Engineering Council.

Hope, G (2005), Making a bag. *5TO7 educator*, 4 (8): National Curriculum section, D&T.

Moyles, J (1989) *Just playing*. Buckingham: Open University Press.

Pluckrose, H (1984) Learning and teaching art and craft skills in Fontana, D (ed) *The education of the young child* (2nd edition). London: Open Books, p256.

Rogers, M and Clare, D (1994) The Process Diary: developing capability within National Curriculum Design and Technology, in *Conference proceedings*, International Design and Technology Education Research Conference (IDATER94). Loughborough University: Department of Design and Technology.

Wells, G (1986) *The meaning makers*. London: Hodder & Stoughton.

5 PLANNING TO TEACH DESIGN AND TECHNOLOGY

The four main sections of this chapter will focus on the importance of good planning to maximise children's opportunities for creative designing.

In this chapter you will learn how to

- *plan schemes of work and well-structured lessons from first principles, having taking account of differentiation and inclusion and health and safety.*

Planning from first principles in design and technology

Although there are published schemes of work available (e.g. the Qualifications and Curriculum Authority (QCA) scheme or Nuffield Primary Solutions, plus support materials such as lesson plans and worksheets, published, among others, by DATA and LDA), you need to know how to plan a scheme of work as part of your professional capability and because, even if you use a published scheme, you will need to adapt it to the needs of your children. These schemes are designed with the 'average' class in mind. You may have a high proportion of children with special or additional educational needs or, for any number of reasons, your class may not have the prior experience of designing and/or making that the scheme assumes. Thus you need to understand how to plan a scheme of work that is suited to the needs of your class.

So, faced with that blank sheet of paper, where do you start?

Guiding principles

There are two aspects to planning, which can sometimes appear to be conflicting.

First, you need to start from the *children* – their current needs, interests and prior learning. This approach to teaching was current before the National Curriculum was introduced and is often called 'child-centred learning'. For many long-serving teachers, *Excellence and Enjoyment* (DfEE, 2003) appeared at first to be offering a return to child-centred approaches. There is, however, a subtle difference. *Extended Schools* (DfEE, 2005a) is based on the government initiative *Every Child Matters* (2004). The child-centred approaches to teaching that developed from the theories of Rousseau and Dewey were based on the premise that *each child matters.*

Reflective task

What is implied in the difference between the two words each and every?

Part of the reaction against the child-centred approach, and which led to the introduction of the National Curriculum, was that the emphasis on individual freedoms and choices meant that it seemed to be increasingly difficult to ensure the quality of educational provision. Access to a nationally agreed curriculum was seen as the right of every child to equip them for their future needs as an employable member of society. At the time of its introduction, the National Curriculum was seen by many teachers as eroding their own freedoms and professionalism. Although clear on the need to begin from where the child is now in their understanding and interests, the child-centred approach was less clear on where education would take the child to. Like all journeys, knowing the destination enables arrival. The National Curriculum provided that clear destination and the framework for getting there.

Secondly, therefore, you need also to start from the *curriculum* – the National Curriculum tells you what children should be taught in each Key Stage and the Attainment Targets tell you the expected achievements at each level. The normal range for Key Stage 1 is from working towards level 1 to working within level 3. For Key Stage 2, this may extend to level 6 for the highest achieving children in Year 6, but it is equally possible to have children still working within level 1 right through Key Stage 2. It is not a year-by-year programme. The QCA scheme was designed to provide teachers with such a programme. It was constructed from schemes of work written by teachers that worked well in their classrooms. Although widely accepted and used throughout the UK, the QCA writers themselves intended the scheme to serve as a springboard from which teachers would be able to design their own schemes, and they have been surprised at the way it has been adopted and applied with little adaptation. The soundness of the scheme has been demonstrated by this enthusiastic uptake and by its endurance. However, many schools now feel it is time to move on and that *Excellence and Enjoyment* is encouraging them to be more creative with their curriculum and make more explicit cross-curricular links than has been the case for some years.

Practical task

Read **Excellence and Enjoyment** *(DfEE, 2003) pp5–6, beginning at 'Learning – a focus on individuals', and p39, the introductory Summary.*

How does this relate to teaching and learning design and technology?

See below, 'differentiation and inclusion'.

Planning cycles

Planning can be considered to be at three levels, with different review cycle lengths:

- *Long-term plans* – whole school level, covering all year groups across whole school year, review cycle of several years' duration (often 3 years) led by design and technology co-ordinator in consultation with the senior management team, overseen by the school governing body;

- *Medium-term plans* – year group/class level, covering year group/class across whole school year, review cycle usually annually, led by the year group co-ordinator/class teachers in consultation with design and technology co-ordinator, overseen by senior management team;

- *Short-term plans* – class level, covering class across one week, review cycle weekly, written by class teachers, overseen by design and technology co-ordinator and/or year group co-ordinator.

Both long-term plans and medium-term plans can be described as schemes of work, which can be confusing. In the following discussion, the term 'schemes of work' will be used to refer to medium-term plans for several weeks' work. Students on school placement experience are usually given copies of the medium-term plans from which to plan lessons. A student on final school experience placement might, for example, be asked to develop a scheme of work on a specific topic to cover six lessons across the duration of the placement.

To satisfy the requirements of the National Curriculum for design and technology (see Chapter 2), each scheme of work must ensure that:

1 Children are engaged in developing ideas, planning, making products and evaluating them.
2 This is achieved through the application of each of the areas of Knowledge, Skills and Understanding for the appropriate key stage (but not every element needs to be applied in every scheme).
3 This Knowledge, Skills and Understanding is to be taught within the context of the Breadth of Study (investigating familiar products, focused practical tasks, design and make assignments).

These principles still apply in cross-curricular work, so that practical work in geography or history (for example, making a model of a Plains Indian tepee) will be unlikely to satisfy the requirements for design and technology.

Reflective task

Why would making a model of a Plains Indian tepee not satisfy the requirements for design and technology? (Think about the nature of design, innovation, creativity.)

Could it form any part of a scheme of work in design and technology?

How would it relate to investigating familiar products?

Could it form part of the research for a design and make project or would the children's evaluation of this solution to a specific survival problem be that it works so well that they cannot improve on the design?

Could it form part of the research for a design and make project in which the survival problems were very different? (How different? As different as the moon or only as different as where they live?)

In which case, would they not want to look at several solutions, perhaps a range of portable homes from around the world, and be making a model of the Plains Indian tepee as a way of investigating the principles behind the construction of such portable homes?

This design and technology approach is rather different to making a model of something the children are learning about in history or geography.

See below for sample scheme of work for design and technology: portable homes.

Schemes of work

Schemes of work need to have:

- **title**

- **aims**

- **objectives**

- **links to previous and future learning**

- **lesson outlines**

- **health and safety implications**

- **differentiation**

- **organisation of activities**

- **key vocabulary**

- **resources**

- **assessment methods**

These may not necessarily occur in this order as the scheme of work is probably written in a week-by-week grid format, but all these elements should be found.

A sample scheme of work for both Key Stage 1 and Key Stage 2 can be found in Appendices C and E. The sample lesson plans for both key stages in Appendices D and F are lessons from these sample schemes of work.

TITLE

This should include:

- **class and/or year group, dates for delivery (e.g. Term 2, weeks 1–4);**

- **links to National Curriculum for design and technology and to other areas of the National Curriculum;**

- **reference to published scheme, if appropriate (e.g. QCA 2a).**

AIMS

This initial statement links the scheme of work to the long-term plans and the school's policy documents for design and technology. In these documents there will be statements such as *To develop children's creativity*, but these need to be made much more specific at medium-plan level, e.g. *To develop children's creativity in designing an artefact for a specified user*. The aims of the scheme of work will be statements that reach across several lessons, and perhaps even subjects.

OBJECTIVES

Objectives are a little tighter than aims. There are usually several inherent in the scheme of work and are specific to the work that the children will be doing.

For example, in a scheme of work involving textiles, leading towards making a small placemat as a festival gift, the objectives might be:

- **to enhance children's knowledge, skills and understanding of printing techniques;**

- **to develop children's knowledge of fabrics to enable informed choices;**

- **to develop children's sense of pattern and colour;**

- **to design and make a suitable gift for a female parent/carer.**

LINKS TO PREVIOUS AND FUTURE LEARNING

This places the scheme of work in relation to the long-term plans. For, example, for a scheme of work on portable homes:

> Building on: Year 1, Term 3, Where I Live
> Further developed in: Year 5, Term 2, Structures

It can also link the design and technology work to other areas of the curriculum:

> History – Plains Indians' tepees
> Geography – Mongolian gerts

LESSON OUTLINES

At this level these need only to be a brief statement of the lesson content. They need to state whether the activities in which the children will engage are focused practical tasks or design and make assignments. They will indicate health and safety implications for specific lessons, where differentiation will occur, how activities will be organised (especially if the planning involves several adults or more than one class working at the same time), the key vocabulary that needs to be taught and the assessment methods to be employed.

HEALTH AND SAFETY

There is a separate section on health and safety in this chapter. All schemes of work must include specific risk assessment details.

DIFFERENTIATION

Most design and technology activities are differentiated by expectation and outcome for the majority of the class. However, if you have groups of children for whom it is appropriate to plan a different range of activities (if, perhaps, the children from a hearing-impaired unit join the mainstream classes for practical activities) then these need to be specified in your medium-term planning. The needs of individual children within the class are more appropriately recorded in lesson plans. There is a separate section on differentiation and inclusion within this chapter.

ORGANISATION OF ACTIVITIES

Will the design and technology lessons be whole class lessons delivered to all children at the same time, or will they be spread across a whole day/several afternoons and children engage in them in small groups? Will a TA work with these groups or will the TA supervise the rest of the class while you teach the design and technology? The answers to these organisational questions need not be the same for every lesson in the scheme. If, for example, the children need to learn something new that is vital for the success of the project (for example, experimenting with combining different shaped cams with followers of different lengths), then this might be better done in a small group with an adult to facilitate discussion to enable understanding. The availability of resources or health and safety implications of particular techniques, tools or equipment might also influence organisational choices.

KEY VOCABULARY

There will be certain key terms that you want all children to be familiar with and using correctly by the end of the project. These may be process words as well as names of tools and equipment, for example,

design processes (*evaluate, investigate, experiment, develop*);
material properties (*flexible, mouldable, translucent, opaque*);
tools (*set square, tenon saw, bench vice, batik bath*);
hand skills (*stir, beat, whisk*);
health and safety (*secure, thermostat, goggles*).

RESOURCES

To ensure that the school has everything that you require for this scheme of work, make a list of every resource (tools, equipment, materials and adult support) that you anticipate needing and find out how to order anything the school does not have. Most suppliers used on a regular basis by schools can deliver within days but may charge extra for small or short date orders. Think too about storage of half-finished work (especially if likely to be dripping glue or paint) and where and how completed work will be displayed. If worksheets, help or instruction sheets will be needed by the children, then ensure a copy is stored with the scheme of work, and kept for future reference/re-use when you teach this scheme of work again. There is nothing so frustrating as planning to repeat a scheme of work and not being able to find the really good help sheet that you found or designed for it.

ASSESSMENT METHODS

You are unlikely to be looking at the National Curriculum level descriptors on a regular basis in design and technology in the way that you might in literacy and numeracy. Design and technology learning is much less high-stakes. However, you will need to decide how and when you will assess the children's capability in order to give the next teacher an accurate assessment of the children's capabilities. Thus you need to decide at medium-term planning stage how you will assess and report the children's success. You might decide that assessment of children's capability will come at the end of a project and that interim assessment will be at class or group level, with specific notes on any individuals having particular difficulties. Assessment in design and technology is discussed in greater detail in Chapter 7.

Well-structured lessons

Well-structured lessons enable children to engage with the topic and develop their own creative solution to the task. Lesson plans for design and technology should contain the following, although not necessarily in this order or under these specific headings:

- **Title**
- **Aims**
- **Objectives**
- **Learning outcomes**
- **Implications from prior learning**
- **Resources**
- **Organisation of activities**
- **Health and safety**
- **Differentiation**
- **Key questions and vocabulary**
- **Lesson outline**
- **Assessment methods**
- **Evaluation of teaching and learning**
- **Implications for future planning**

Sample lesson plans D and F for both Key Stage 1 and Key Stage 2 can be found in Appendices D and F. These are illustrative of the lessons from the sample schemes of work for both key stages that can be found in Appendices C and E. For the Key Stage 1 scheme, it is Lesson 5 that appears here; Lesson 1 can be found in *5to7 educator*, March 2006 (Hope, 2006).

TITLE

This should include: date, class and year group, a simple title to the activity (e.g. Puppets, Lesson 3), supporting adults, National Curriculum links, and links to other areas of the curriculum (e.g. part of project on Romans).

AIMS

The statement of lesson aims places the lesson within the medium-term plan and connects it with the long-term plans. The statement you make here should answer the question 'How does this lesson fit into the grand scheme of things?' Although pitched at what one might describe as meta-level, it is important to clarify to oneself how the lesson being taught will contribute to children's overall learning and development.

OBJECTIVES

Objectives originate at scheme of work level, which may be a sub-set of the medium-term plans. Some schools do not list aims and objectives separately; however, the kind of thinking inherent in identifying aims and objectives is foundational to all lesson planning. Design and technology lessons are not just practical work, as 'craft activities' might be. In this sense it is well to be wary of books of children's craft ideas that seem like nice things for children to make. Always think from aims and objectives to activity, and not the other way around.

LEARNING OUTCOMES

These are lesson-specific: What will the children learn in this lesson that will contribute towards them achieving the objectives of the National Curriculum and of the scheme of work into which the lesson fits?

IMPLICATIONS FROM PRIOR LEARNING

No lesson exists in a vacuum, even if it is just one in a series that the student teacher has been asked to plan. You will need to know what the children have done (or will be doing) prior to your lesson. The answer to this might have health and safety implications for what you plan to do. For example, if you plan to use saws, do they already know how to use a bench hook or bench vice or do you need to teach them?

Note, too, that it is implications from prior *learning,* not implications from prior *teaching.* You will need to have assessed the children's learning before planning this lesson. This will probably be by informal observation through assisting in the class teacher's lesson. If there are important health and safety implications in the lesson you are planning to teach, make sure you have assessed the children's capabilities/sense of responsibility relevant to the techniques you are planning and decide the level of supervision they will require in your lesson.

The lesson may well be part of a cross-curricular project and this too needs to be recorded in your plan.

RESOURCES

Ensure that all of these things that you and the children will need are ready in plenty of time. Make a list. It is frequently part of a TA's job to prepare resources, but do not assume this to be so and you should clarify with them that this is part of their role.

ORGANISATION OF ACTIVITIES

This is where you specify how you will arrange the room, site the potentially hazardous equipment/activities (and who is supervising them), arrange how you will organise the distribution of equipment and materials, how/to what extend children will move around the room (from one activity to another?), collecting of resources at the end of the lesson and the cleaning of tools and equipment. This is the kind of thing that happens automatically in established classes and with older children, but that you will need to prepare in detail with younger children and if you are unfamiliar with the class and their routines. Year 6 children will tell you what they usually do and organise it for you – but you will quickly have chaos with Key Stage I unless you plan all these aspects meticulously, and make them crystal clear to the children.

HEALTH AND SAFETY

Refer to the separate section on health and safety in this chapter and list the main points that you will need to consider in relation to this lesson. Include reminders to brief adult assistants.

DIFFERENTIATION

As stated above in discussion of planning schemes of work, most design and technology activities are differentiated by outcome. However, children with specific special educational needs that impinge on their ability to access the lesson will need to be planned for separately. For example, if you have a child in a wheelchair, is it possible to store the things their table needs close to their place so that they do not have to keep asking others to fetch things?

Food technology will require differentiation for children with specific allergies or dietary requirements/taboos. You will need to consider how you provide alternatives for these children (make ingredient choices available for all, and quietly direct the child towards the appropriate choice for them, perhaps?). The same principle applies to other activities that might offend parental beliefs (e.g. Jehovah's Witnesses do not wish their children involved in Christmas activities). These beliefs and wishes *must* be respected. It is the child's right to have their family's beliefs honoured by others.

KEY QUESTIONS AND VOCABULARY

These are, of course, not just for that final 5 minutes when they have tidied up at record speed. They are your anchor points that will remind you what you were hoping the children would learn about designing in the course of the activity. You can use them to introduce the task (*I will be looking for those who are able to …*), re-focus children as they work (*I've found a really good example here of what I was saying about …*), challenge them (*Tell me, how will that achieve our goal of …*) and so on. They will also, of course, provide the basis of the review of learning objectives in the plenary and that 'who's ready to go home' device that lowers congestion in the cloakroom by allowing children out as they can answer such questions as *What do we call a … ?*

LESSON OUTLINE

Introduction: Think through carefully and record how you will introduce the activity. If you have some examples to show children, when and how will you introduce them? If you have some props (e.g. a teddy who needs a new chair) where will they be at the start of the lesson? If you are using an ICT resource (whiteboard or data projector) ensure that this is ready to show with the minimum fuss.

Main activity time: How will you ensure children remain on-task? (See 'Key Questions and Vocabulary' above). How is each activity/group to be arranged? This will be different for a group activity as opposed to individual work. Teachers tend to organise all group or all individual work, unless they have a TA, taking small groups in turn for a specific different activity), but there is nothing to prevent you from setting up a mixture of group and individual work within the main classroom. This is especially so in Key Stage 1 where two groups of children can work with construction kits whilst others work with you on design and make activities. This enables you to better supervise those who are thus engaged and give help more easily to individuals as they need it, rather than have the children waiting a long time for your help.

Clearing away and plenary: Clearing away practical activity work is always messy, noisy and potentially hazardous. Allow 10 minutes to tidy away and give children 5 minutes' warning of the end of activity time. If you are allocating jobs to children (collecting resources, etc.) write this in your plan if you are inexperienced in teaching design and technology. Also plan what the children who do not have jobs will be doing. The plenary does not need to be long. It can just be an affirmation of how well the class has worked, who has done particularly well, what the aims of the lesson were and an announcement of what they will be doing next time. Plan additional questions in case the tidying up goes particularly smoothly. There is nothing worse than a class who are ready for playtime in 5 minutes' time and it is useful to be able to say *When I was planning this lesson, I thought about some things to ask you, if we had time at the end.* and then refer to your key questions and vocabulary.

ASSESSMENT METHODS

Although this needs to be in line with the decision made within the scheme of work, you will, additionally, make informal assessment of particular aspects of the lesson. Perhaps, despite having used a particular technique in their previous class, many of the children could not manage to apply this in a new context. Hand skills such as sawing (or even sewing) need constant practice to perfect and if children only experience a few opportunities to experience these techniques, they will not develop their skills. You might decide, therefore, to either adapt the following lesson to give children more practice in the skills they need, or set up a small activity table so that they can take turns practising before the next lesson. This, of course, will have implications within your planning of other lessons. (Assessment in design and technology is discussed in greater detail in Chapter 6.)

EVALUATION OF TEACHING AND LEARNING

Your lesson is so well planned, success is inevitable. Or is it? How will you judge its success? Your early attempts at teaching design and technology might be judged by your feelings of relief at survival, but inevitably, this stage must lead on into focusing on the children's learning. The criterion of successful teaching is not your own performance, but that of the children. How well did how many achieve what you were hoping they would achieve? Which leads on to ...

IMPLICATIONS FOR FUTURE PLANNING

What do you need to remember that will help you plan the next lesson? This could be anything from thinking about a different way to arrange the furniture to how you introduce next week's task. This could also include children who found it difficult to behave appropriately alongside those with whom they were placed, so that you can move them to another part of the room next time. You need to jot this down immediately the lesson ends (on a sticky note that you affix to your plan is easiest), because by the end of the next lesson you will have forgotten. Many students write vague notes here simply because, by the time they get home and sit down to write up their notes, they have forgotten the detail of how the lesson went. If you were happy with the lesson, say so, and say what you will do next time to build on your success. Make sure, too, that if you need to organise adult support for the next lesson, you not only write that here but you act on it immediately and make the arrangements quickly before your chosen adult arranges to do something else at that time. Never rely on an adult helper 'always' being there. If you will need an extra pair of hands, book them early and make sure their owner knows they are essential to the success of your lesson.

Differentiation and inclusion

Ensuring that all children are able to become involved in the lesson and feel a sense of personal achievement should be the goal of all teachers. *Excellence and Enjoyment* (DfEE, 2003, p39) stresses that learning must be fitted to different children's needs.

Practical task

Read pages 39–45 of Excellence and Enjoyment *(DfEE, 2003) and consider how the following relate to teaching and learning design and technology:*

- *the relationship between assessment and learning (assessment for learning: See Chapter 6);*

- *the child as an individual;*

- *inclusion and support for children with special educational needs in mainstream schools;*

- *provision for gifted and talented pupils;*

- *support for pupils from minority ethnic groups (discussed in Chapter 9);*

- *transition from Foundation Stage to Key Stage 1, from Key Stage 1 to Key Stage 2 (discussed in Chapter 4).*

As indicated, three of these points are the subjects of other chapters, points 2–4 are discussed here.

The child as an individual

This chapter began with a discussion of guiding principles underlying planning (the needs of the child and the requirements of the curriculum) and you were asked to reflect on the difference between the words *each* and *every*. *Excellence and Enjoyment* (DfEE, 2003) reflects the interplay of these issues – *Learning must be focused on individual pupils' needs and abilities* (p39) – and acknowledges that child-centred education has not gone away, despite 20 years of rhetoric against it: *Every teacher knows that truly effective teaching and learning focuses on individual children, their strengths, their needs, and the approaches which engage, motivate and inspire them* (paragraph 4.6). However, this is a curriculum-centred view of the needs of the child and a target-led view of educational attainment. This is also reflected in *Higher Standards, Better Schools for All* (DfEE, 2005b). In her Foreword, then Secretary of State Ruth Kelly claims one of the central tenets of this White Paper to be to *tailor education around the needs of each individual child so that no child falls behind and no child is held back from achieving their potential.* Although the White Paper mainly discusses this in relation to literacy and numeracy attainment for primary school pupils, there is the potential to develop a more personalised curriculum for all children in all subjects. This could mean the end for slippers in Year 6 and a move towards a more creative approach to teaching that springs from your class's genuine interests.

Inclusion and support for children with special educational needs in mainstream schools

The QCA document *Planning, Teaching and Assessing the Curriculum for Pupils with Learning Difficulties: Design and Technology* (QCA, 2001a) is one of the set of guidance booklets that apply the Performance Descriptors (P scales) P4–P8 to learning within foundation subjects. P scales are designed to:

- **support summative assessment at end of school year or key stage;**
- **track individual pupils' progress towards National Curriculum level 1;**
- **identify and record pupils' lateral progress (i.e. across subject areas).**

Thus P scales are used to assess the learning of those pupils who are still working towards achieving level 1 of the National Curriculum Programmes of Study, regardless of age or key stage. *Using the P Scales* (QCA, 2005) provides an introduction to the use of P scales across the curriculum. Pupils working at P1–P3 are considered unable to access the National Curriculum Programmes of Study, but those working within p4–P8 are considered able to access the Programmes of Study in modified form. Children working within Levels P1–P3 are unlikely to be within mainstream schools at Key Stages 1 and 2. Both *Planning, Teaching and Assessing the Curriculum for Pupils with Learning Difficulties: Design and Technology* (QCA, 2001a) and *Using the P Scales* (QCA, 2005) can be downloaded from the QCA website **www.qca.org.uk**.

The following is a summary of the main points of the QCA (2001) document.

For children with learning difficulties, design and technology:

- **provides opportunities to make choices within accessible and personally meaningful practical learning experiences;**
- **applies knowledge and understanding from across the curriculum;**
- **gives pupils a sense of achievement and improves their self-esteem;**
- **enables them to take ownership of their work and a greater responsibility for their own learning;**
- **develops pupils' social awareness, the ability to consider the needs and preferences of others and capability to work as member of a group;**
- **allows pupils to work at their own pace and level.**

Teachers may need to modify the programmes of study for design and technology but they are reminded that activities in which the design and the outcome are decided by either the teacher or supporting adult are *inaccurate interpretations of design and technology and reduce the opportunities for pupils to develop capability* (p7). The intention is that pupils with learning difficulties should experience all three aspects of the Breadth of Study for design and technology, but at their own level. Thus, suggestions are made for how pupils might evaluate products, practise and consolidate particular skills and knowledge through focused practical tasks, and undertake design and make assignments. Sensitive ways to ensure pupils' success are suggested, including:

- **working on shorter, more focused design and make assignments, where success is guaranteed and pupils can be proud of what they have designed and made;**
- **undertaking design and make assignments that relate to their own strengths, interests and hobbies;**
- **asking pupils to adapt, make improvements or add a new feature to the design of an existing product rather than inventing something new;**
- **giving pupils choice within a range of alternative solutions or similar materials;**
- **using a range of support techniques for recording and developing design ideas;**
- **using the support of others (children and support staff) to help pupils take part safely in practical work;**
- **using ICT applications, such as specialist software, CAD-CAM to produce quality products.**

While much of the Key Stage 1 Programme of Study for design and technology is relevant to pupils with learning difficulties, some parts of the Key Stage 2 Programme of Study may be too challenging intellectually or too demanding physically. It might be more appropriate to use materials from Curriculum Guidance for the Foundation Stage. Teachers need to provide opportunities for pupils to work at their own level within the activities in which the rest of the class are engaged.

The Performance Descriptors (P scales) for design and technology can be found in *Planning, Teaching and Assessing the Curriculum for Pupils with Learning Difficulties: Design and Technology* (QCA, 2001a) **www.qca.org.uk/8798.html**. It is unlikely that children within mainstream primary schools will be working below P scale level 4, especially in Key Stage 2. There will also, of course, be children within Key Stage 2 who are working at levels more usually associated with Key Stage I. The same principles outlined above with regard to children working within the P scales will apply to these children. Teachers' planning must ensure that all children within the class are catered for and their needs met.

Equally challenging are children with social, emotional and behavioural difficulties. *Supporting School Improvement: emotional and behavioural development* (QCA, 2001b) provides the following table of desirable traits:

Learning behaviour	Conduct behaviour	Emotional behaviour
1 Is attentive and has an interest in schoolwork 2 Has good learning organisation 3 Is an effective communicator 4 Works efficiently in a group 5 Seeks help where necessary	6 Behaves respectfully towards staff 7 Shows respect to other pupils 8 Only interrupts and seeks attention appropriately 9 Is physically peaceable 10 Respects property	11 Has empathy 12 Is socially aware 13 Is happy 14 Is confident 15 Is emotionally stable and shows good self-control

Practical activities such as design and technology can become very challenging to teach if one or more of the children in the class have difficulties with a number of these traits, especially conduct behaviour. The health and safety of the child, other children and adults, including yourself, must be paramount in your mind and if you have any doubts about your capability to diffuse a potentially hazardous situation or deal with one that has already arisen, then seek help and support. Never feel that you should be able to cope with a particular child's challenging behaviour and that you are failing if you cannot. Even teachers of many years' standing need and seek help and advice to deal with particular children's behaviour. It is important to remember that it is the *behaviour* that is challenging, difficult or inappropriate, not the child.

- **Keep sharp tools, including scissors, out of sight as well as reach when not in use.**

- **Teach safe procedures whose importance is stressed and insisted upon, e.g. state clearly how many children are allowed at the glue gun table. Children with social, emotional and behavioural difficulties appreciate routine and structure in order to get their bearings within the lesson framework. If they know the right place and right way in which certain procedures and techniques are to be tackled, they will generally abide by the rules, and insist everyone else does too.**

- **Praise early – a child with social, emotional and behavioural difficulties is usually very insecure, which is why they react badly to changes of teacher or to a student teaching the class. This praise needs to be specific and relevant to the learning objective of the task and take the form of a dialogue interaction between yourself and the child, not just a cursory 'well done'. Affirming the worth of their initial idea, the way they have begun to develop their design, the** sensible way in which they are using tools, etc., will help to re-assure and minimise the likelihood of disruptive or dangerous behaviour later. Remember – being creative and solving problems is risky. For the sake of the smooth running of your lesson, a child whose insecurity expresses itself in disruptive or violent action needs re-assurance and support early.

- Playing music whilst children are engaged in practical tasks can lower heart rates and help to maintain a happy atmosphere. Choose the music with care, though. It needs to be calming and without a strong beat or you will find everyone sawing or banging in time to it. Children believe playing music in class to be 'special', almost teacher being naughty – so suggesting you will have to turn it off if they cannot work well with it on can be a good ploy. Key Stage I children (especially Year I) love singing, so you can invent special 'working songs' – design and technology themed 'this is the way …' verses to the tune of Here We Go Round the Mulberry Bush are within even the poorest musician's capability. These can be sung at the beginning of a session, as children move to their tables, tidy up or other moments that you know your more challenging children will find difficult. It gives them a secure framework in which to function in shared social action.

- Aim to divert and diffuse, do not become confrontational. If the child will not take their work to the sawing bench and insists on taking a saw to their own table, gently discuss with them the reasons for the rule. The child often feels more secure with unfamiliar equipment at their own workspace than being amongst the jostling queue in an unfamiliar part of the classroom, so consider having this on a table close to where they sit, even though this feels counter-intuitive with regard to safety.

- Act calm, however stressful the situation has become. Children are often frightened by the strength of their own emotions and need to feel that you are still in control (of the rest of the class at least!). As far as possible, divert other children's attention away from any disruptive behaviour.

- Have an 'all stop instantly' signal, that is loud, sharp and attached to your person – not a rain stick that is somewhere under the clutter on the teacher's desk. Design and technology activities have the potential to become very dangerous very quickly and you may not have time for social niceties. This is one of the few occasions on which you are justified in shouting in the classroom – but only sufficiently to stop the hazardous activity. Do not continue with any activity that becomes hazardous. Calmly state that you will have to stop the activity because it is too dangerous. See the section on health and safety in this chapter.

Children with physical disabilities

Health and safety in design and technology are a special issue with regard to children with physical disabilities, especially since children will have greater freedom of movement around the room in comparison to other lessons and there will be a more diverse range of tools, materials and equipment. See the section on health and safety in this chapter and apply the principles on avoiding risks and hazards with respect to the teaching of children with impaired physical capabilities.

Having said that, design and technology can be a source of delight and pride for children whose ability to access other areas of the curriculum is restricted. Education is not just a futures event – preparing children for adult life. Design and technology education is not just about fitting children for the technical workplace. Making products in which to take pride and finding joy in the making is a fundamental human need. Enriching childhood should be a basic aim of all education.

TO THINK ABOUT

- **Consider where you store basic equipment such as scissors or glue.**
  G. in his wheelchair needed to be next to the Fire Exit door as this was the only flat access to the classroom. Mrs P. moved her shelves so they were near to this door.

- **Find out whether wrist braces should be on or off during practical activity.**
  L.'s physiotherapist said that 5 minutes using scissors every day without her wrist brace could improve the muscle tone in L.'s hand.

- **Think about position of bench vices around children likely to fall over.**
  Although the bench vice was attached to a side table, S. only missed it by inches when his weak foot caught under him as he manoeuvred around the room holding his work.

- **Different kinds of scissors are available to help children with poor hand control but experiment yourself with different ways of holding standard scissors, that may make children feel less self-conscious about their difficulties.**
  Try using thumb and fourth finger, thumb clutching one side of scissors in the palm with other fingers operating the other side.

- **Triangular pencils enable good grip for writing but this is the wrong grip for shading.**

- **Adapt task for visually handicapped by including texture, sound, taste or smell in design specification. This will also give you insight into the cues the child is using to make sense of and control their environment.**
  J. did not choose the brightly coloured paper Mr T. had expected but spent time feeling each of the papers before choosing some wallpaper off-cuts with slightly raised pattern.

- **Have hearing buddies for hearing-impaired children with prearranged and clearly understood actions or signs for stop (hazard), stop (teacher talking), work more quietly, etc. Remember that some children may have low level hearing impairment.**
  M. can cope well in other lessons but the background noises of sawing, banging, scraping of chairs and generally higher level of conversation noise will make distinguishing sounds (including his teacher's voice) difficult.

Practical task

Food technology

What difficulties would be encountered by the following children in accessing food technology activities and how could you reduce these barriers to learning?

G. *in his wheelchair;*
L. *with paraplegia wearing a wrist brace;*
S. *with paraplegia that affect his right leg, especially his foot;*
J. *with visual impairment;*
M. *with a hearing difficulty.*

Provision for gifted and talented pupils

DEFINITIONS

Gifted   = children who are working at a higher academic level than their peers
Talented = children who show particular high ability in art, music, PE

This leaves design and technology in a strange position, since it is not strictly an 'academic' subject yet it is missing from the list of subjects for which children are to be identified as 'talented'. The QCA's *Guidance on Teaching the Gifted and Talented: Design and Technology* (2001c) describes the highly able in design and technology as 'gifted' but, as examination of the list of likely capabilities of such gifted pupils reveals, this is mainly of application to the secondary school, rather than to primary pupils. The most helpful, yet obvious, statement describes those especially talented in design and technology as pupils who show 'performance at an unusually advanced national curriculum level for their age group'. Added to this means of identifying such pupils are:

- **the outcomes of specific tasks;**

- **evidence of particular aptitudes;**

- **the way pupils respond to questions;**

- **the questions that pupils ask themselves.**

Might it be too impertinent to ask if the writers of this guidance know themselves about identifying potentially gifted designers? Given that the aim of the government initiative is to foster the potential of gifted and talented pupils, guidance to aid the identification of such latent talents needs to be more specific. The following comment is, however, helpful:

> *The pupils who are gifted in design and technology may be a very different group from those with gifts and talents in other subjects. The breadth of designing and making means that some of them will have abilities in a specific area – for example working with food, using computer-assisted design (CAD) or high-quality making – but not in others.*

But, again, note that the context is more typically secondary than primary. Given that early identification is important to foster talent, how do you identify a good designer or talented maker? OFSTED (*Providing for gifted and talented pupils: an evaluation of Excellence in Cities and other grant-funded programmes 2001*) comment that the procedures used to identify gifted pupils have been variable and suggest the development of subject-specific approaches and encouraging the skills of independent learning early in the pupil's school life as two of the ways in which to improve the identification of gifted and talented pupils.

Practical task

Read the QCA document Guidance on Teaching the Gifted and Talented: Design and Technology *(2001) which is available on-line at* www.nc.uk.net/gt/design/.

How far is the guidance offered specific to the teaching of gifted and talented pupils, as opposed to describing what good practice for all pupils should be?

The National Academy for Gifted and Talented Youth (NAGTY) **www.warwick. ac.gifted/** is in the process of building a Guidance on Pedagogy page. The current page on pedagogy offers a brief but apposite statement on teaching gifted and talented pupils – once you have identified them, of course.

Ofsted (2001) makes the observation that:

> Good teaching for gifted and talented pupils has the essential characteristics of good teaching for any pupil but it is particularly dependent on the teachers' own specialist expertise and scholarship.

Having a secure knowledge of the subject, the best teachers were aware of possibilities within the lesson and were confident, providing imaginative contexts and able to devise creative challenges. Their lesson presentation was flexible and they were able to respond to the needs of their gifted pupils, often through more advanced ways of thinking, showing pupils how to tackle complex tasks, using their knowledge and experience to approach a new task. (This sounds like gifted teaching, regardless of the presence of gifted pupils.) These gifted teachers also had:

- **the capacity to envisage and organise unusual projects and approaches which catch pupils' attention and make them want to explore the topic;**

- **the ability to deploy high-level teaching skills in defining expectations, creating a positive classroom climate for enquiry, asking probing questions, managing time and resources, and assessing progress through the lesson;**

- **the confidence to try out new ideas, to take risks and to be prepared to respond to leads which look most likely to develop higher levels of thinking by pupils.**

They provided
- **tasks which help pupils to develop perseverance and independence in learning through their own research or investigation, while ensuring that they have the**

necessary knowledge and skills to tackle the work effectively on their own;

- demanding resources that help pupils to engage with difficult or complex ideas;

- **ICT** resources to extend and enhance pupils' work and the opportunity to present the outcomes to others.

They were also, incidentally, working predominantly in non-mainstream settings – master classes, summer schools, etc. How far do you think the freedom from the demands of the set curriculum allowed the teachers to display these skills? How far were the teachers self-selecting – having a passion for their subject and interested in sharing this with gifted and talented pupils?

Health and safety

Health and safety is concerned with the assessment of hazards and risks, in order to protect people, environment *and* property, *of which people are the most important.* (Hope, 2004b, Chapter 6). The health and safety of the planet depends on good design choices too, of course (a topic that will be considered in Chapter 9, but the focus in this chapter is on teachers and children in classrooms.

It is imperative that teachers work within the requirements and procedures of the school, Local Education Authority and national risk assessment frameworks. For student teachers going in to schools on school experience placements, it is likewise imperative to take advice from mentors and class teachers regarding any activities that such requirements and procedures should cover, and also to check personal insurance position. In these days of an increasing litigation culture, such matters need to be considered seriously, not to mention the possibility of permanent physical damage to the child in question. Having children sustain serious injury whilst you are in charge of the class is traumatic. If unsure about the safety of anything – ask – and err on the side of caution.

- The **NAAIDT (National Association of Advisers and Inspectors for Design and Technology)** publish a booklet *Make it safe!* that provides guidance on good practice as well as making clear the responsibilities of teachers in design and technology lessons.

- **DATA** have a certification scheme for safe working practice in design and technology education, which may be available through your institution's design and technology education department, if a tutor has the relevant qualifications to certify your competence.

- The **British Nutritional Council** have a safety with food technology certificate and, like the **DATA** scheme, details are available on their website.

The advice that follows in this chapter, inevitably therefore, is for guidance only and cannot be quoted in defence in the event of accident. It is, however, in line with guidelines listed above.

Responsibility

The ultimate responsibility for health and safety in a school rests with the governing body, the headteacher and senior management team. However, each class teacher is responsible for their own safe working practices and that of other adults under their direction, as well as children. Assessments of risk should be a matter of course in planning design and technology lessons and students on first school experience placement should not teach design and technology without the class teacher present. DATA offers insurance cover to members of the association.

Do not teach any potentially hazardous technique or activity unless you know:

- **how to use the equipment and materials to be used both by the children and other adults;**
- **the location of the first aid box, what you are allowed to use and who the designated and trained first aiders are;**
- **fire safety procedures, including the location of fire alarms, fire extinguishers and fire blankets;**
- **the school's procedures for reporting accidents and hazards.**

Defining risks and hazards

Hazard = the potential of something (such as materials, substances, methods of work, machinery, equipment, etc.) to cause harm, including ill health, injury, damage to property and the environment.

Risk = the likelihood that an undesired effect from the hazard may occur.

LEVEL OF RISK

Likelihood: based on working knowledge and experience:

- *High*: **certain or almost certain to happen, resulting in injury or damage, difficult to avoid; could be activity carried out frequently which is not itself a high risk if only occurring occasionally;**
- *Medium*: **likely to occur; infrequent but regular activity;**
- *Low*: **very little risk of occurrence; unlikely to recur.**

Severity: based on the consequences of the accident:

- *High*: **would result in fatality/serious amputations/permanent disability;**
- *Medium*: **would result in other major (over 3-day) injury;**
- *Low*: **requires first-aid treatment only.**

Assessing risks and hazards

RISK ASSESSMENT CHECKLIST

What is the hazard?

- Slipping/tipping hazards (e.g. poorly maintained flooring, spilt fluids, furniture used inappropriately)
- Fire (e.g. from flammable materials)
- Chemicals (e.g. batteries)
- Moving parts of machinery and hand tools (e.g. blades)
- Ejection of parts or materials (e.g. from drills, moulds)
- Electricity (e.g. extension leads)
- Dust (e.g. sanding) and fumes (e.g. soldering)
- Noise (e.g. hammering)
- Poor lighting
- Insufficient space
- Poor storage (including of bags, coats, etc.)
- Manual handling

Who might be harmed?

- Person directly involved
- Others sharing workspace
- Staff in position of responsibility
- Persons with disabilities/SEN
- Cleaners and maintenance personnel
- Visitors

Is the risk adequately controlled?

- Check legal compliance, e.g. regulations covering items such as guarding machinery, PAT (Portable Appliance Test) testing
- Take precautions against the risks from the hazards you have identified
- Be sure that you have received adequate information/instruction/training in hazardous tools/techniques/materials
- Provide adequate information/instruction/training to other adults as well as to children and specify safe procedures
- Check that your precautions comply with known safety standards or Code of Practice
- Ensure that what you are doing represents good practice.
- Reduce risks as far as is practicable and consider carefully what is 'reasonably practicable' within the classroom context

HIERARCHY OF RISK CONTROL

- **Avoid the risk altogether – for all methods, substances, etc. that are harmful, ask why they are used, are they really needed, what benefit do they offer.**

- **Combat the risk at source – e.g. where floors are slippery, treat the surface rather than provide a sign.**

- Adapt the work to the individual, rather than the individual to the work.

- Give priority to measures that protect the whole workforce (adults and children).

- Ensure people understand what they need to do, from how to operate safely, to how to report concerns.

- Promote a positive health and safety culture – the prevention, avoidance and reduction of risks.

WHAT COULD YOU REASONABLY DO YOURSELF TO REDUCE THE RISKS YOU HAVE IDENTIFIED?

- Remove the risk completely.

- Try a less risky option.

- Prevent access to the hazard (e.g. by guarding).

- Organise work to reduce exposure to the hazard.

- Issue personal protective equipment.

- Provide welfare facilities (e.g. washing facilities; first aid).

- Report accidents.

A safe learning environment

To minimise risks to pupil safety, the learning environment should be safe, comfortable, hygienic. This includes ensuring that there is sufficient working space for the intended activity, that the furniture is of a suitable height and type and that the room is well lit and adequately ventilated. It is important also for the teacher to plan how and where tools, equipment and children's work (both finished and un-finished) should be stored. Plastic mushroom trays, for example, make excellent storage trays as they are light, stackable and can be easily washed. A ready supply, free of charge, can be obtained from local stores and restaurants. If you ask your local Indian or Chinese take-away or restaurant to save them for you, you will soon have more than enough (incidentally building good relationships with a source of first-hand knowledge about the food technology of their cultural heritage).

For every design and technology activity, you need to consider the following.

ARRANGEMENT OF FURNITURE

- Movement around tables (especially if some children are standing) and across (will children need to stretch too far to reach equipment?).

- Will you use chairs/stools or will everyone stand to work, bearing in mind this might mean taller children bending over tables?

- Access to resources (e.g. one-way system around the room? Only two at the glue gun table at a time?).

PROTECTIVE CLOTHING

- **Coveralls – old shirts are not really ideal. If not provided through the normal school budget, the PTA may be willing to buy proper plastic aprons for all or make them available for parents to purchase through School Shop. Insist that all children remove sweaters and roll up shirt sleeves before starting work.**

- **Plastic gloves (especially for tie-dying and printing!).**

- **Goggles/glasses should not be necessary for most activities in primary school, but might be desirable for woodwork. It also stops arguments at the workbench – the child who wears the goggles saws the wood!**

SAFE STORAGE

- **Appropriate racking with clear labels (words plus pictures/examples of actual item) that provides protection for sharp edges/points, non-metallic storage box for batteries, etc.**

- **Appropriate sorting of materials into easily accessible boxes (large sheets stored separately to scraps, recycled materials sorted by type, etc.).**

- **Weight and size of resources considered when making storage decisions.**

- **Counting/checking return of equipment (e.g. know how full scissor rack was at start of every lesson).**

- **Clear, established routine for fetching and clearing away (including managing access of potentially dangerous tools/equipment – especially true in Key Stage 1; I have taught Year 1 children who could not be trusted with scissors being left on show in the classroom).**

This last point is very important. Younger children have little idea of danger and want to explore everything. Even some Key Stage 2 children will not realise the danger of pointing the staple gun into mid-air and firing it. Children will readily see the potential of sticks of dowel as impromptu swords and you will need to stop the whole class and stress the dangers as soon as you spot the first child doing so. Say that you understand X's desire to play with the dowel like this, but who can think why you have to stop them. It is better to have a quick, sensible whole class discussion about safety that promotes responsible action *towards each other* than for the children to think that you are a typical grown-up spoilsport.

EQUIPMENT, PROCESSES AND TOOLS

- **Identify and act to minimise the hazards and risks involved in processing materials (whether holding, cutting, joining, mixing or heating).**

- **Be aware of specific dangers and safety issues connected with hot, sharp or electrical tools or equipment. Children can use sharp needles from Year 3, provided they have developed sufficient skill with sewing in Key Stage 1.**

- **Check all tools and equipment for safety and good working order before allowing children to use them.**

- **All electrical equipment must be PAT conformant. This can be seen by the presence of a yellow triangular certificate glued to the side. Check that the certificate is valid before use. Do not bring in electrical equipment from home – not even your blender, bread maker or steam iron.**

- Any electrical equipment must be plugged into a wall-mounted socket of the appropriate voltage rating. Extension leads must have automatic cut-outs and leads must, of course, go around the edges of the room. Extension leads can be used only for temporary usage equipment, which is fine for the design and technology lesson in which everything will be cleared away afterwards. The extension lead should not be left unattended for any length of time, so if it is needed again the next day, unplug it overnight.

MATERIALS AND COMPONENTS

- Especially for Key Stage I, be careful of small components (beads, construction kit parts, etc.) that may be put into mouths and swallowed. Be sure to warn children of this every time these components are used.

- Choose appropriate storage systems, especially for small components (e.g. screw-topped plastic jars).

- Be aware of dangers associated with some recycled materials that may be donated to the school and which are consequently inappropriate for children's use: anything made of sheet metal, including drinks cans, unless to be used whole; glass and plastics that easily shatter; containers whose previous contents you are unsure about or that originate from pharmaceutical, medical or agrochemical industries; toilet roll tubes; anything else that you feel unhappy or uncertain about.

- Sometimes schools are given bags of fabric of uncertain age and cleanliness. It may be worth the bother of washing and ironing, if not, politely refuse, saying that the school has enough fabric for its need right now. Unsorted bags of wood, complete with splinters and rusty nails, should be refused, as must old electrical equipment, whether working or not – solder may well contain traces of arsenic, and dead and cracked components may contain heavy metals. Undischarged capacitors can give nasty electrical shocks, even if the equipment has been switched off for some time. The older the equipment, the more potentially hazardous.

Practical task

Risk assessment exercise: glue guns

Suggest a design and technology activity in school for which you might want to use cool melt glue guns. Identify and evaluate the risks and hazards involved in organising the activity.

Consider the specific circumstances in which glue guns might be harmful (you might consider these to vary according to the age, experience, capability of the children).

Decide what needs to be done to minimise these risks and hazards.

Food

The advice on safety so far has not mentioned issues relating to food technology, since it is easier to discuss these separately. Obviously, all the points mentioned above need to be considered when dealing with food but other points are also important:

- **Hygiene: children's hands *must* be washed with germicidal soap before touching any foodstuffs – and touching of body parts after washing is strictly forbidden.**

- **Storage of food: all foods should be stored appropriately – perishables in the fridge, dry ingredients in wall cupboards, dispose of anything that reaches its sell-by date, dispose of all dry ingredients if mice or cockroaches are suspected around the storage area.**

- **Allergies to foodstuffs: ensure that you know that children will not handle ingredients to which they are allergic.**

- **Storage of utensils: all knives and other sharp or heavy tools to be kept high up out of child reach or in lockable cupboards.**

- **Aprons: separate ones for food technology – definitely not the same apron as for painting! Ideally these should be plastic and sponged down with germicidal liquid after each use. If fabric, wash (along with all tea towels) after every use. Soak all cloths used for surface wiping and washing up in germicidal solution overnight. Use separate hand towels and tea towels (ideally use disposable paper towels for hand drying).**

- **Hot plates and ovens: Children in the primary school will not, of course, be putting food in the oven themselves or stirring things in saucepans on the hob, but there is no reason why Key Stage 1 children cannot make items that need cooking. They need to be reminded of safe working around heat sources (*What does mummy tell you at home?*) and that they will not be touching anything hot. Make sure the adults do not leave tea towels to dry off over a half-open oven door!**

- **Knives: Key Stage 1 children should have access only to blunt knives for spreading. Key Stage 2 children can use sharp knives provided they are taught the correct way to do so (watch television chefs!). Making a salad can give plenty of practice of this if lots of carrots, celery and radish are included.**

- **Washing up: children should be encouraged to wash up and clear away as part of their food technology experience. Many children are encouraged to do such chores at home and have relevant skills and understanding. However, be aware of the potential hazards of caustic ingredients in washing up liquids and powders. Minimise risk by purchasing a brand that is recommended for sensitive skins. Heavy, sharp or breakable items should be put to one side for an adult to deal with separately.**

What happens if a child is allergic to certain ingredients or is not permitted to eat them for health or religious reasons? The easy way to ensure that this does not happen is to send home to all children a list of ingredients they will be handling and/ or eating as a 'permission slip to participate'. Do not risk 'no news is good news' – in case, unknown to you, the child who is allergic to the main ingredient has just forgotten to get the slip signed. If the food technology work is spread over several days or weeks (a group at a time with a TA, for example), it gives those who forgot the permission slip the chance to take home another one ready for next time.

The need for hygiene in preparation of foodstuffs cannot be stressed strongly enough. Children with runny noses and coughs should not be allowed to participate and this should be stated clearly on the permission slip. This ban only creates distress if food technology is a rare treat and these simple hygiene rules are not made clear to the children. If food technology happens regularly (or if one group per week cook whilst the others are doing something else equally exciting) then waiting a week until the cold has passed is not a problem. There is, however, the problem of the children who are never clean, with permanent cold sores, ingrained fingernails or nits in their eyebrows. If time permitted, they could be asked to help get everything ready and 'discover' that some things have been put away dirty and need a good wash – hot water and washing-up liquid will deal with the finger-nails. Teachers are not, however, permitted to attempt to wash a child's face, apply antiseptic cream or remove nits (or part hair to look for them). Do not, on any account, tackle parents about their standards of hygiene. One of the senior management team in the school will have responsibility for child welfare and a word with them about your concerns will clarify the school's position on these issues.

HEALTH AND SAFETY AWARENESS CHECKLIST

This is a suitable finding-out activity for school experience placement. It is not an exhaustive list covering all aspects of health and safety but is designed to raise your awareness of the practical outworking of some of the points raised in this chapter:

- **Ask to see a copy of the school's health and safety policy.**
- **Ask about the governing body's Health and Safety Committee – how often does it meet, what is its remit, do members observe/comment on safe working practices in design and technology lessons?**
- **Who has a first aid certificate?**
- **How should accidents be reported?**
- **What are the procedures in case of accident? Who should you call first?**

In the school:
- **Who is responsible for the storage and auditing of potentially hazardous tools/ equipment/materials?**
- **Where/how are potentially hazardous tools/equipment/materials stored, e.g. iron, saws, craft knives, food technology equipment?**
- **How are adult-use-only tools and equipment kept out of reach of children (including ovens)?**
- **How/where are food technology ingredients stored?**
- **Where are cleaning materials stored and who has access to them?**

In the classroom:

- Where are potentially hazardous tools/equipment/materials stored?

- Where/how are these set up for use by children?

- How are potentially hazardous activities organised and who supervises them?

- How are tools/equipment/materials for less-hazardous design and technology activities arranged prior to/during a lesson (e.g. on a side table, centrally accessible on group tables, etc.)?

- How do children move around the room during design and technology lessons (e.g. are there special class rules in place)?

- How are the safety implications of the needs of children with **SEN** or **AEN** taken into account?

- What signal does the teacher use for 'all stop' in the event of a potentially hazardous situation arising?

- Whose responsibility is it to clear up after messy activities that might present hazards to others?

If you are planning to teach the lesson, then change each question in this last list to begin with 'How will I …?'

The last word:

       Remember

           Prevention is better than cure!

Planning to teach design and technology:
a summary of key points

In this chapter, you have learnt about:

_____ long-, medium- and short-term plans *that ensure meaningful progression of tasks and activities across several lessons to enable children to develop their design and making skills;*

_____ *how to structure your lessons to enable children to gain maximum benefit from the opportunities they are offered, to engage with the topic and develop their own creative solution to the task;*

_____ *ensuring that all children are able to become involved in your lessons and feel a sense of personal achievement;*

_____ *health and safety: assessing and minimising the risks and hazards inherent in practical activities in the classroom during design and technology lessons.*

Appendices

The Appendices relating to this chapter appear on pages 209–14.

Appendix C: A scheme of work for Key Stage 1: Year 1 Growing Things
Appendix D: A lesson plan for Lesson 5 of this scheme
Appendix E: A scheme of work for Key Stage 2: Year 5/6: Portable Homes
Appendix F: A lesson plan for Lesson 1 of this scheme

References

DfEE (2005a) *Extended Schools*. London: Department for Education and Employment. (Based on the government initiative *Every Child Matters*, 2004).

DfEE (2003) *Excellence and Enjoyment: a strategy for primary schools*. London: Department for Education and Employment.

DfEE (2005) *Higher Standards, Better Schools for All*. London: Department for Education and Employment.

Hope, G (2004) *Teaching Design and Technology 3–11*. London: Continuum

Hope, G (2006) The needs of seeds, *5то7 educator*, 5 (3): National Curriculum section, DORT.

NAAIDT (National Association of Advisers and Inspectors in Design and Technology) (1992) *Make It Safe*. Reading: NAAIDT Publications.

OFSTED (2001) *Providing for gifted and talented pupils: an evaluation of Excellence in Cities and other grant-funded programmes*. London: OFSTED.

QCA (2001a) *Planning, Teaching and Assessing the Curriculum for Pupils with Learning Difficulties: Design and Technology*. **www.qca.org.uk**

QCA (2001b) *Supporting School Improvement: emotional and behavioural development*. **www.qca.org.uk**

QCA (2001c) *Guidance on Teaching the Gifted and Talented: Design and Technology*. **www.qca.org.uk**

QCA (2005) *Using the P Scales*. **www.qca.og.uk**

Websites

www.nc.uk.net/gt/design/ for DfEE (2001) *Guidance on Teaching the Gifted and Talented: Design and Technology*.

www.warwick.ac.gifted/ National Academy for Gifted and Talented Youth (NAGTY).

6 ASSESSMENT, EVALUATION AND CELEBRATION IN DESIGN AND TECHNOLOGY

This chapter considers not only the assessment of children's achievements in design and technology by teachers, but also the development of children's own ability to evaluate the progress and final success of their design project, and the ways that such success can be celebrated.

This chapter, therefore, covers three topics:

- *assessment for learning in design and technology;*
- *evaluation within the design process;*
- *celebration of achievement.*

Note about terminology: The words assessment *and* evaluation *have overlapping meanings. However, within education, the word* assessment *is more often used for interactions that are* teacher → pupil's ideas/work *and* evaluation *for pupil → other pupil(s)' ideas/work. This is the usage of the two words that will be employed in this chapter.*

Assessment for learning in design and technology

The purpose of assessing children's learning in design and technology is to enable teachers to help children towards higher levels of achievement, as defined by the National Curriculum Level Descriptors. As indicated in the title, this section is about assessment *for* learning, not just assessment *of* learning. There is a world of difference within those two words. Assessment *of* learning does not imply that the child will be taught anything more as a result. It implies completion: the course has run, how much does the pupil know? The emphasis in this chapter is assessment *for* learning: what are the next steps in the pupil's learning to be?

You need to be aware of the problems inherent within assessment-led teaching. This is already a problem in literacy and numeracy due to league tables and it is vital that this does not become the case for creative subjects. One problem inherent in published schemes of work or support materials for the QCA schemes, is that the assessment criteria are too prescribed. Be wary of statements that specify too precisely what the children should or will have achieved within a lesson or scheme of work. Designing is by its very nature creative and it is dangerous to suggest that only certain outcomes to design tasks can count as successes. Often adult designers do not know what the answer to the design problem will be:

> *But how will you look for something when you don't in the least know what it is? How on earth are you going to set up something you don't know as the object of your search?*

To put it another way, even if you come right up against it, how will you know that what you have found is the thing you didn't know? (Plato, *c*.500 BC)

Case study

Escaping the Minotaur

Zara, Year 3, making a model of the Maze to help Theseus escape from the Minotaur:

Zara made a simple box 'maze' and cut-out Minotaur figure, but then made a river outside the castle walls with a crocodile in it and a boat to help Theseus escape from the crocodile:

Zara (pointing): **This is for the crocodile to come in (blue card).**
Lee: **It's a Minotaur.**
Zara: **No, a crocodile is in the garden; I'm doing a boat, walls and a door.**

Later: Zara is playing with it – walking the Minotaur about inside the maze.

Is this off-task or highly creative?

How would you assess Zara's work?

For fuller discussion of this question see Hope (2004).

Teachers need to distinguish between assessing the *product* and assessing the *process*. A product or even a class set of products may be produced to a high standard of workmanship but the children may have been given few design choices. The teacher may have provided templates or the children may have been assisted by an adult who believed that the teacher wanted well-finished products without understanding that in the teacher's mind, the *design process* was more important. This can be a particular problem for children with special educational needs, who can inadvertently be denied choices over the design of their product because their assisting adult makes all the design decisions for them and talks them through the making process. The National Curriculum Level Descriptors describe generic skills and design processes, so assessment of children's design capability needs to focus on process skills.

Modes of assessment

Assessment comes in a range of combinations:

	Diagnostic	Formative	Summative
Informal	?	?	?
Formal	?	?	?

INFORMAL *v* FORMAL ASSESSMENT

Informal assessment is the kind that teachers do moment by moment throughout the school day. It includes everything from using children's answers to questions as feedback to gauge understanding of the task that has just been set, to keeping notes on children's progress or marks given for achievement. It may or may not be linked to the teacher's intention to move the child forward in their learning. Formal assessment is characterised by reference to external and recognised criteria, and is usually performed via a set-piece task, such as an examination. Formal assessment does not occur in design and technology in the primary school. The National Curriculum provides Level Descriptors against which teachers in primary schools are required to assign levels to children's work through informal assessment. This does not mean that this assessment is not informed by national guidelines, rather that no formal tests (such as the National Tests) were administered to ascertain the children's attainment.

DIAGNOSTIC, FORMATIVE AND SUMMATIVE ASSESSMENT

- **Diagnostic assessment tells teacher and pupil where they are starting from.**

- **Formative assessment tells them where they have got to and where they need to go next.**

- **Summative assessment tells them what destination they have reached.**

Diagnostic assessment is the assessment that the teacher undertakes at the start of a topic to ascertain pupils' prior knowledge, skill or understanding. In design and technology this will be conducted informally. It might be as simple as asking the class *Did you use saws in Mrs S.'s class last year?* or *How many of you were able to use the batik with Mrs W.?* It may also be the observations that are made, often in the first weeks of term, that give teachers the sense of the overall capability of the class. In design and technology it is less likely to be a set task by which the teacher assesses the children's capability, in the way in which one might do so at the beginning of a new maths topic, for example.

Formative assessment may be teacher–pupil, pupil–pupil and pupil–self. The aim of formative assessment is to inform on progress in order to enable further progress and learning. Formative assessment is only formative if it is also informative. Thus a tick list of 'task complete' is a poor tool for formative assessment. There needs to be also a qualitative comment about the way in which the child tackled the task for the record to be of use in planning future work. Such notes are always useful as they give a more accurate record of the capability of the children than relying on an overall impression of busy-ness.

Formative assessment, at its heart, is the analysis of children's learning that enables the teacher to know what the child needs to learn next. Subjects such as literacy and numeracy, which have clear targets set through the National Strategies, lend themselves readily to accurate assessment of pupils' progress. For other subjects, including design and technology, the criteria are less closely defined and the teacher has to develop their own sense of what this means for the children in their class.

Barlex *et al.*: (2000) summarise the purposes of formative assessment as:

- **to let the teacher know how well the student is doing;**
- **to let the student know how well he/she is doing;**
- **to help the teacher and student work together in helping the student improve;**
- **to tell others how well the student is doing;**
- **to tell others what they can do to help a student improve.**

Summative assessment provides a summary of children's learning. This is most clearly exemplified in the end-of-year report to parents. It may also be directed towards celebrating the achievements of the children, perhaps in the form of an End of Project Certificate (see below, Celebration of Achievement).

National Curriculum Level Descriptors

The National Curriculum for design and technology has a single Attainment Target for which Level Descriptors are given (from levels 1–6 for primary school pupils) and it is suggested that you have a copy of these Level Descriptors to hand as you read this section.

The Level Descriptors of the National Curriculum for design and technology are meant to be read holistically. If you pick out sentence by sentence and compare each statement level by level (each one on planning, for instance) you will find it difficult to see how each sentence, standing alone, represents progression. It is as you read the whole of each Level Descriptor that you gain an understanding of the standard of work that is expected at each stage.

Practical task

Apply the Level Descriptors to the designing and making of at least one child whom you are able to observe in school. If possible, do this activity with several children across different classes or across key stages.

Alternatively or additionally:
Apply the Level Descriptors to the designing and making of one child you know well outside of the school context. This could be your own child, or the child of a neighbour, friend or a family member.

Although written to support the 1993 National Curriculum, *Expectations in Design and Technology at Key Stages 1 and 2* (SCAA, 1997) is a useful document which contains exemplars of achievement at the end of Years 2, 4 and 6, that can be a useful indication of national expectations. Access to exemplars are invaluable for less experienced teachers to see what the Level Descriptors mean in terms of real children's work and act as a means by which all teachers can check the validity of their own judgement. Sarah Ward (2001) reported that she had been judging her class's work by far too high a standard until she went on a course and compared the work of her children with that from other schools. It is difficult to interpret words in a document unless you have seen examples of what is meant.

It is easy to become accustomed to the work of one's own class or school and not be aware of how this really relates to children of the same age in other schools in the local area. Relating your own class's achievements to national expectations is significantly aided by seeing exemplars. Many schools keep portfolios of work labelled with National Curriculum levels to assist teachers in this process and have informal or formal arrangements with other local schools to moderate each other's assessments. This is especially important at transfer (either at end of Key Stage 1 or Key Stage 2) and consultation on assessment between Year 6 and secondary schools builds trust and respect. It can be quite hard, for experienced teachers even more than their less experienced colleagues, to consult with colleagues from different key stages as there are inevitably feelings of defensiveness and fear of criticism. These fears need to be overcome as there is no point in being protective over territory or defensive of personal opinion or position if it will not, in the long run, benefit the children we teach.

For interesting international comparisons see the New Zealand Curriculum Exemplars for Technology which can be viewed online at **www.tki.org.nz/r/ assessment/exemplars/tech/index_e_php**. New Zealand Attainment Levels are not the same as the UK Level Descriptors, so the examplar shown as level 3 on **www.tki.org.nz/r/assessment/exemplars/tech/structures/pdfs/sm_3a_ e_pdf** represents expectation for 11-year-olds (i.e. UK Year 6). The New Zealand National Curriculum for Technology is downloadable from **www.minedu. govt.nz/web/downloadable/dl3614._1/tech-nzc.pdf** and makes interesting comparative reading.

What counts as evidence?

Looking at the national curricula and assessment methods of other countries can enable us to be reflective on our own practice and presumptions. David Barlex, Malcolm Welch and colleagues devised the following set of questions to find evidence of performance in the areas of achievement for the Elementary Science and Technology Curriculum of Ontario, Canada (reported in Barlex et al., 2000):

A. Understanding of basic concepts:
   What concepts are important?
   Where is there evidence of understanding?
   How extensive is this understanding?
   Can I now assign a level?
   Do I need to look outside the big task for evidence?

B. Inquiry, design and 'safe use' skills:
   What are the skills?
   Where is there evidence of their use?
   How effective is their use?
   Can I now assign a level?
   Do I need to look outside the big task for evidence?

C. Relating of science and technology to each other and to the world outside school:
   What connections are important?
   Where is the evidence for the connections being made?
   What is the significance of these connections?
   Can I now assign a level?
   Do I need to look outside the big task for evidence?

D. Communication of required knowledge:
    What communication took place?
    What range of communication media were used?
    How effective was it?
    Can I now assign a level?
    Do I need to look outside the big task for evidence?

Reflective task

What underlying differences are there between the Ontario curriculum and the one in the UK?

Does it nevertheless suggest a model that might be useful to teachers in UK schools?

For instance, if each of the Knowledge, Skills and Understandings statements were substituted as titles for each section, would this cover all the aspects of design and technology or would parts of the Breadth of Study be left out?

The Ontario curriculum is based on the Nuffield Foundation scheme that uses 'Small Steps – Big Task' rather than focused practical tasks and design and make assignments, and there are subtle differences. You probably also noticed that there is a section on science–technology links, because this is an elementary science and technology curriculum, rather than a design and technology curriculum. However, the wording in C could be changed to 'Relating of design and technology to other curriculum areas and to the world outside school' for UK use, along with changing the 'big task' to 'design and make assignment' in each list.

Assessment of children's capability could be through a combination of:

• **discussion with children of their ideas and progress of the project;**

• **drawings;**

• **photographs of work in progress;**

• **the final product.**

While conducting research into children's design capabilities, I found that the easiest means of collecting data on work in progress was to have a notebook constantly to hand and to make quick sketches as well as verbatim records of comments that children made, combined with photographs. The children became so used to this method of recording their work that they would come and say *I have just done something I want you to draw in your book* or *I've just thought of … Can you write that down*. These Year 2 children became metacognitively aware of their own design thought because they wanted it to be recorded in the book. Their design skills and processes were being valued in a way that was not usually the case with practical activities in schools.

Likewise, Maggie Rogers and Dominic Clare's Process Diary (see Chapter 4) is not only a means by which children can assemble their own record of their work in progress, but can be a rich source of assessment data for the teacher.

Recording summative assessment

The simplest means of recording whether or not children have achieved expected National Curriculum levels at the end of a project is by devising a form such as the one shown here, used by South Avenue Primary School in Sittingbourne, Kent. On such a checklist there is no need to record the individual achievement of every child. If your teaching is aimed appropriately for the majority of the class, then most children will have achieved the learning objectives. What you need to know for your future planning (assessment *for* learning) is:

- **who has achieved a higher level and will need additional extension work or greater challenges next time;**
- **who is not working yet at the same level as the majority of the class and who will therefore need extra support or adaptation of the next project.**

In the boxes on South Avenue Primary School's End of Unit Assessment there is space to write the levels at which both these sets of pupils are achieving. Teachers may well want to make more detailed notes on specific pupils, which can, of course, be written on the back of the sheet. The sheets are used as a summary sheet in conjunction with the DATA Primary Technology Lesson Plans, which provide assessment criteria and recording sheets for each of the units of the QCA schemes of work.

Design and Technology – End of Unit Assessment

Date: Class: Expected Level: 1 2 3 4 5

All children have achieved this level with the exception of those stated below:

Names:

Children achieving above stated level

Children achieving below stated level

Evaluation in the design process

Self-evaluation is also a form of formative assessment and is one of the meta-skills of designing. It involves the ability to evaluate one's own learning and progress towards a predetermined goal.

Children evaluating their own work

Evaluation is an integral part of designing but young children are not sufficiently aware of their own thought processes to realise that evaluation is a natural part of everyday decision-making and problem-solving. Teachers can help children to begin to become aware of their thinking by sensitive debriefing and open-ended questioning about their thought process. Too often children are asked to make semi-formal evaluations of their work without having been taught the skill of reflecting on process.

Garvey and Quinlan's article 'Why don't I just throw it in the bin?' in DATA's *Journal of Design & Technology Education* (1998) highlights the problems inherent in such a situation. Year 2 children were asked to draw designs for lamps on paper ahead of engaging with materials. When the teacher questioned whether the products they had designed would work, the children perceived the drawings of their designs as 'wrong', hence the question that forms the title of the article.

Reflective activity

How do teachers value and support children's work in progress and encourage them to develop evaluative skills?

Consider the role of:

- *open-ended questioning (e.g What could you use to join these two parts?)*

- *scaffolding (e.g. Shall I show you what I might do?)*

- *guided participation (e.g. Let me hold that like you want it to go and you stand back and look at it ...)*

in opening up and broadening out children's problem solving and thinking and modelling skills.

End of project evaluation

What I could have done better if ...

> The teacher had let me do my first idea instead of having to think of another two;
> I hadn't had to work with Shani;
> I could have worked on my own;
> There had been enough saws to go round;
> Sam hadn't nicked my bit of balsa;
> I'd remembered to bring in my new felt pens;
> We had been given some better colours to choose from ...

If it does nothing else, the end of project evaluation forces all these wayward thoughts underground. Children dutifully write about how they would approach the project again, given the chance, complete with pictures. How much of this activity is for the child's benefit and how much is to satisfy the teacher's desire for them to have something in their books, is open to question.

Especially for younger children, and if children had maintained a Process Diary throughout the project, a simple 'happy sheet' can be used to record their overall reflections at the end of a project.

Did you enjoy designing your jewellery?	☀	☺	☺	☹
How easy did you find it?	☀	☺	☺	☹
Did you enjoy making drawings for your jewellery?	☀	☺	☺	☹
How easy was this?	☀	☺	☺	☹
Did you enjoy learning new techniques?	☀	☺	☺	☹
How easily did you master them?	☀	☺	☺	☹

'Happy sheet' for end of project evaluation

The questions can be adapted according to the nature of the project and the age of the children.

Children evaluating each other's work

Pupil—pupil formative assessment is often referred to as peer review. This can be a useful strategy in encouraging children's design thinking as it forces them to externalise their ideas. Often children have only a hazy notion about what they will make or how their idea will satisfy the design criteria. Being asked to tell someone else their idea forces them to be more precise and puts their ideas under scrutiny. However, the vague instruction 'tell your partner what you intend to make' will not help clarity of thinking. The teacher needs to give specific questions to be answered and to actively support those children who will find this activity difficult. Five minutes of unproductive chatting will not move children's design thinking forward, and it is more than likely that their thoughts will lose momentum.

Sarah Ward's (2001) article 'The planning, delivery and evaluation of a moving pictures project' is a case study by a reflective practitioner. Verbal evaluation by children of each other's work was part of her original planning but although Sarah had intended to do this as a plenary at the end of the last session, the children were busy engaged in the task and so she let them carry on and did the evaluation the next day. This allowed time for each child to come to the front and demonstrate their picture. There was then an opportunity for the rest of the class to say what they liked about it and make suggestions for improvements. The teacher then gave children a choice: do you want to make these changes? They did and worked purposefully in making the improvements suggested by the other children. The key to the success of this approach was in the way the evaluations were set up. The teacher stressed the importance of constructive comments only. The children were in charge of their own agenda, pace and reflective process.

Key Stage 2 children can present their group ideas for scrutiny by other groups.

Case study

4M St Peter's Primary School: Menu for 'Healthy Lunches Restaurant'

Lesson 1: Designing lunches
Introduction (10 mins): whole class discussion – reviewing knowledge about healthy food and balanced diet. Explanation of task: class menu: show set menu pages of menus from Beijing Inn and Flyovers (scanned images shown on Interactive white board). Each group to devise healthy set menu for three-course lunch plus drinks to become one page of class menu.

Group work (four groups of six children) (30 mins): using recipe books as research source, devising menu for three-course lunch plus drinks, to provide healthy balanced meal. To think about: range of colour texture and taste. Recorded as list on flip chart sheet in felt pen to aid presentation.

Feedback (20 mins): each group presented menu to class, justifying choices. Suggestions made by rest of class recorded in pencil on flip chart sheet.

Lesson 2
In computer suite – designing set menu cards (30 mins): Working in pairs, using clip art and Word Art, designing set menu card for group menu. Each pair typed in words for one course; TA and class teacher assisted assembling group document, swapping files via floppy disks. Each pair then used Word Art and clip art (borders and pictures) to design attractive menu card. It was not expected that any pair would finish and most had not. During PE after lunch, the TA loaded all the work onto the class laptop ready for evaluative discussion.

Lesson 3
After PE (20 mins): Everyone's work shown on interactive white board (through Print Preview – the TA made one long Word document). Class discussion – what next as class (emphasised this was not comment on individual work). Decided to

put together one set menu from each group to make one menu book. The computer technician who called in to watch the show suggested they could be printed out as A5 and put back-to-back into an A4 laminator pocket and she offered to take the children in 4s to do this next week.

Lesson 4
Early finishers began to design covers as the computer technician assembled the printouts ready for laminating. The covers were completed in after-school Computer Club.

Celebration of achievement

PRAISE AND ENCOURAGEMENT
This should be part of every lesson but beware of empty praise or false sympathy. It is not helpful to tell a child that it does not matter that their model has just fallen apart and their afternoon's work has been wasted. No teacher would say this about a child's writing or maths, so it should not be said about their design and technology work either. Children appreciate a genuine discussion about the success or shortfalls of their ideas. The design might be failing because the materials they are working with will not support their ideas. This frequently frustrates Year 5 and 6 children who want a greater realism in their work. The originality of children's ideas needs congratulating, whilst acknowledging the limitations in the attempt to realise them.

AN END OF PROJECT CERTIFICATE
This is especially useful for projects that are made by a group of children or become part of a display, so that not every child has something to take home. A simple means of producing these is to take digital photographs of work in progress as well as the finished product and insert these into a certificate proforma. Microsoft Works includes a Task Wizard that produces good-looking certificates, as do many other software packages. You can create and save a range of these, containing a suitable range of appropriate comments for each project. As well as providing the child and parents with recognition of their achievement, it also provides the teacher with an aide memoire when writing the end of year report. This is especially useful as a record of group projects, as each child's contribution can be praised.

PUBLIC RECOGNITION
Recognition within and beyond the school can come through:

- **displays in corridors, lobby, library, hall, etc., especially when parents are visiting for other events;**
- **assemblies;**
- **open doors – invite parents/carers to come to a special viewing of their children's work laid out on tables in the classroom half an hour before end of school;**
- **school fête/bazaar – but be aware of ethics of selling school work – would you sell a child's story?**
- **special design and technology events;**

- competitions – enter all local and national design competitions; being placed is a bonus;

- local events and places of interest – see your school's work in the post office or local library to commemorate the new bridge, motorway tunnel or 200 years of cotton spinning;

- Design and Technology Week (contact **DATA** for help and ideas);

- local newspapers – invite them to all significant events in the life of the school.

There has been a continuing thread relating children's present understanding and achievements to your planning for their future learning in design and technology. Simplified models of assessment process and design process placed side by side enable comparison between the teacher's planning and assessment cycle and the child's designing (refer back to Rob Johnsey's (1995) MEM and EAI cycles in Chapter 2, page 20).

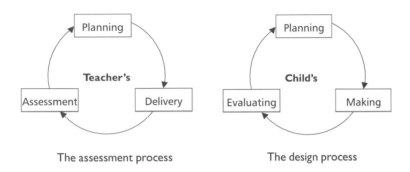

The assessment process   The design process

Reflective task

Why do you think these are so similar?

Relate your answer to Rogers and Clare's design process spiral (see Chapter 3). This was based on Kolb's learning spiral which underpins concepts such as the 'spiral curriculum' in which topics are revisited frequently at ever-deepening levels.

Assessment, evaluation and celebration: a summary of key points

In the three topics that this chapter has covered:

_____ *assessment for learning in design and technology;*

_____ *evaluation within the design process;*

_____ *celebration of achievement;*

References

Barlex, D *et al.* (2000) Developing an approach to assessment for the elementary science and technology curriculum of Ontario, in *Conference Proceedings*, International Design and Technology Education Research Conference (IDATER2000). Loughborough University: Department of Design and Technology.

Garvey, J and Quinlan, A (1998) Why don't I just throw it in the bin? – Evaluation and self-esteem. *The Journal of Design & Technology Education*, 2 (1).

Hope, G (2004) 'Little c' creativity and 'Big I' innovation within the context of design and technology education, in *Conference proceedings*, DATA International Research Conference 2004, Sheffield.

Johnsey, R (1995) The place of process skill in making in design and technology: lessons from research into the way primary children design and make, in *Conference Proceedings*, International Design and Technology Education Research Conference (IDATER95). Loughborough University: Department of Design and Technology.

Rogers, M and Clare, D (1994) The Process Diary: developing capability within National Curriculum Design and Technology, in *Conference Proceedings*, International Design and Technology Education Research Conference (IDATER94). Loughborough University: Department of Design and Technology.

SCAA (1997) *Expectations in design and technology at Key Stages 1 and 2.* London: SCAA (Schools Curriculum and Assessment Authority).

Ward, S (2001) The planning, delivery and evaluation of a moving pictures project. *Journal of Design & Technology Education*, 6 (3).

This chapter outlines the subject areas usually covered in practical activities within design and technology lessons. There are many excellent books to support individual projects and topics, as well as those that provide a comprehensive treatment of the subject areas. The aim of this chapter is to provide an introduction to this subject knowledge and to consider it in terms of classroom pedagogy, rather than in terms of providing you with a range of techniques or information that is readily available elsewhere.

The subject content of design and technology is considered under the following four headings:

- *artefacts, systems and environments: contexts for practical activity in design and technology;*
- *materials, components and tools: cutting, shaping and joining the range of materials and components suitable for primary children, including textiles;*
- *engineering: covering buildings, structures, vehicles, mechanisms and control;*
- *food technology: production as well as preparing, presenting and eating.*

Artefacts, systems and environments

The first National Curriculum for design and technology introduced primary teachers to three terms with which they were unfamiliar, *artefacts, systems* and *environments*. These dropped out of subsequent documentation since they had intimidated rather than supported teachers struggling to get to grips with the new subject. If these were introduced again now, they would probably be less problematic and possibly be helpful in extending teachers' thinking about design and technology education beyond 'cutting and sticking'. With no apologies, therefore, the first section of this chapter on subject content examines these three categories.

Definitions

Artefacts are single products: shoes, pizzas, chairs, tables, necklaces, ships, bridges, houses, etc. The word 'product' is commonly used as an alternative term.

Systems are combinations of components, mechanisms and their connections. Systems may be:

- **physical, e.g. the hydraulic braking system of a car;**
- **electrical, e.g. your house lighting system;**
- **electronic, e.g. computer systems such as the internet; telecommunications networks;**
- **economic, e.g. the banking system or the retail trade;**

- social, civic, commercial, political, etc.

Artefacts can contain systems, for example, ships and houses contain communication, fuel, water and electrical systems.

Systems can contain artefacts, for example, electrical systems contain switches, light bulbs, motors, power supplies.

Systems can contain subsystems that contain artefacts and/or artefacts that contain systems, for example, the National Grid, the Rail Network.

Environments are the contexts in which systems and artefacts are used or operate. At the highest level the whole planet is the environment for all human technological activity. At a smaller scale, a large trading estate and the supply systems and support services that the companies use comprise an industrial environment. The local high street or out-of-town shopping centre is also a technological environment, using support services of delivery and postal companies, cleaning, building services and maintenance, security, public transport and car parking, etc.

The New Zealand National Curriculum for technology places these three levels of technological engagement centrally in its definition of technology:

> *Technology is a creative, purposeful activity aimed at meeting needs and opportunities through the development of products, systems, or environments. Knowledge, skills and resources are combined to help solve practical problems. Technological practice takes place within, and is influenced by, social contexts.*

Practical task

Consider the progress of one product (artefact) you bought recently (an article of clothing or entertainment, perhaps) and draw a concept web to identify the systems that supported the delivery of the artefact to your hands. Include the unseen computer systems involved in stock ordering and sales too.

Are there parts of the environment surrounding the shopping experience that are not included? The ambience of the shopping mall, the park and ride bus service, the eating places nearby, availability of cash machines?

Where would you place these on your diagram?

What about the impact of the place you bought your artefact on other shopping areas, local housing, transport networks, employment opportunities, the landscape, water supply, drainage and sewage treatment, rubbish and waste disposal?

All of this and more comprises the environment surrounding your purchase.

Key Stage 2 children can begin to appreciate the issues affecting the natural environment but will be simplistic in their solutions (e.g. ban all cars from the high street). In Upper Key Stage 2 you can begin to discuss with children how the systems interconnect within the environment.

How would you adapt this activity for a Year 6 class who live close to a brown-field site that is earmarked for a new retail park?

Materials, components and tools

Materials are cut and shaped in order to be made into something. *Components* are combined with materials or other components to make something. Some things can be either materials or components depending on context.

It is usual to refer to something that has been changed in the course of construction as a material and things that do not change as components but there seem to be no hard and fast rules on this.

Materials

Various terms are used to describe materials available for design and technology:

• **Resistant materials (as opposed to mouldable)**

Resistant materials are those that require joining by some technique other than simply pressing them together. For instance, card and paper require either gluing or notching and slotting.

• **Mouldable materials**

These materials are those like clay that can be made into shapes by hand and can be pushed together (or with addition of water) to join. Pastry is an edible mouldable material.

• **Sheet materials**

These include anything that comes in large flat pieces, such as card, paper, corroflute, foam.

• **Frame materials**

These are all those structural materials that do not come in sheets, such as dowel and square section wood, wire, straws, etc.

• **Recycled or reclaimed materials**

This category includes all the packets, cartons, tubs and tubes (not toilet roll ones) that you collect in the classroom and also the wool, fabrics, wood off-cuts, polystyrene shapes, etc. that kind parents bring in and all the offcuts and scrap that you can collect from commercial and industrial sources locally. Be careful about health and safety with some of these, however.

• *Fabrics*

Although the word 'material' is often used for cloth in ordinary speech, it is advisable to use the word 'fabric' with children to avoid confusion. The word 'cloth' is usually applied to woven or close-knitted fabrics. There are three kinds of fabric: woven, knitted and felted. See later section in this chapter on Textiles.

There are also:

• **Decorative materials**

These are materials such as shiny paper that is used to give an aesthetic appeal to the product.

• **Ingredients**

These are the materials of food technology (see Food section of this chapter).

• **Plastazote and other heat-mouldable foams**

These can be cut to shape and placed in a warm oven to become mouldable. Upper Key Stage 2 only.

And, of course, there are some multi-purpose and unclassified materials that do not neatly fit into any category (e.g. pipe-cleaners).

Components

These are items that are not cut or shaped in order to be made into something:

• **all the small, ubiquitous joining components: paper clips, treasury tags, split pins, etc.;**
• **decorative items used whole: beads, sequins, feathers, etc.;**
• **electrical parts: batteries, bulbs, switches, motors, buzzers;**
• **mechanical parts: wheels, cams, gears, elastic bands, rotor blades, etc.;**
• **syringes and bottles used for pneumatics and hydraulics (the tubing is usually classified as a component of the system, rather than as a material);**
• **construction kits are component-based construction systems;**
• **food ingredients that stay whole (e.g. currants) are also, strictly speaking, components, not materials.**

Tools for cutting materials

• **Scissors**

Key Stage I children may use rounded end scissors only. Separate fabric scissors need to be sharper and not blunted by use on card and paper. Heavy duty snips must be kept separately and can be used safely by Key Stage 2 children. There is progression in the skill of scissor use that is not immediately apparent to adults who intuitively adjust the pressure and twist of the blade almost as soon as they begin to cut the material.

Most children will have mastered basic scissor use by the time they enter Key Stage I. However, you will observe children attempting to pull sideways with scissors rather than cutting, especially on thick or tough materials. You will also observe that if the scissors' central rivet has become loose, this will present children with difficulties as they are not able to control the sideways movement and the cutting motion simultaneously.

Left-handed scissors and snips are essential classroom equipment. The school should keep a stock of scissors that are adapted for children with poor muscle control. These come in a range of designs and are available from specialist suppliers.

- **Craft knives**

These are for adult use only. Store out of reach of children. Use them with a metal safety ruler and a safety mat. It is also best to avoid small hand-held cutters with rolling blades.

- **Other cutters**

Pinking shears, fancy-cut scissors, 'magic safety cutters' and Rototrim paper cutters with safety guards can be used by children.

- **Bench hooks, vices, saws**

Year 2 and above may use these in small groups with supervision. Teach sawing technique and allow children to practise (focused practical task) before cutting parts for the final product.

- **Making holes**

For card, use a hole drill, single-hole punch or 150cm nail on to a scrap of carpet tile. A ballpoint pen or sharp pencil on to a ball of modelling clay is effective for thin card. In lolly sticks and thin wood use a heavy-duty hole punch. Year 6 may use a hand drill if mounted in a drill stand. A bradawl is for teacher use only. See Chapter 4 for additional advice on hole-making.

Shaping mouldable materials

- **Play dough/salt dough**

(2 mugs flour, I mug salt, I tablespoon cooking oil, water with food colour to mix — add slowly and have extra flour ready if necessary)
This material is cheap, can be made by children, can be 'cooked' in slow oven or microwave, painted and varnished when cooled. For Key Stage 2 — it can be used as a focused practical task material for designing biscuits, shaped rolls and pastries. The children can enjoy experimenting with a range of techniques and shapes, rolled and pulled by hand or cut with pastry cutters and blunt knives, or combinations of both. They can then decide the form of their products ahead of mixing the real ingredients. This kind of work is one way in which to introduce a genuine design element into food technology. The salt dough products can be left out overnight to dry, be compared to

the final products and could even be varnished and sent along to a Foundation Stage class as play props for a class shop or home corner.

- **Clay**

Since most primary schools do not have a kiln, this is air-drying clay, which must be stored correctly or it will dry out. Place a damp sponge in the bag with the clay to maintain humidity and check frequently. Products must be varnished soon after drying or they will crumble to dust. PVA mixed into powder paint is adequate. Water-based varnishes are also suitable, if rather most expensive and time-consuming, but give a better finish.

- **Modelling clay**

This can be used for focused practical tasks for clay work. It is also useful for holding wheels on axles, for weights and counterbalances in mechanisms, as a base for unstable structures of all sorts, and has many other applications.

- **Papier maché**

Use slightly watered down PVA glue rather than cold water paste, as the latter can cause itching and rashes. PVA also takes less time to dry. About five layers of newspaper are needed, so covering the base (balloon, plastic pot, etc.) alternately with newspaper and plain newsprint paper enables children to keep count of their layering. As a focused practical task for something more interesting, provide a range of bases (shallow, deep, round, oblong, etc.) to cover in newspaper in preparation for designing a papier maché product to be made from tissue paper and other flat materials including dried leaves, sequins, scraps of hand-made paper, etc.

- **Modroc**

Key Stage 2 children can work well with Modroc. It requires a tray of water per small group and clear instructions just to dip the Modroc and not to squeeze it out and thereby lose all the plaster. As always with a new technique, some practice is needed to get good results, so a suitable focused practical task could be to cover a yoghurt pot. This can become a product in its own right later by gluing seashells or other small items to the surface and varnishing.

Joining materials and components

- *Glue*

PVA is cheap and safe but takes time to dry and children can get impatient. Use paper clips or clothes pegs to hold parts together whilst waiting. Avoid wallpaper paste – avoid as it contains fungicides, and other cold water starch-based pastes can cause allergic reactions. Rubber-based glues are not suitable for general classroom use. Glue guns should be cool melt only and may be used by Key Stage 2 in small groups with supervision.

- **Card triangles**

Jinks' corners are a system of card triangles and plastic jigs for holding square dowels at right-angles to each other whilst small card triangles are glued on (named after David Jinks who devised this simple system). They work best in conjunction with cool melt glue guns, since waiting for PVA to dry holds up the production line. Advantages of using the Jinks system are:

- the card triangles help the stability and rigidity of the structure;

- the plastic jigs ensure that corners are right angles;

- even if children saw the dowel at somewhat other than a right angle, the card triangle will compensate;

- children can make rigid structures that would otherwise prove beyond their capability.

- **Needles and thread**

See below under Textiles.

Progression

MATURATION OF HAND MUSCLES

Many Year 1 children still have more cartilage than bone in their hands and so have insufficient strength yet too much flexibility for some design and technology processes. They also find it difficult to hold a thin pencil and make accurate marks with it, even when they can see perfectly well where the marks should be. Poor-looking products and the inability to produce neat work may, therefore, be a result of slower physical maturation of the hand. Sometimes, therefore, children appreciate the attention of an adult to mark out, hold and even help cut out parts of their work and the child's pride in the finished product will be just as great as if they had done it all by themselves because the adult has helped them to achieve success.

ACCURACY

Estimating size and how much material is required to make something is a skill that is learnt across the primary years, as is accuracy of measurement. Key Stage 1 children tend to want to place whatever they draw onto a piece of paper or card either centrally or part way up and a little in from the edge of the paper. This is because they cannot predict the final size of what they draw. They need to be given a small enough piece of card so as not to be wasteful, but not so small as not to allow for the child's inability to draw to fill the sheet.

Case study

Hand puppets in Year 2

The children in 2B were given a small piece of card exactly the right size onto which to draw round their hand to make a template for a hand puppet to be made from felt. Instead of placing one hand on the card and drawing round as Mrs H. expected, the children drew a free-hand arc in the middle of the card and cut it out. The finished products had to become finger puppets. The children learnt to sew and were very proud of their results. Mrs H. learnt to not to be so mean with card and to make her instructions clearer.

PRACTICE EFFECTS

No one makes a perfect job of a new skill first time, whether it is wallpapering your bedroom or sawing a piece of wood. Many teachers cannot saw wood straight and yet seem to expect that children will do so on the first attempt. Allow children time to learn and practise new skills but do not insist on the first attempt not becoming the final product if the child was successful first time – the rule of beginner's luck can be applied.

BEING TRUSTED WITH TOOLS

Student teachers often ask at what age particular tools and techniques can be used by children. This is always difficult to answer without first-hand knowledge of the children, the setting, the level of the supervision or even the student's own capability and confidence as a teacher and with the specific activity planned. A confident student who did A level art might feel extremely comfortable teaching Year 4 children batik in small groups, whereas another with a science background might feel happy making kites but not doing batik. As a general rule, the less well you know the children, the less risks you should take, regardless of your previous experience with the tools, the techniques or teaching. More detailed health and safety advice is given in Chapter 5.

Differentiation and inclusion

CUTTING

Several different kinds of scissors are available that are adapted for children with physical disabilities. 'Magic safety cutters' can be used to cut curved as well as straight lines accurately, even by those with little movement in their fingers. Store sharp implements out of sight of children whose social, emotional and behavioural difficulties make them likely to throw, stab furniture or threaten other children.

SHAPING

Many children with physical and social, emotional and behavioural difficulties enjoy the feel of soft, squidgy materials and the sense of control over its shape. However, some children on the autistic spectrum may find the sensation repulsive, as may some older girls who do not like to get their hands messy. Both situations must be handled sensitively and the teacher must decide whether to offer alternative activities or devise a way into the activity for these pupils.

JOINING

All joining techniques involve some measure of accuracy which will present problems for children with visual or physical impairment. Support should be given by an adult or another child holding parts while they are glued together. For children with severe problems, the child can hold one part and the assistant manoeuvres the other. What is important is that the child makes the design decisions and directs the assistant.

GLUE GUNS AND OTHER DANGERS

It is unfair to a child to ban them from an activity or process that the rest of the class are using because they 'cannot be trusted', even if you really believe that to be so. You need to arrange for the child to be adequately supervised by someone they respect so that they can access the curriculum along with the rest of the class. Banning children from activities that they see the rest of the class enjoying will only cause resentment. If you cannot arrange adequate supervision, arrange for the child to be elsewhere doing something else interesting. Most children enjoy extra computer time and this could be set up as a treat for good work/behaviour in a previous lesson – but wait until the child has left the room before you introduce the exciting design and technology work. If, when they return, they are disappointed at what they have missed, perhaps they could have their turn at lunchtime? Although this impacts on your break and preparation time, spending time yourself on a one-to-one basis with a child who is difficult in a group or class situation helps to build a relationship that the child values and will be less likely to risk breaking by poor behaviour in the future.

Differentiation and inclusion is discussed in more detail in Chapter 5.

Textiles

Textiles include fibres, threads, fabrics and cloth, rugs, carpets, tapestry and other wall hangings, curtains and blinds, sails of boats and ships, belts to drive industrial machinery, umbrellas and tents (including the huge ones now frequently seen as roofing for out-of-town designer outlet centres).

- **Textiles can be produced, decorated and joined using a range of techniques, not just 'sewing'.**
- **Fibres include wool, cotton, flax (linen), silk, nylon and polyesters, glass fibre.**
- **Threads are made from fibres by twisting.**
- **Fabrics can be felted, knitted or woven.**
- **Cloth is an ambiguous term, usually applied to clothing fabrics.**
- **Flock and stuffing materials (e.g. cotton wool and Kapok) are also included in textiles; these may be by-products of manufacturing processes (e.g. shoddy is made from woollen waste).**
- **Also included under textiles are fastenings (such as hooks and eyes, buckles, buttons, zippers), decorative items (such as studs, toggles, embroidery), 'fancies' (ribbons and bows) and fabric components (such as elastic, draw cords, belts and Velcro).**

PRODUCTION OF TEXTILES

Children can discover and appreciate how threads are made through:

- **Taking a variety of threads apart: chunky knitting wool is easiest to begin with. Provide magnifiers for thinner threads.**

- **Visiting museums in areas where thread is produced (e.g. Manchester Museum of Industry and Science), where rope-making took place (Chatham Dockyard, Kent), or demonstrations of hand-techniques at places of interest or themed events such as Medieval Fayres, etc.**
- **Inviting local craftspeople and hobbyists to bring into school, and demonstrate, spinning wheels.**

SPINNING

If you live in a sheep-farming area, collect the pieces of fleece that fall naturally from the sheep in springtime, or obtain a genuine fleece. This can be combed and spun, using a traditional stone or clay whorl. It can also be used to produce felt, as can shoddy.

PRODUCING CORDS

Stand two children some distance apart (at least 2 metres), each holding a pencil at arm's length. Tie the end of a ball of wool to one pencil. A third child takes the wool between and around the pencils, about a dozen times, finishing by tying to the second pencil. The two children holding the developing rope need to keep the tension constant in order to make a neat cord. The two ends are then twisted in opposite directions until the rope begins to twist back on itself (this point is discovered by lessening the tension). The two children holding the ends are going to bring the two ends together, under tension, whilst third child helps to keep the two halves separated and tensioned. Once the two ends are together, the third child lets go and the two halves will automatically wind into one cord. This sounds complicated when written down, but Year 3 children can do this efficiently once shown how. Once they have learnt this focused practical task, they can design and make belts in a range of colours, incorporate metallic thread, string beads onto the cord before final twisting, design and make fastenings.

OTHER TYPES OF CORD MAKING

These include plaiting, finger knitting (one- and two-handed), crochet, French knitting and so on. Try these in a range of threads, including soft copper wire. Year 4 can learn to plait and to do single finger knitting. Two-handed finger knitting, crochet and French knitting can be learned by Upper Key Stage 2.

POM-POMS

Simple enough, even for Year 1 with adult support, including cutting thread, starting off and final cutting through thread and tying. Give children thick wool, quadrupled into thick cord to make the production possible within a single lesson. These can be made into Easter Bunnies and children can design and make wheel-barrows for them to deliver small chocolate eggs.

WEAVING

The most attractive way of teaching weaving is around a paper plate (see diagram).

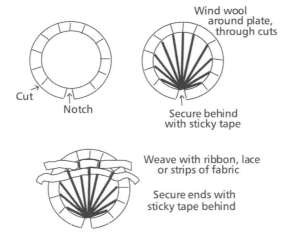

Weaving on a paper plate

Although this is technically quite easy for Key Stage 2 children, children should still have the opportunity to make a practice plate before deciding on colours and decorations (beads threaded onto the ribbon, perhaps). The plates can become, for example:

- **hot air balloons with addition of basket;**
- **fish (turn through 90 degrees and add fins and tail).**

Decorating textiles

TIE-DYING
Protect all clothing and hands (plastic gloves should be secured at the wrist with an elastic band); preferably work outside on an unfrequented grassy area, well supervised. Organise the hanging and drying place before starting.

PRINTING
Good links with art and design here, and with local history if you are working in a textile manufacturing area. Protect hands with plastic gloves and protect clothing.

This can range from simple to complex, for example:

- **vegetable printing: try peppers, onions and Brussels sprouts cut in two, leaves and twigs as well as the conventional potatoes and carrots;**
- **sponges, wood and other found objects, including scrunched-up fabric;**
- **batik and other wax techniques (Upper Key Stage 2 with close adult supervision);**
- **combine these techniques with tie-dying; printing with bleach will take colour out of fabric – try this on strong-coloured cotton fabric as well as tie-dyed cloth.**

Needles, thread and sewing

At the beginning of Year 1, children will be able to:

- **thread beads and buttons onto shoe laces;**
- **thread shoe laces in and out of sewing cards.**

During Year 1, children can learn to:

- **use Binca to make straight running stitches in a range of patterns using large blunt needles;**
- **use tapestry needles to sew beads and buttons to felt, with adult help.**

During Year 3, children can learn to:

- **make cross stitches on Binca;**
- **use tapestry needles to sew together felt, fur fabric and other loose-weave fabrics.**

By the end of Year 4, children can learn to:

- **choose and cut an appropriate length of thread for the purpose;**
- **thread a large needle;**
- **sew beads and buttons to felt;**
- **sew together felt, fur fabric and other loose-weave fabrics with minimum adult assistance.**

In Year 5, they will still need help with:

- **threading tapestry needles;**
- **making a knot in the end of thread before starting;**
- **fastening off ends of work.**

They will need to practise:

- **making stitches the same length;**
- **keeping stitches in a straight line;**
- **keeping fabric unpuckered as they work.**

In Year 6, they will still need help with:

- **threading crewel and other smaller-eyed needles;**
- **pinning work together before sewing.**

They can learn and practise:

- **a range of decorative stiches (chain stitch, feather stitch, etc);**
- **using simple paper patterns for small items with multiple parts (e.g. bags with gussets, soft toys).**

Each of these items needs to be taught as a focused practical task. Clearly some of the skills (e.g. threading a needle) will be incidental to the main task and will need to be practised across several projects. Making cross stitches on Binca, on the other hand, could be a focused practical task for a project in which children design a small place mat as a festival gift.

Health and safety needs to be considered with use of sharp needles and pins in the primary school. Never hold needles and pins in your own mouth in front of children Provide a small sponge for needles and pins to be pushed into between use. Count how many are in each sponge at the start and check that the same number return at the end of the lesson. It is better to teach children the correct way to store and use sharp needles and pins than for them to suffer the frustration of trying to work in close-weave cloth with blunt needles.

Case study

The Millennium Tapestry

In the months leading up to the turn of the millennium, many schools across the UK were involved in the Millennium Tapestry Project, and you may find a school near you which has their tapestry still on display. Halfway Houses Primary School, a first school (ages 4–9) on the Isle of Sheppey, has theirs hung proudly in the school hall.

Every child in the school took part In the design competition. Year 3 Edward Chawner's picture map was chosen as the basic design, to which many other children's ideas and features were then added. These were scaled up onto the metre-square backing by teacher Carole Day. The tapestry-in-progress lay on tables in the communal area outside the Year 1 classrooms and groups of children came to work on it whenever there was an adult available for help and supervision. Little squares of Year 4 knitting became sheep, Year 3 plaiting and cording became hedges, Year 2 made felt collage houses, Year 1 made figures from pipe cleaners and Year R came in small groups and threaded a bead or two. Boats, yachts, shops, the school, all were commissioned to different classes as the need arose. Year 4 children came at lunchtime to work on the more complex parts, such as the Sheerness Clock Tower and the King's Ferry Bridge. The librarian came in at 8.30 each morning to sew things on and added whimsies of her own – like a rabbit-shaped button. Carole Day made a convict escaping from the prison!

It was an intensive whole school project that was designed and made by children, with adult support and guidance. As with all such projects, it could not have been completed on time (or as successfully) without staff giving up their lunch breaks.

Engineering

Of all topics in design and technology, engineering has the closest links with science. The subject area includes buildings towers and masts, which may also support moving parts, such as cranes, gantries and fairground rides. Engineering also covers vehicles, including ships, and all forms of mechanisms and control of movement and environments (e.g. air conditioning systems).

Contexts for learning about the structure of buildings

The range of building styles across the globe and across history is determined by the materials as well as the skills and knowledge in handling those materials that are available.

Taking a walk around London, Liverpool, Edinburgh, or any city that has a long history of investment of innovative design will reveal a wealth of structural techniques utilising a mixture of stone, brick, steels and glass. The 'Gherkin', the latest addition to the London skyline, is an exciting and innovative building that makes a bold statement about contemporary architecture and, whether seen from outside Liverpool Street Station, the top of St Paul's or from the considerable distance of Alexandra Palace, it contrasts starkly with the square-edged buildings that surround it. The Gherkin exemplifies the change in architecture, the way materials can now be handled, flexed and joined, and the way in which buildings can be perceived. The arch, the cone and the dome are no longer the only curved shapes that feature in city skylines.

When looking at simpler structures, Berber tents, Viking longhouses or Inuit igloos, for example, the term 'primitive' is not just derogatory, it confuses simplicity with a lack of sophistication. Many simple homes are ideally suited to their location, climate and locally available materials. The ubiquitous 'modern' concrete block of flats has proved inappropriate in many hot and cold climates around the world. Evaluations of buildings as structures must take the local climate into consideration. Likewise the internal structure, including the use of roof and basement spaces.

Links with maths and science

Stability of structures is dependent on the interaction between the strength and weight of the construction materials, the joining techniques chosen and geometry. A visit to a medieval church can help children to understand the problems: thick heavy walls are propped up by buttresses that can barely resist the outward thrust of the roof. In the classroom, this can be demonstrated by taping two rulers together at their ends and standing them between two lightweight books on a shiny table. Pressing down on the apex of the rulers will make the books slide away from each other, just as the church walls are doing.

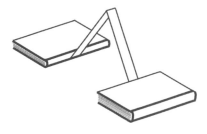

Thrust demonstration

Exploration of the problem can then ensue, with the stipulation that the smallest possible number of extra parts should be added. The range of responses (adding extra books, sticky-taping the rulers to the books or the table, etc.) can be discussed and related to real buildings. The triangular roof truss is only one answer among many but is the most economical on time and materials. Children can build a variety of roof trusses from art straws, card struts, construction kits, etc., to ascertain the best technique for the materials:

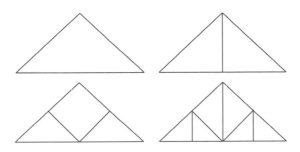

Experiments with roof trusses

This could be linked to investigations of real buildings (historical and modern) and considerably enhance such historical model-making as Tudor houses. It could also be linked to observations of temporary structures such as cranes, or open structures such as transmitter masts.

Bridge-building can also extend children's understanding of structure and of the use of folding and rolling of thin sheet materials to increase strength without increasing weight.

Practical task

Take some sheets of ordinary A4 photocopy paper and devise as many ways as you can of bridging the gap between two books without the paper sagging down onto the table.

Further ideas for structural problem-solving: using newspaper

All these must be able to stand up by themselves unsupported by human hand, feet, etc. and sticky-taping to the floor or furniture is strictly forbidden.

• **Years 1/2**

Frosty the Snowman is in his house on a hill on one side of the valley and Icy the Shopkeeper has his shop on the next hill. Yesterday there was a big thaw and now there is a lake in the valley between them. How can Icy deliver Frosty's shopping? He cannot go round the lake, of course, that would be too easy (and cheating!). Build a model to show them the solution. If you know the story of the Lighthouse Keeper's Lunch, this might give you some clues.

- **Years 2/3**

Can you make something strong enough to sit on? Note: simply making a pile of newspapers is not allowed!

- **Years 3/4**

You will need a small lightweight ball for each group. Can you make a three-dimensional marble run, whose starting point must be more than 30cm in all directions, including height, from its finishing point? Provide rulers to check distances.

- **Years 4/5**

Can you make a bridge to span a distance one and a half times the length of the longest piece of newspaper? Provide a paper 'river' the right width for each group.

- **Years 5/6**

Can you make a shelter large enough for the tallest person in the group to sit under? It must stand up on its own after they get out! See sample scheme of work for Year 5/6 and lesson plan for Year 5/6 in Appendices E and F at the end of the book.

Moving things

This section will focus on wheels, axles, pulleys, cams and gears, which can not only form part of a topic on transport but can also be used to control wind-up toys and automata. See Chapter 8 on Crossing curricular boundaries for ideas for linking science and design and technology in a topic on Fairgrounds.

MOVING THINGS WITHOUT WHEELS

How can heavy loads be moved without using wheels? Sit the class around a large plastic box containing real bricks and see what they come up with. Discuss pushing, pulling, friction, inertia. Have handy some rope, crowbar or other lever, broom handles to serve as rollers. Connect with skis, skates, sledges. Do these work on shingle as well as snow? How could we find out without going to the beach?

WHEELS AND AXLES

Either the wheels revolve on the axles and the axles are fixed to the chassis or the wheels are fixed to the axles and the axles revolve in sockets or brackets on the chassis: a whole lesson of focused practical tasks exploring ways of attaching wheels to axles to chassis (recycled boxes and cartons).

The simplest solution is to push the axle through the box and push on wheels. The wheels can be prevented from coming off the axles with a small ball of modelling clay or an elastic band wound round and round the ends. An elastic band also makes a good spacer between the chassis and the wheel to prevent rubbing.

To put axles and wheels below body of chassis, use:

- **triangles of card, glued to the sides of the chassis, protruding below with holes for axles;**
- **straws or plastic tubing glued to the underside of the chassis for axles to pass through;**
- **clothes pegs, glued to the underside of the chassis so that axles can pass through the semicircular cut-outs intended for the clothes line.**

Wheels do not need to be on the outside of the vehicle. Slots can be cut in the underside of the chassis and any of the above techniques adapted to accommodate them.

What to use for wheels:

	Advantages	Disadvantages
Pre-cut wooden wheels	De luxe class	Expensive
Plastic wheels	Bright and colourful	May come in limited range of sizes
Card wheels	Cheap	Flop about through being too thin and fixing spacers between demands accurate gluing
Cotton reels	High stability	Wide and not much clearance height, improved with addition of pipe lagging
Plastic washers, out-cuts, etc.	May be a donated item	May be too small or have different sized central holes
Recycled jar lids	Good range of sizes, free	Need washing before use; need at least four of each sort
Tins, yoghurt pots, etc.	As above; the little yoghurt-based drinks bottles are useful	As above, plus may be too large.
CD-ROMs	Large, shiny, recycled	Large hole in centre
Beads	Spherical shape adds interest	May be too small
Balls: air-flow, tennis, ping-pong	Spherical shape plus larger size	Expensive unless reclaimed from PE store; making holes in tennis and ping-pong balls needs to be done by adult

OTHER MOVING PARTS

For Key Stage 1, building a basic vehicle with wheels that really turn, that resembles a specified vehicle for a specified purpose (Cinderella's Coach, Mr Grumpy's Car, etc.) is sufficiently challenging. In Key Stage 2, children can add moving parts to their vehicles to turn them into tip-up trucks, cement mixers, crane lorries and so on. Provide a range of toy vehicles (children with younger siblings can bring these from home) so that children can examine how the mechanisms work. Videos and pictures can also be useful to demonstrate how the moving parts connect and interact.

Case study

The impact of steam power

4L were spending a whole term studying Victorian Lancashire. An outing to the Manchester Museum of Science and Industry was planned for the fourth week of the project. Because the focus at the start of the project was on clothing, cotton production and the mills, Ms L. took the precaution of equipping all the adults with cameras to help the children remember the engines they had seen, as well as arranging for all the children to have a ride on the train. She was pleased that some of the children had made the connection between the way the mill engines worked and the locomotive engines. The children made linear to circular motion converters (see below) to help them understand how the pressure from the steam boilers turned the wheels in the factories and on the locomotives. Ms L. discovered that Victorian fairgrounds were powered by steam stationary engines and that her father had a recording of a fairground organ. She remembered Tess of the D'Urbervilles working in the fields to the tireless demands of the steam-powered threshing machine. The children used their mechanisms as the basis of a range of two-dimensional tableaux illustrating the impact of steam power on life both in the towns and in the countryside.

Mechanisms and control

The kinds of control technology that are discussed in this section are mechanical, pneumatic and hydraulic, electrical and electronic control. See also in Chapter 8 on crossing subject boundaries the sections on Science and Information and Communication Technologies.

Mechanisms can be used:

- **to link materials or components to make or allow for movement;**
- **to change one type of movement or motion to another;**
- **to change direction of movement or motion;**
- **to change angle or orientation of movement or motion.**

MECHANICAL CONTROL

- **Paper engineering**

The simplest way for children to start learning about making their own mechanisms is with paper and card. A folded piece of paper makes a hinge that can be used as part of a pop-up mechanism inside a card.

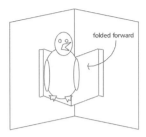

folded forward

Paper engineering

Teach children to fold paper and card along a ruler to get a sharp and accurate fold. Key Stage 2 children can score card before folding: a blunt dinner knife is a good tool for this. Learning to put folds in different places provides children with a range of techniques that can be adapted for different contexts and purposes, including cranes and tip-up trucks.

Puppets, figures or animals can be given moving joints by attaching parts with split pins. Do make sure that the holes are crisply cut and not too near the edges of the material.

• **Construction kits**

These provide a wealth of opportunity for intuitive learning about mechanisms. Mobilo, for example, allows the construction of houses with hinged doors as well as being ideal for building a whole range of both simple and complex vehicles, including fire engines with ladders that can swivel and fold up and down. For more on construction kits see Chapter 3.

In order for children to learn to make hinged joints, construct a series of demonstration boards that can form the basis of focused practical tasks to learn the basic configurations.

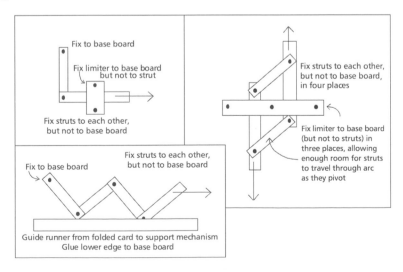

Basic hinge joints

Practical task

Obtain a pop-up book that you can take apart to examine the mechanisms. Make copies of these in card and list other applications for the same mechanism. For example, a card circle rotating on a split pin can be used as a wheel on a vehicle, for a word wheel to show days of the week, or to change circular to linear motion (see below).

Children can make their own pop-up books, either as a group or class, with each child designing and making one page. These can be for their own enjoyment or that of younger children, or (as South Avenue Primary School in Sittingbourne decided) to link to learning French. Each group made a pop-up book of different vocabulary groups (colours, animals, etc.) to add to the class library.

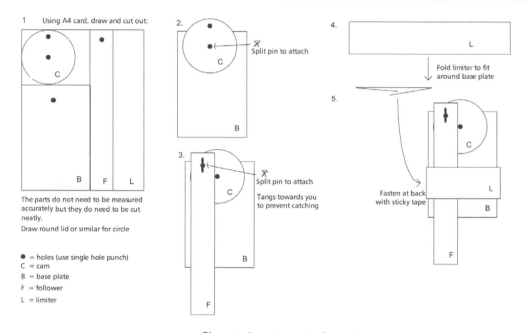

Changing linear into circular motion

• **Changing linear into circular motion**

This is the basic mechanism behind pistons in engines and pumps, sewing machines, etc. The activity described here would need to be a whole lesson focused practical task for Year 4/5.

As well as teaching children how to make the basic linear–rotary converter, teach the correct vocabulary: base plate, cam, follower, limiter. For your own learning, make this from scratch. For children, you may want to provide this photocopied onto card for their first attempt. Once they understand how the parts fit together, they can experiment with different-sized circles, placing the holes and split pin in different places, different lengths of follower and positions and widths of limiter. Two small tweaking adjustments may need to be made for smooth motion: a slight concave curve down the length of the follower to clear the head of the split pin through the centre of the circle, and do not make the limiter too tight. Size, rigidity of the card and the smoothness of the holes also contribute to success.

PNEUMATICS AND HYDRAULICS

Pneumatics use air power and hydraulics use water.

Pneumatics is less messy but the air will compress and so will not deliver as much movement or force as was put in. Hydraulics is more effective but leakage and spills can ruin the children's work. Children should have the opportunity to experiment with both and decide for themselves which they feel would be most appropriate for their design. They need to be aware that the choice to use hydraulics could mean damage to someone else's work as well as (or instead of) their own.

To be successful, pneumatics needs a large volume of air at the input end. Empty plastic bottles are ideal but they need to be made of fairly flexible plastic, so those designed for flexing in use (washing up liquid, paint, glue) are a better choice than drinks bottles. They will successfully inflate balloons and lift syringes that can be attached with rubber bands to plastic tubing to convey energy from input to output and move the intended mechanism. A focused practical tasks lesson spent experimenting with different-sized bottles alongside comparisons with hydraulics will be well worth the time. It should precede any designing of products, which can be:

- **two-dimensional pictures with moving parts – these can be free-standing or wall-mounted. The mechanism is mounted on the back of the card, so the card needs to be quite thick;**
- **three-dimensional boxed projects – the mechanism is mounted inside the box, so the box needs to be large enough to get hands inside to assemble the mechanism.**

ELECTRICAL AND ELECTRONIC CONTROL

There are strong links here with work in science, and design and technology can provide the focus for understanding electrical circuitry. When initially teaching children about circuits, refer to motor racing toys, such as Scalectrix. Children readily understand this analogy for electricity going around the circuit and it enables them to understand that the electricity needs to go through all the components on its way around. The children first experience building a circuit in Key Stage 1, with a battery, bulb, switch and two wires, which can be laid out on the table in a circle. In Key Stage 2, they can build circuits with switches that allow for choices (red light or green light). A useful aid to understanding electrical switching can be computer simulations of trains going around a track that requires the player to make choices about which points to open to send the train to visit different stations.

Children can use their circuits to light torches, lighthouses and vehicles. A project on homes could involve children making rooms for a block of flats (quantity of same-sized boxes needed) that included a light in each room. The furniture can include a cupboard for storing/hiding the battery. Do check that the battery output does not exceed the rating on the bulbs or you will have instant disappointment as the bulbs all blow. Most bulbs used in schools are 2 amp and AAA batteries will power these.

Ensure that you understand serial and parallel circuitry (see Johnsey et al., 2000, pp95–102) and have tried out the intended circuits yourself before asking children to do so.

- **Switches**

Switches control flow of current – on or off – but they can also be used to choose between alternatives. Children should make their own switches and explore a range of ways in which electrical current can be controlled before being asked to incorporate switching into control projects.

- **Motors**

Projects based on wheels, gears and cams, from vehicles to automata, can be powered by motors:

- The structures need to be quite strong and work well before a motor is attached. An electrical motor will continue to apply force until any resistance is overcome, usually through breakage.
- If used to control to vehicles, it is better to attach a pair of long wires to a remote control (hand-held switch) rather than mounting the switch on the vehicle. Heavy-handed turning on and off of the power (especially if the vehicle is about to crash) could wreck, in moments, many hours of hard work.
- Mountings for motors need to be secure but the adhesive must be weaker than the material. Better for glue to break than the vehicle or structure.

- **Sensors**

Sensors can be used to control responses to light, sound, movement, temperature and even humidity. Basic burglar alarm systems can be designed and built by children, although teachers soon tire of buzzers sounding whenever someone enters the room. Combined with motors, sensors can open and close doors, raise and lower a portcullis (if anachronism is acceptable), turn and rotate parts of structures and whole vehicles. Consider buying ready-made control boxes (see Information and Communication Technologies in Chapter 8 on Crossing curricular boundaries) for children to use in combination with their own home-made switches and customised switching devices.

- **Buzzers**

Use buzzers sparingly to avoid irritation.

Food technology

With the greater emphasis on the role of school in educating for healthy lifestyles, food technology has seen a revival in its perceived importance within education. This section of the chapter will suggest approaches to teaching food technology through evaluating foodstuffs, examining production chains, researching the history of food preparation and, of course, cooking.

Food technology is considerably more than 'cooking'. It is designing something to eat for specific people in specific circumstances. Examples might be:

- **sandwiches for class picnic;**
- **biscuits for Red Nose Day;**
- **fruit salad as part of a healthy lifestyle menu.**

Food technology covers four main areas: production, preservation, preparation and consumption.

In all four areas, children can learn *about* technology and *through* practical technological activity. Health and safety issues with regard to food technology can be found in the Food section of Health and Safety in Chapter 5.

Production

Many schools have garden areas in which children can grow their own flowers, herbs and vegetables. The Sample Scheme for Key Stage I in Appendix C provides a starting point for ideas for considering the design aspects of growing things, for example, designing a multi-level self-watering propagator from recycled materials, e.g. stackable takeaway trays (see Hope (2006)).

Suitable seeds to sprout include:

- **mustard and cress;**
- **bean sprouts (mung beans are the usual kind, but any dried beans will do, though NOT red kidney beans as these are poisonous when uncooked);**
- **wheat, pearl barley, unpolished brown rice;**
- **left-over seeds from gardening – broccoli, cabbage, carrot, lettuce, herbs and other crops that can be eaten raw;**
- **alfalfa, fenugreek and other more unusual sprouts can be bought from seed suppliers.**

As well as obvious links with science, history topics provide opportunities for menu-planning. For example, Wartime Foods offers scope for children to design an austerity menu. Shortages meant that substitutes had to be used for some ingredients and rationing meant just that. The children can research the wartime ration allowance for a child for a week and create a healthy menu. This can be compared to their own food consumption for a week.

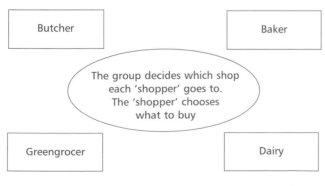

Shopping activity

A group design activity could be to have a selection of 'shops' from which to collect food cards – boxes on a front table will do, but better to have different labelled places around the room. To make this more authentic, you could give each group a set of ration cards. Each shopper chooses two foods. You will need to have several cards for most common foods (e.g. milk and bread). You could even have 'Garden' as an extra option, as people grew a lot of their own foods in wartime. Each group must then try to plan a menu around the foods they have bought.

Try to obtain a copy of Marguerite Patten's *We'll eat again* (published by the Imperial War Museum in 1985 but reprinted several times since). Marguerite Patten was Home Economist in the electrical industry before the war, demonstrating elaborate and lavish menus, but as food supplies became short she joined the Ministry of Food to give advice and demonstrations on providing good wholesome and attractive meals with substitutes and rationed ingredients. She continued to work and write about food and publish recipe books well into the 1980s. The book is a valuable resource as it was written by someone who was directly involved in the war effort to feed the nation and reads with the directness of personal experience. Needless to say, the recipes work, although some of them taste rather strange due to the substitutes used.

Many foods have travelled the world and are now grown in places far removed from their place of origin. Both history and geography are combined in considering the impact of the discovery of America by Europeans:

- **From the Americas: avocado pears, beans (lima, runner and haricot = baked), blueberries, chocolate, maize (sweet corn, popcorn and cornflour), peppers (sweet and hot capsicums, green and red chilli), potatoes, pumpkins (and other squash), tomatoes, tortillas, turkey** …

- **To the Americas: apples, aubergines, bananas, cows, pineapples, okra, wheat (pizza, burger buns, brownies, muffins and pasta)** …

- **A design task could be to see what can be made with, or without, this combination of ingredients.**

Preservation

Before the advent of refrigeration and frozen foods (link with science and history), a whole range of techniques existed to preserve surpluses in order to survive times when food was less plentiful and to stop food from deteriorating before it was needed. Some of these techniques are suitable for children to try in school. Avoid processes that require high heat and do not use sharp knives below Year 4.

● **Drying**
Apple rings, onion rings, mushroom slices, halved plums and herbs all dry best hanging on kebab skewers: design a drying cupboard/rack for them.

● **Flavoured vinegar or oil**
Onion, chilli, herb, garlic can be added to oil/vinegar in a screw-top jar. Leave for one month. Design and make salad dressings (to go with the home-grown sprouts) by

experimenting with combinations of the oils and vinegars (include plain oil and vinegar as a choice too).

● **Lemon, orange or grapefruit curd**

Curd can be made in a microwave — experiment with flavours.

● **Jams and chutneys**

These are too hazardous for primary children as they involve high heat, but there are no-cook jam recipes available. Children could cut up the ingredients, however, and leave the cooking to an adult. Designing their own pickles and chutneys would be an interesting project.

● **Jelly**

Although mainly eaten today as a dessert, covering foods in aspic or calf's foot jelly was a means of preserving food for a few days, usually with a layer of fat on top. Brawn and other cooked meats are familiar products that are set in jelly and children can taste and analyse these. Designing and making should be limited to setting fruit in jelly, to avoid food poisoning. Gelatine can be purchased in a range of flavoured and unflavoured powders, based on vegetable and animal products. Children can try making each of these and then designing a dessert based on one of them. As well as fruit juice, various milk products (including condensed, evaporated, buttermilk and yoghurt, as well as ordinary milk) can be substituted for some of the water (but not fruit juice and milk products together). Children can design healthy and attractive puddings based on layering different kinds and colours of jelly and fruit. Use transparent plastic cups (allowing jelly to cool before filling) and think about tipping the cups to different angles to make interesting sloping layers.

● **Curd cheese**

Fun but smelly! Heat 1 litre of milk to just below 40 degrees, add the juice of one lemon and stir gently. Curds and whey will separate. Strain and add salt and a range of sweet and savoury flavourings. This could be the basis for designing 'bites' combining different small biscuits with sweet and savoury curd cheese and topped with fruit and/or salad vegetables (or your home-grown sprouts).

● **Yoghurt**

It is easiest to start with evaporated or sterilised (UHT) milk, otherwise boil 1 pint of milk and stir in 4 tablespoons of real milk powder (not coffee whitener). Again the milk needs to be just below 40 degrees. Stir in one large tablespoonful of commercial natural yoghurt. Pour into a Thermos flask and leave in a warm place overnight. Note: the first batch is always runny (use for jelly making). Your subsequent batches will be thick and creamy. Children can design their own yoghurt-based dessert that can include fruit (your own dried fruit?), crushed biscuits or breakfast cereals, sweet sauces, small pieces of that home-made jelly, etc.

● **Freezing**

Despite the fact that freezers are ubiquitous, making ice lollies in a range of flavours, colours and shapes is still fun for children. This is an ideal design opportunity for Key

Stage I and can easily be linked to science. Use the small-size dessert tubs rather than ice cube trays, as lolly sticks stand up better in these. The children will be able to supply these from their lunch boxes (good recycling).

Preparation

This topic has already been touched on in the suggestions for preserving foods. This section examines those areas of food technology that one might most readily describe as 'cookery'.

Hygiene needs to be a high priority in food work. Think about:

- **work surfaces – if working in an ordinary classroom on general purpose tables, one solution is to cut open large plastic bin bags and sticky tape them inside-out across the tables and then wipe over with sterilising fluid (white bags seem to suggest cleanliness rather than black ones);**
- **storage of ingredients (up high, away from dust, dirt and pests) and utensils (child-proof cupboard, especially for Key Stage I);**
- **washing hands and scrubbing finger nails; sterilise nail brushes after use;**
- **wipe down aprons; tied-back hair; no watches or jewellery on hands or wrists – enforce this rule strictly;**
- **washing up, including sterilising cloths and tea towels.**

This is far more rigorous than the cleanliness you might apply in your kitchen at home, but remember, you are not in your kitchen at home.

FOOD AND SAFETY
- **All electrical equipment used in classrooms must be PAT tested and this includes equipment you bring into school, even though you may use it at home every day (see page 106).**
- **All portable electrical equipment must be stored unplugged; unplug ovens after use too.**
- **Storage of equipment and utensils must be out of reach of children.**
- **Keep children away from hot ovens, hobs, saucepans, etc. – and do not leave tea towels hanging on oven doors to dry.**
- **Teach children how to hold and chop ingredients. Demonstrate the correct way to hold both food and knife (tips of fingers tucked back, hinging motion of knife with point touching table).**
- **Ensure children know safety rules around handling food.**

Despite that long list of dos and don'ts, food in school is fun. You do need to be very organised, especially if working in the ordinary classroom. Rearrange the furniture (e.g. semicircles of seats around your demonstration table, children sent to work standing up at own tables). Ideally, the tables should be correct height for children to work standing up but this is frequently not possible.

Food technology can also be readily linked to other areas of the curriculum, as in the following example.

Pumpkin pies

Pumpkins are often available really cheaply after Hallowe'en which is not too far away from American Thanksgiving Day, which can be linked to history, geography and RE.

Peel the pumpkin and cut the flesh into cubes and steam/cook in the microwave. Allow to cool until warm enough to eat and allow children to try a cube so that they have experienced the taste of plain pumpkin. Provide forks, small bowls and a range of 'flavourings' to be mashed into portions of the cooked pumpkin. These can be both sweet and savoury – salt and pepper, butter, olive oil, plain yoghurt, peanut butter (watch out for allergies), sugar, honey, orange juice, apple sauce, mixed spice, ginger, etc. The children can then try all the flavours (provide small spoons and paper towels plus glasses of water to clear the palate between flavours). The children note their preferences and choose which they will use to make pumpkin pies. These are made in the same way as jam tarts but putting on a lid (like a mince pie) allows some personalisation and identification marks, e.g. maker's initials pricked into the lid with a cocktail stick.

Consumption

Once the food is made, then it obviously needs eating. However:

RESPECT CHILDREN'S REFUSALS

Food prepared in design and technology does not have to be eaten. Accept wastage of food in this circumstance in the same way as you accept using up other resources, such as card and glue. Some foods may be taboo due to religious beliefs or because families are vegetarian. Restrict food technology in the school (especially cakes) during Ramadan if you have even one Muslim child; it is simply unfair. Foods may be unfamiliar and children are very conservative about trying new foodstuffs. Children may not be aware of how some foods are made and seeing this for the first time may deter them from eating them. They may not be willing to try foods that other children have prepared. This may be for social reasons (not being friends) or related to perceived levels of personal hygiene, even if everyone has washed their hands.

FOOD AND HEALTH

Although clearly linked to healthy eating strategies and fears about growing child obesity and Jamie Oliver's School Dinners, it is important that in the promotion of healthy options, teachers do not actively criticise children's tastes and food choices. You need to be sensitive to the circumstances of home, where food choices might be governed by financial difficulties, inadequate kitchen facilities, parental work patterns or even that no one can cook. Send a checklist of ingredients home beforehand for parents to sign, to ensure that no children have allergies that you do not know about, and insist – no note, no cooking.

PRESENTATION

Ensure that food that is prepared as part of food technology is presented in an attractive way. Clear the tables and cover with plastic table cloths. Decorating the table (including a flower arrangement) could provide a design activity while waiting for food to cook or set and creates a sense of occasion. Small portions can be served in plastic cups or dessert tubs, but choose plain coloured ones rather than those which obviously come from own-brand bulk-buys. However, serving food in pots featuring favourite cartoon and computer game characters is a strategy that food manufacturers use successfully to persuade young children to eat their products, so try this with your food technology products too. There should be plenty of these available for recycling from children's lunch boxes.

FINALLY

All the food technology projects suggested in this section have *design* at their heart. There is an inherent fear of wastage, spoilage and failure in allowing children to experiment with food products but as Ridgell (1994) says, *They may encounter failure, which is an important learning experience when designing food products*. Although preparing food is the design task that children see most often demonstrated at home, parents' need to produce good quality food quickly with minimum wastage does not allow children to experiment with ingredients and processes. Old-fashioned cookery or home economics lessons did not do that either. Food technology in school can provide children with the opportunity to experiment and make design choices and 'failure' is not important — it is not their dinner that has been ruined.

Resources and ideas

As well as devising ideas of your own, use the wealth of ideas that can be found in books and magazines aimed at supporting your teaching of the key stage in which you are working. Some books with good ideas for each subject area can be found below, along with books that cover several areas.

Do not dismiss older books as a source of ideas. For example:

> Frisch, U (1977) *Pictures to play with*. London: Faber.
> Philpott, A R (1972) *Let's make puppets*. London: Evans.
> Robinson, S and P (1962) *Simple fabric printing*. London: Mills & Boon.
> Smith, R G (1975) *Paper for play*. London: Evans.
> Snook, B (1974) *Making birds, beasts and insects*. London: B. T. Batsford.

All of these and similar books are out of print but may be available through libraries and second-hand book shops, boot fairs and other sources. Despite the changes in emphasis and the ways in which children are taught, many of the activities in these older books can be adapted for a modern generation.

In all of the books listed above, the authors stress that their ideas are intended for children to try out, adapt and use as starting points to explore new ideas of their own. Ulla Frisch, for example, says in her introduction: *[the pictures] are tailored to the needs of the children who use them and many can be made by children with the minimum of adult help* (p9). Many of her ideas are readily adaptable for Key Stage I classroom displays:

- **Washing Day: landscape with real clothes pegs to hang up dolls' washing (the clothes having been designed and made by the children)**

- **Carpet Picture: a floor mat for toy cars, etc., that can be a class textile project. Take Frisch's advice to *Keep the picture fairly simple; the children's imagination will supply the rest* (p49). This could be made by Key Stage 2 for Year I, for example. There is no need to sew everything – Upper Key Stage 2 children can use rubber-based glue sensibly with adult supervision. Younger children can design the mat and cut out the pieces ready for an adult to pin to the backing cloth and machine-sew later. It could feature the local environment to develop geography skills at the same time as design and textile capability.**

Subject content for practical activity:
a summary of key points

In this chapter you have learnt about:

—— *Artefacts, systems and environments as three levels of engagement with technological activity that form contexts for practical tasks in design and technology.*

—— *A range of techniques for cutting, shaping and joining materials and components suitable for primary children, along with appropriate tools.*

—— *Engineering structures within the built environment, ways of exploiting linear and circular movement, not only for vehicles, but also for mechanisms and control systems, which can be linked to electrical and electronic devices.*

—— *Food technology as a separate topic, which stresses the importance of enabling children to make design decisions within the production, preservation, preparation, presentation and consumption of food products.*

References

Hope, G (2006) The needs of seeds, *5TO7 educator*, 5 (3). National Curriculum section, D&T Education.

Johnsey, R, Peacock, G, Sharp J and Wright, D (2000) *Primary Science: Knowledge and Understanding*. Exeter: Learning Matters.

Ridgwell, J (1994) *Working with food in primary schools*. London: Ridgwell Press.

Patten, M (1985) *We'll eat again*. London: Imperial War Museum.

Ministry of Education, New Zealand (1995) *Technology in the New Zealand Curriculum*. Wellington: Learning Media.

Buildings and structures

Blythe, K (1996) *Children and technology,* Chapter 5. Oxford: Nash Pollock Publishing.

Cole, M and Darby, D (1991) *Tritech Series: Vehicles, bridges, fairgrounds, cranes.* Crediton: Southgate.

DATA (2004) *The Design and Technology Subject Leaders' File,* Section 5.9. Wellesbourne: DATA.

Richards, R (1990) *An early start to technology.* London; Simon & Schuster.

TTS (1995) *Technology Topics Series: Houses and structures.* Derbyshire: TTS.

www.sodaplay.com/

Moving things

Blythe, K (1996) *Children and technology,* Chapter 6. Oxford: Nash Pollock Publishing.

Richards, R (1990) *An early start to technology.* London: Simon & Schuster.

Tarquin publishers sell a range of books of automata and working toys and models.

Mechanisms and control

Blythe, K (1996) *Children and technology,* Chapters 6 and 7. Oxford: Nash Pollock Publishing.

DATA (2004) *The Design and Technology Subject Leaders' File,* Section 5.8. Wellesbourne: DATA.

Hann, K (1998) *Science and technology at the fairground.* London: Pictorial Charts Education Trust.

Parkinson, E and Plimmer, D (1995) *Mechanisms.* Bradford: Resources for Learning.

Parkinson, E and Plimmer, D (1995) *Sensing and control.* Bradford: Resources for Learning.

www.flying-pig.co.uk/

Textiles

DATA (2004) *The Design and Technology Subject Leaders' File,* Section 5.6. Wellesbourne: DATA.

Food

DATA (2004) *The Design and Technology Subject Leaders' File,* Section 5.7. Wellesbourne: DATA.

Ridgwell, J (1994) *Working with food in primary schools.* London: Ridgwell Press.

www.nutrition.org.uk/

Series of books on each subject area

Collins Primary Technology series (199) written by Eileen Chadwick. A series of booklets for each of Key Stages 1 and 2 based on stories and rhymes (e.g. London Bridge, Teddy Bears' Picnic) or specific topics (wheels, the post) with teachers' guides and assessment books. Published by Collins Educational, London.

TTS (1995) *Technology Topics Series (colour and light, houses and structures, people, playground and toys, transport, weather, wind and sun).* Derbyshire: TTS.

8 CROSSING CURRICULAR BOUNDARIES

When the National Curriculum for design and technology was introduced, it was felt strongly that primary teachers would be able to embrace this new subject and incorporate it into their established pattern of working, which at the time was project-based and cross-curricular. Part of the process of the introduction of the National Curriculum was the near eradication of the project-based approach. As many primary schools return to a more cross-curricular working it is important to ensure that the insights into the teaching of learning to design quality products that have been gained over the past 15 years do not evaporate.

In this chapter, you will learn about building secure and valid cross-curricular links to:

- *language and design;*
- *more maths than measuring;*
- *science and technology;*
- *information and communication technologies;*
- *the art of design;*
- *humanities united;*
- *music-makers.*

Finally, this chapter discusses the implications of thinking about the whole curriculum holistically and the place of design and technology as a driver within the context of cross-curricular thematic pedagogy.

Language and design

Language is not just *creative*, it is also *created*. It is *designed* by users for users, in the same way as anything else that humans create and use. Here are two examples to support that statement:

1   Two minutes after leaving the house, Ray rings back home:

   Ray: It's Big Bin Day.
   Gill: Yes, I know.
   Ray: It's Odd Leggedy Day too.
   Gill: Yes, I know that too.

'Big Bin Day' is probably obvious – Big Bin (as opposed to Little Bin who lives in the kitchen) will be emptied today. Odd Leggedy Day? On alternate weeks the recyclables are collected, by Odd Leg Lorry, rather than Big Bin Lorry. Apart from having a non-standard word, the phrase has a family story attached to it (from attempting to explain 'alternate' to a non-English speaking maths student). No doubt you too have similar odd family words, because humans are constantly creating and designing new language. Adolescents have the highest output of new words as they create and define their own peer group sub-culture.

2   The following terms were selected from Daniel Pink's *A whole new mind* (2005):

- knowledge economy;
- concept age;
- kiddie garb;
- that same Target trip;
- a Taco Bell counter jockey.

Pink's book says important things about the possible economic future of America but, like Odd Leggedy Week, the language has been designed in a family context, in this case the shared culture of the United States. Part of Pink's thesis is that the right hemisphere of the human brain supplies context to the left hemisphere's text, including understanding of metaphor.

And if a picture is worth a thousand words, a metaphor is worth a thousand pictures (Pink, 2005, p50). This only becomes true, however, if the concepts behind the metaphors are familiar enough not to need decoding by the left hemisphere. You probably used the left hemisphere for the Taco Bell counter jockey, whereas 'kiddie garb' was handled quickly and efficiently by the right.

Language is not sited purely in the left hemisphere as once thought and the conceptual, metaphorical, visual, the major contexts for language and design seem to be found alongside each other in the right hemisphere. In the Preface to the 2001 edition of *Drawing on the right side of the brain*, Betty Edwards talks about her surprise in discovering the transfer of skills between drawing and other areas of human reasoning.

The fluidity of language within accepted rules is in some ways parallel to the way adult design professionals use drawing to model and develop design ideas. Likewise, the emergent writing of young children demonstrates a similar fluidity between written and drawn form, that uses a combination of pictorial items and symbols (letters, numbers and invented ciphers) to meaningfully place-mark and develop ideas.

The benefits of linking language development with design and technology, say Clare Benson and Julie Mantell (1999), are:

For pupils:

- **a real need and purpose;**
- **relevant contexts;**
- **the opportunity to apply and practise language;**
- **enjoyment and motivation which encourages higher levels of language.**

For teachers:

- **planning for meaningful contexts;**
- **assessment opportunities for use and application of language;**
- **best use of time.**

As Benson and Mantell point out, language is broader than literacy (1999, p3). It also involves speaking, listening, discussing, negotiating, communicating through a range of media (including writing) and reading.

Kay Stables and Maggie Rogers of Goldsmiths College, University of London, conducted research in Middlesbrough for the Design Museum's Handling Collections Project. The aim of the study was to ascertain the extent to which design activities enhanced literacy skills. Year 2 and Year 6 children in schools across Middlesbrough took part in the study. Some of the results were reported by Maggie Rogers at the Third International Primary Design and Technology Conference (CRIPT) in June 2001, subsequently published in the *Conference proceedings*. In Year 2, the most significant progress across the project (September to June) was in understanding of genre, but there was progress in writing for the reader, spelling and language structure among literacy skills, and for design and technology: addressing the task and generating and developing ideas. In comparison to children who did not take part in the project, the greatest difference was in their ability in identifying and specifying users and needs, and in evaluating own processes. The Year 6 children also showed significant progress in writing for the reader, communicating, evaluating own processes and identifying and specifying users and needs. There was also a marked improvement in their punctuation, in comparison to children who did not take part in the project. Overall, it was concluded that there was a significant growth in personal capability and that design and technology and literacy are mutually enhancing.

Starting from stories – using fiction as a basis for design and technology work

Almost any story can stimulate design and technology work without too much contrivance. The central character always needs something or the context can be exploited. Alternative endings can be devised and appropriate props designed and made.

Examples might be:

- disguise the mirror as something else (alternative ending for *Harry Potter and the Philosopher's Stone*);
- a model of Cinderella's coach to take her to the palace;
- Seven League Boots for Puss in Boots or other fairy tale character (Terry Jones' *Fairy Stories* is a rich source of alternative characters solving perennial problems);
- three-dimensional model of the Minotaur's maze to help Theseus get in and out safely;
- buildings in the Emerald City (*Wizard of Oz*).

Practical task

Choose a picture book appropriate for the key stage in which you are working and develop some ideas for design and technology work based on that story.

Hint: It is easier to begin from a picture book than one with no pictures. There are plenty of books with excellent illustrations suitable for Upper Key Stage 2, including Greek myths, Shakespeare, Hiawatha, etc.

Identify

- *a client/user/person who needs something, preferably not illustrated in the book – this may be readily suggested by the text or you may need to be inventive (e.g. Harry Potter example above);*
- *how you will describe what this item is to the children – do not be too specific – avoid closed descriptions that leave few design choices (as Cinderella's coach might if you just show the children a picture in a book);*
- *how you will explain the dilemma the user faces (Puss in Boots needs you!)*
- *what resources the children will need (don't forget the string for Theseus' Maze);*
- *content of current children's programmes, computer games, films, books for connections or distractions (Theseus' Maze unexpectedly tapped into some Year 4 boys' obsession with a particular computer game);*
- *how you will store/display the results – is there space in the classroom for a whole Emerald City? Perhaps the single portion cereal boxes might be better than family size?;*
- *health and safety issues.*

What specific design and technology learning will the children gain from this activity? Look back to Chapter 5 and refer to the National Curriculum for your key stage.

Non-fiction texts

One unexpected by-product of the National Literacy Strategy has been that children are being exposed to a range of genres of non-fiction texts at a much earlier age and with more directed teaching than was previously the case. Although non-fiction books were widely available in classrooms, children were not given specific teaching on how to read them nor were they expected to produce non-fiction text of their own, apart from writing 'news' or a few sentences about a topic studied in other lessons. Children are now being taught how to read and create labelled diagrams, lists (including bullet points) and tables, and to cope with a wide range of page layouts, including boxed text, columns, indents, different fonts, colours and sizes of print.

This means that children understand the idea of drawing a diagram to show how something might work, can produce a list of materials needed for making their product or write instructions for someone else to make it. It also means that this can be done as independent work during literacy hour, as it will count towards literacy targets, and enables design and technology time to be used for practical activity rather than more writing and drawing. This also applies to evaluation of the products the children have made. It would be far more exciting and meaningful than drawing their product in their design and technology books and write 'What I could do better next time' to create an advertisement or to work together to devise a commercial complete with jingle, sound effects and drama to 'sell' their product to the rest of the class, or to contribute to a class web page about the whole project.

And finally, before moving to other areas of the curriculum, do not forget that books are part of technology. Children can design:

- **small books for other children;**
- **scrapbooks and portfolios to show their own work to best advantage;**
- **pop-up books that use simple paper engineering mechanisms such as sliders, levers, wheels and hinges;**
- **books with surprises, such as lights and buzzers.**

More maths than measuring

Reflective task

What do you think about mathematics and design?

If it can be said that language is designed, then what about mathematics. Is it invented or discovered?

Is there an objective universe out there that obeys mathematical laws and which humans are struggling to discover, or is mathematics a human creation which is being constantly adapted and redesigned as it is found not to fit the universe as observed?

Are some parts of mathematics arbitrary (e.g. currency), others fixed, for example π (the ratio between the radius and circumference of a circle), and others relational (e.g. a litre of water is 1000 cubic centimetres and weighs 1 kilogramme)?

What about irrational numbers? Is this a real category or dependent on the number system used? For example, we usually count in base 10 and π is irrational (cannot be expressed as a ratio of two numbers) but if we were counting in base π, then 10 would be irrational.

The more you think about it, the more designed mathematics seems.

A child's most basic mathematical sense is the sense of self in space and in relationship to other objects and people. This is fundamental to a sense of distance, scale and proportion and leads on to the development of hand–eye co-ordination. Although these skills begin in a baby's first few weeks of life, they continue to develop throughout the primary school years. They are as fundamental to design and technology as they are to mathematical (and also to PE) skills.

Correlated to the self–object relationship is object–object relationships. In their early months, babies are able to tell whether an object has disappeared behind another and to be surprised if objects appear in unexpected places (hence their enthusiasm for games of peep-boo). Through playing with small toys such as cars and animals, children learn spatial awareness and develop the ability to estimate comparative size, especially in conjunction with contexts such as garages, farms, zoos, etc.

Turning things around in the mind's eye develops from turning them around in the hand. Through manipulating objects in their hands, young children learn to do so mentally. Observations of the look of things from different angles develops children's sense of symmetry and angle of rotation. Construction kits enable children to develop their ability to visualise objects from different viewpoints with components added or removed. This sophisticated mental skill is essential to designing. Children who have plenty of early exposure to toys of this kind are frequently more able to model three-dimensional design ideas in their heads and to imagine how components can be joined and fitted together. The ability to reliably choose the right part of a construction kit for the desired function (side strut for chassis of space ship, for example) depends on the ability to estimate length, breadth, width and angle of rotation. It is a small step from here to be able to do the same with card or wood, and to measure sizes and angles exactly.

An understanding of the importance of scale and proportion can be developed by providing small toys as clients or users for projects. Making an apartment block for a selection of class toys, for example, can be a whole class project in which each group designs and makes one room for one of the toys. The seats, tables and beds must be of an appropriate size for the toy to use. Teachers need to ensure that the boxes provided for this purpose are large enough for the toy sit on the furniture without hitting its head on the ceiling. A surprisingly easy mistake to make, and yet we are so often quick to criticise children for getting scaling wrong.

Measuring accurately is far more important to children when they have a practical purpose in mind and it will really matter if they do not. Year 3 children can measure in centimetres and rule lines if given opportunities to practise (focused practical task) to prepare them for their final piece.

Case study

Mosaics

Class 3N were studying the Romans in history and tessellation in numeracy. Mr Norris immediately saw the potential for a history- and maths-related activity that provided genuine design opportunities: mosaics. It would also foster co-operation and groupwork. It seemed an enjoyable, if messy, activity for the summer term, when much of the work could be done outside. He planned for it to be spread across a week, with the messy parts on Tuesday, Wednesday and Thursday.

Monday

In the history lesson Mr Norris provided squared paper for designing and colouring individual paper mosaics. In Lesson 2 on Tuesday, the children would combine their ideas into one single group design. Some negotiation would be necessary but Mr Norris felt this all helps build co-operative skills.

Tuesday

It began to drizzle part-way through lunchtime. Mr Norris pressed on with his plans and Lesson 2 began with each group mixing plaster of paris in bowls on plastic sheeting on their tables, to cast a plaster base in a large shallow tray, onto which the group's design would be copied once it had dried. As the children cleared up, Mr Norris had to shout at Ryan: Do not pour leftover plaster down the sink!

Each group then designed a motif or pattern by combining their separate ideas from Monday's lesson. They were restricted to having the same number of colours as there were children in the group, in roughly equal proportions. The noise level was high as arguments ensued and Mr Norris was feeling fraught by home time.

Wednesday

It was raining hard and the forecast was no better for Thursday, so Mr Norris decided to spread the rest of the messy work across one whole day to make it manageable in the classroom. Each child rolled out a large thin slab of clay according to the need for their colour (Mr Norris had prepared gauges cut from thick card to ensure these were all the same thickness). The slabs were divided into 1cm squares (using notched strips of card as measuring devices) and scored very deeply. The children painted the whole slab with one colour (as agreed on Tuesday) with a mix of powder paint and PVA glue. Mr Norris encouraged the children to mix their own paint to get a good range of colours. The slabs were left until the paint had just dried and then Mr Norris cut through the score lines with a craft knife. When these tessare were dry, they were sorted by colour into trays (six children during the wet lunch break) ready for each group to make their mosaic in the afternoon. Each group had to transfer their design onto their plaster cast by tracing the design onto greaseproof paper, making pinpricks through the lines and rubbing charcoal over the greaseproof paper onto the plaster, just as the Romans did.

Since the children had worked sensibly in the morning, Mr Norris decided that the whole class would complete their mosaics that afternoon. No arguments now, as the children concentrated hard on sticking tessera on to a base with thin plaster and, finally, filling in the gaps with more plaster.

Thursday

Each group nominated a 'varnisher' who painted the whole surface of the mosaic with water-based varnish to give a good shine and seal any unpainted clay edges. While this was happening, Mr Norris conducted a class evaluation of the project.

...here was glorious sunshine!

What points do you think were raised and discussed in 3N's whole-class evaluation?

Science and technology

Students frequently ask where the borderline between art, and design and technology lies, but far less frequently the difference between science, and design and technology. Is this because it is clearer or is the opposite the case? When does practical science (e.g. investigating flight) become design and technology (designing and making a kite)? Does it matter? Northern Ireland, in common with other countries, e.g. Canada, links science and technology as a curriculum area.

The insights of science make for good design and technology. However, the aims of the two subjects are fundamentally different (see Chapter 1, FAQ 3: *Isn't technology just applied science?*). As explained there, the aim of science is to understand the world and to uncover the principles on which it functions, seeking to abstract general rules and principles on which to build theories. Technology applies the discoveries of science, and combines them with ways of working that are akin to art and to holistic pragmatic understandings, with the intention of applying them to specific and particular problems. Science looks for the right answer or theory, whereas technology looks for the best solution for the current situation. The aim of science is not to produce a washing machine, neither is the rotating tub washer the only means of getting clothes clean.

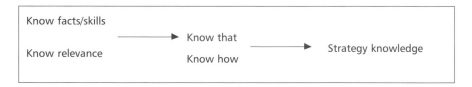

Ryle (1949) divided knowledge into knowing how and knowing that, from which the following model (Hope, 2001) is developed:

Know facts/skills		
Know relevance	Know that	Strategy knowledge
	Know how	

A model of knowledge

In discussing design problems with children, this converts to the following three questions:

- **What do you know/can you do?**
- **How does that apply to this problem/what else might apply?**
- **How will you use that knowledge/skill to solve this problem?**

Scientific knowledge and understanding forms part of the knowledge base required for the solution to some, but not all, design problems.

Science is needed for:
- **projects that are based on engineering principles, e.g.**
  - **designing moving vehicles, whether planes, boats or land vehicles;**
  - **working with mechanisms such as levers, pulleys, cams, gears, making cranes, gantries, lifts, etc.;**
  - **electrical control projects;**

- **projects that are based on biological understanding, e.g.**
  - **designing healthy menus;**
  - **homes for pets.**

Science is needed for some:
- **cooking (changing materials);**

- **structures (intuitive understanding of forces and tension).**

Science is not needed for:
- **most textile work;**

- **paper and card work;**

- **thinking about finishes and aesthetic appeal of any project.**

The level of scientific understanding can be intuitive. There is no requirement for scientific principles to be stated explicitly. For instance, the effect of friction on axles and wheels can be understood by young children, who will use such words as *sticky*, *rubbing* and so on. The word *friction* can be introduced to them to aid the development of understanding through extension of vocabulary and terminology but the focus of a design and technology activity would be to solve the problem of how to reduce the friction so that the vehicle's wheels work better. The theme might be taken up as a science topic later or it could be discussed in the plenary of the design and technology lesson.

Science, technology and reading (Association for Science Education, 2000) is a book of practical science activities based on poems (with full colour illustrations for each) that also has some sound design and technology ideas. For example:

- *Cow's Shoes* (pp42–3) could be used as an alternative to the **QCA Slippers project. The Key Activities section lists essential questions for shoe evaluation and design, leading into a description of a scheme of work that could enable Year 6 children to explore and design shoes, sandals or slippers. An interesting extension (or alternative?) activity is suggested at the end:** *design footwear for other creatures, for example, elephant 'wellies' or polar bear 'slippers'.*

- *Night Rides* (pp.54–5) could fit with and extend the **QCA's Torches:** *Older children could be challenged to design and make an illuminated display to advertise a good cause. Mount it on a frame to attach to a model or picture of a bus. Make a large card cut-out to give the children an idea of scale.*

- *Woolly Saucepan* (p110) could help Key Stage I children focus on suitability of materials for designing on the basis of their properties rather than visual characteristics: *they could design objects made from silly materials such as a 'chocolate saucepan' or a 'jelly chair'.* Young children love exploring the incongruous. This could be a 'virtual focused practical task' or part of text-level work in the literacy hour.

Design and technology can provoke scientific questions and reflections. For example, in a project on Fairgrounds in which the children are asked to make merry-go-rounds, swings, slides and ferris wheels:

- **Merry-go-rounds:**
  What makes the merry-go-round turn?
  What forces start and stop things moving?

- **Swings:**
  Why does the swing not swing for ever?
  What other devices use a pendulum?

- **Slides:**
  What force pulls you down towards the ground?
  On a helter-skelter, which force pushes you out sideways as you slide down?

- **Ferris wheels:**
  Why do the seats always stay level as the wheel goes round?

There is great scope in a Fairgrounds project for incorporating work on electricity that the children will have covered in science. For instance, merry-go-rounds can be powered by small electrical motors.

- **Roller coasters can become a focus of both scientific investigation and design and technology problem-solving:**

  - **What makes the roller coaster loop the loop?**
  - **What forces are involved here?**
  - **Can you design a roller coaster using a construction kit? Card? Plastic tubing?**
  - **Which works best? Why? (Use a marble or bead to be a 'car' as these will have almost zero friction themselves.)**

  Once children are convinced that the plastic tubing works best, then they can experiment with angles, slopes and size of loop. The results can be attached to a board (see Hann, 1998) which can be painted in true fairground colours.

This Fairground project can be linked to ICT too (see below under Information and Communication Technologies).

Practical task

Do you know the answers to the science questions in the Fairground example? If not, consult a science book such as **Primary Science: Knowledge and Understanding** *by Johnsey, Peacock, Sharp and Wright (2000).*

Likewise, design and technology activities can develop from science topics. For example:

- **growing things: see Appendix C Example scheme of work for Key Stage I;**
- **materials and their properties: essential knowledge for good design choices; changing material properties can be linked to food technology – setting, freezing, melting, boiling, reacting, aerating;**
- **electricity: see the Fairground project example above, put lights and motors in vehicles, on cranes, traffic barriers, etc., see also the section on electrical control in Chapter 7;**
- **forces and motion: again, see the Fairground project example above, but also for any vehicles, including boats;**
- **light: pinhole cameras, kaleidoscopes, periscopes;**
- **sound: musical instruments (see below under Music-makers), loudspeakers, string telephones – give children the opportunity to design several ideas for both of these and compare solutions);**
- **space: link this to flight and design aeroplanes and rockets;**
- **ecosystems: see Chapter 9.**

Information and communication technologies

It is likely that if you were to ask someone to name a technological product, they would be more likely to name an ICT product or system than anything else. In many people's minds ICT is 'technology.' In many countries, technology education at public examination level implies learning about advanced mechanical, electrical and electronic systems, especially associated with computer control. In the first National Curriculum of 1991, ICT was part of design and technology. Splitting the two has transformed ICT into a tool for working across the curriculum, and its role in design and technology has diminished.

The opportunities for learning *about* and *through* ICT in design and technology, however, are manifold, especially as highly sophisticated ICT tools have become cheaper and more widely available. As well as software, internet, CD-ROMs, digital cameras, video and DVDs, etc. as resources to support design and technology teaching and learning, this section discusses computers as technological systems.

Using internet, CD-ROM and other software resources

RESEARCHING

Unlike history, geography or other subjects with a large proportion of facts that can be transmitted through words, the use of ICT as a research resource for design and technology appears at first to be limited. Children need to try things out themselves, not look for purely factual information. However, CD-ROMs and internet access have transformed the way in which children can search for information on any topic. Keep adding sites to your Favourites and encourage the children to do so too. Teach them to open a new folder for each subject or topic and store their web links tidily. They will then build up a bank of useful sites for information on every topic they study, whilst also building ICT skills.

EVALUATING EXISTING PRODUCTS

Some products are too large (skyscrapers, bridges, etc.), expensive (jewellery, caviar, Porsche) or scarce (Tutankhamun's treasure) to collect and bring into the classroom but this does not preclude access to viewing the whole range. The '1000 images on one CD-ROM' genre can be invaluable for creating PowerPoint presentations on specific subjects. Many Key Stage 2 children will happily go through these in a wet lunch break looking for all the photos of, say, cars, and saving them to a new folder. They will be delighted when they see the teacher using the pictures they found. The same applies to web resources. Much of the initial digging can be done by the children. Some Year 6s may be happy to spend a lunchtime a week providing the service to teachers of younger children. Teachers then need only to collate and organise it.

- **Bridges, cranes and other large structures – you can't take a bridge apart to see how it's built but you can search the internet for every kind of bridge ever built.**
- **Buildings – assemble the whole history of housing, look at skyscrapers, modern buildings based on curves, interior design – move through a building on screen.**
- **Space topics – rockets, shuttles and space stations as well as views of stars and planets to set the mood and inspire imagination.**
- **Shopping – how has the internet changed buying and selling? (Incidentally, Key Stage I teachers, does the class shop reflect these changes? Does it have an electronic bar-code reader and PIN number entry credit card payment or are children playing 'pennies at the corner store'?).**
- **Advertising – link to media studies, healthy food campaigns, deconstruct the advertainment industry.**
- **ICT itself – changes and upgrades, mobile music, video phones, etc. – every company has an internet presence and so it is easy for children to research these topics and become discriminating viewers and readers of advertising hype and informed users of technology.**

Digital cameras, video and DVDs

Recording the critical moments in children's learning experiences causes them to reflect and enhances meta-cognitive learning. As well as pictures of commercially produced products, consider slide shows of previous years' products as a valuable resource for future classes, much as Class Books might be. These shows will give children instant insight into the kinds of ideas and products that could be made. They will feel free to make suggestions of how these could be improved, and year on year, standards will go up as each new class seeks to improve on the previous class's performance. These can then become part of the teacher's resource bank for the next project or the next class. It is easier to build design capability and understanding if it is possible to show children good practice, whether their own or that of other children, than to be just talking all the time. A shared understanding does build through talk, but pictures are so much more powerful.

Case study

Working together

Mrs Jones is showing this year's Cherry Class a video of last year's Cherry Class designing a solution to Frosty the Snowman's shopping problem.

Mrs Jones : **Now look at John, chewing his pencil, thinking about what he will make and see how Sam is pointing at his paper and suggesting ideas. Working together; swapping ideas; telling each other what they are planning. Think about whether other people are having good ideas or if you can help them have better ones. I'll just rewind it so we can see that again, because it's really important.**

Things that go wrong can often provide the moments when significant learning takes place, and children can be encouraged to see this as positive and something they want to share with the rest of the class:

Mrs Jones : **Red Group's crane collapsed but they wanted to tell the rest of the class what they learnt. Who can remember what we did to make our bridges stronger? What did we learn about making things with that cardboard? What will you need to make sure you do this time?**

Children can use cameras and video cameras to record their research observations, work in progress or completed to create a personal design portfolio as a PowerPoint presentation for peers, parents or school website. Windows Movie Maker is even easier for younger children to use to assemble sequences of pictures and customise transitions (and also takes up less memory space than PowerPoint). It is designed for making animated films and this is well within the capability of Upper Key Stage 2. An animation topic would be ideal for the last half term of the children's time in the primary school, when they so often feel they have done everything and are just marking time until they move on to the next phase. It brings together so much learning across the curriculum as well as developing skills of independent group working that will be expected in the secondary school environment.

Practical task

Planning a Year 6 animation project

Optimum mixed ability group size: 4. Think about the social dynamics – better to work on this with friends.

Encourage choice of a short story with characters that can be made easily from simple materials (card or modelling clay), whether using a published text or asking children to write their own, perhaps based on familiar text or characters.

Collect shallow boxes (e.g. mushroom boxes from the supermarket) as the stage sets.

Spend the whole of the first lesson planning but have some resources available for children who want to start making the characters. If children are to write their own story then ideas will flow better if they are allowed to create the characters in conjunction with developing the storyline.

Allow children freedom to organise their own work and decide when/who will make scenery, paint backgrounds, make characters, write the script. Keep spoken content to a minimum – a single line for each scene or find suitable music.

Have digital and video cameras available for every lesson and allow children time to practise. They will need to collect clips and shots of their characters in various poses and against different backgrounds for each scene.

Allow plenty of time for practising using Windows Movie Maker. It may help to have some photos on a file for them to practise transitions. Certainly you need to demonstrate some of the techniques. Train the children to save their photos and to save the video every time photos are added to avoid frustrations over lost images.

Create a title page and credits.

Arrange viewing time for other classes and/or parents to see results (could be shown at Leavers' Event).

Control technology

Once children understand how to make a simple electrical circuit, then they can begin to use that knowledge to control technology systems, for example, traffic lights and car park barriers. There is a range of commercially available control technology equipment, for example CoCo3® suitable for Key Stages 1 and 2, that enables children to work either on-screen or to control models they have made. Free-standing models of a clown, lighthouse and a house can be used alongside children's own design work, either as a stimulus or to extend their understanding of possibilities. The traffic lights, pelican crossings and car park barriers could be as features of a roadway system or townscape. Lego® also has a range of control technology products, that can be combined with standard sets of their bricks or form part of themed packs.

Control technology forms an important link into the way that computers work. Children can easily envisage a computer as a giant switching machine and can understand the principle of logic gates linked to keyboard or mouse clicks. Control boxes into which children plug their own circuitry allow children to feel in control of the technology and to think about how computers work. It does not need to be a complex explanation. Understanding the mouse and keyboard as switching devices is sufficient for Key Stage 1. By Upper Key Stage 2 children can begin to understand computer code as a complex system of electrical 'ons' and 'offs' that control gates that 'open' and 'shut' to allow the electricity to pass through in response to user or machine choices.

Do not forget that computers are part of the history of control technology:

- **calculations technology: tally sticks, abacus, Inca knotted strings, ready-reckoners, slide rules, early mechanical and electrical calculators, modern palm-sized solar powered electronic calculator;**

- **navigation and plotting the earth: astrolabes, chronometers, GEOSAT and NAVSAT;**

- **communications: semaphore, Morse code, telegraph and telephone, radio stations, TV towers, satellites, intercom, mobile phones; mail: airmail, e-mail, surface mail, text; radar and sonar, microwaves and ultrasound;**

- **electronic devices: cathode ray tubes, valves, transistors, integrated circuitry and micro-chips, optical fibres, chips;**

- **how computers work, as input–output devices, as binary on–off gated circuitry, as coded messages;**

- **computers in medicine, manufacture, commerce, banking, shops, travel agents, airports and aircraft, the home;**

- **the way in which data are collected and handled, the systems that such organisation represents, the way in which questions are posed, linking with the analysis of texts in literacy lessons.**

Reflective task

How good is your knowledge of the history of control technology?
Use the internet to research the areas in which you feel least secure in your own knowledge.

Also do not discount such helpful things as basic nets for boxes for packaging, which are available in many drawing programs. They can be enhanced on-screen or printed plain for embellishment. These can then be used to gift-wrap items made as Christmas and other festival presents, food technology products, as well as being a design and technology subject in their own right. They can also be quickly produced bases for other products. If everyone should have brought a certain size and shape cardboard box for a project and some have forgotten they can design and print their own on the computer.

The art of design

The word 'design' occurs in the subject area of 'art and design' as well as design and technology. Penny et al. (*Teaching arts in the primary school*, 2002) include design and technology within their remit. The relationship between design and technology, and art and design underlies FAQ 2 in Chapter 1.

Is 'design' in art and design the same as 'design' in design and technology? As a verb, Yes. As a noun, Yes and No.

Verb: As a human activity, designing is designing regardless of context or content. It has only one meaning: to purposefully create something in response to a perceived need, want or opportunity. That opportunity might be to create a new fashion garment, a three-dimensional structure expressing the futility of war, a sonnet, a symphony or a housing estate.

Noun: As a created artefact, the word 'design' has several shades of meaning, which often makes explaining aspects of design and technology difficult. In common parlance, a design is a pattern. This may mean the motif on a jumper or a drawing of a ship. It is a reflection of the enormous capacity that humans have for creative activity. One of the problems with the common parlance use of the word 'design' to mean something that is drawn (probably in a drawing office) before being sent to the workshop to be manufactured by somebody else, is that the two activities, designing and making, are separated in people's minds. This is why planning a product is often called 'designing' and making it is seen as a new, separate activity. This application of the industrial model is not helpful to primary-aged children and their teachers. Unfortunately, in the early days of the National Curriculum for design and technology, few books had been written about primary children doing design and technology, and so the industrial model, which was taught in secondary schools in preparation for entry of 16-year-olds into industry, was transferred to texts aimed at primary teachers. More appropriate is the model of the pre-industrial craft worker, for whom designing is not separate from making and who has built up a repertoire of making and designing skills which he brings to each new task.

Making a quality product that is pleasing to the eye may also involve an aesthetic sense that many would associate with artistic capability. However, this makes the assumption that all art is beautiful and pleasing to look at. Many modern artists have purposely created works that are jarring to eye and senses in order to convey their message. It would be difficult to imagine the furniture industry selling many uncomfortable armchairs. Technological design does not aim to shock or challenge in quite the same way, except in the fashion industry.

The idea that art somehow just flows out from the artist's inner psyche is a false trail. Artists are craftspeople who create images from their repertoire of knowledge, skill and understanding, reaching out from that repertoire to create something new that captures an abstract or ethereal quality. Often they practise the same image repeatedly, constantly searching for perfection of expression. Turner's sketchbooks are available to view in the Tate Britain gallery and some of Constable's are in the Victoria and Albert Museum. Picasso went through several phases in his art and there are repeated images within each phase. Behind each of them were hundreds of discarded sketches and trial runs. Monet destroyed all his practice canvases in case they were sold and diminished his stature as a great artist. Like design and technology, therefore, art requires planning, practice and recording of ongoing ideas.

Another misconception about the difference between art and design and design and technology is regarding purpose. Many detractors of art say that it has no external function, whereas technology has. Much serious art (excluding hobbyists, thereby) is produced for commission or in hope of gaining commission. The rows of portraits in the National Portrait Gallery were not produced to satisfy any artist's inner longing to capture the essence of humanity. Nor did Canaletto keep producing Grand Canals because he loved his home town more than any other place on earth. Few artists have had the luxury of not needing to earn their living from their art, which has meant for most artists that they have had to tailor what they would like to do with what pays. Satisfying the needs and wants of the client, is not, therefore, just true of design and technology. Incidentally, it is a part of art education that is often missing.

Inventors, artists and designers are highly creative individuals and yet creativity seems to be one of the most elusive of human qualities. Some people think it is innate and yet cannot say how we recognise it in small children. Others (including Anna Craft) believe it is within everyone and that it is a matter of degree. A good phrase for creativity is Craft's 'possibility thinking' or 'as if' thinking (Craft, 1997). Another useful term to help in thinking about this is 'dream room thinking'. Design and technology, like art, is essentially to do with encouraging 'dream room thinking' in others. Creative teaching for creative learning was discussed in Chapter 3.

So if art, and design and technology share many characteristics, what is the difference?

- **Technological artefacts are 'useful' in the practical sense that art objects are not.**
- **Technological artefacts are unlikely to have a deeper meaning that is their real purpose.**
- **Art objects are not used to produce other artefacts and have no practical purpose beyond their own existence.**
- **Art objects speak primarily to the psyche, whereas technological artefacts serve to support physical well-being.**

However, Heskett (2002) claims that good design combines both *utility* and *significance*. The Bauhaus movement in Germany, founded by Walter Gropius, believed that form should relate to function and considered design as a vital component of the production process. Pink (2005) considers that the way forward for American designers is to incorporate aesthetic and emotional appeal in the design of any product as a way of circumventing the competitive edge of developing economies with their much lower overheads.

Design for technology, however, has an added element that does not need to trouble the artist: environmental impact. This topic forms part of the subject matter of Chapter 9.

Humanities united

Artefacts and products that have been studied in history, geography or RE can be used as starting points for design and technology, provided children are not simply being asked to make a model of the object they are being shown. For an activity to satisfy the requirements of the design and technology National Curriculum, children must have the opportunity to make genuine design choices and autonomously solve problems. Making model houses from cardboard boxes in the style of a particular historical period does not satisfy these requirements.

The history of technology is an important aspect of studying any historical period. How can we understand the Victorians without reference to the impact of factories and textiles, iron and steel, canals and railways, gas, electricity and sewage works? The same is true of studying the geography of the local area, where history and technology have played a major part in shaping the landscape – mining towns, mill towns and ship building ports cannot escape the technological legacy that has shaped their community. This applies equally when studying other countries. The way in which people cover or decorate themselves and their homes, keep themselves warm, dry or cool, produce, cook and store their food – all these most basic concerns are part of human technology, as solutions to real needs and wants. They are often also exploited as opportunities for decoration, exhibition and celebration, even in so-called advanced industrial societies.

Making games based on the region being studied can incorporate design and technology skills, whilst also re-enforcing ideas learnt during geography. A 'Tour de Jamaica' based on the Tour de France would provide genuine problem-solving design opportunities, both in planning and making the game (including board, counters, dice) and thinking through the practicalities of traversing the Jamaican landscape. A similar idea applied to a historical theme could be 'crossing the prairie with the Sioux'. Working in groups to design, plan, make, trial and evaluate the games as they progress provides opportunities to practise important design and technology skills.

Festivals provide exciting opportunities for participation in carnival, parade, feasts and making decorations and greetings cards.

- **Costumes can be made on a plastic bin-bag base and these are more durable than simply using paper alone. Crêpe, tissue and other paper can then be attached with coloured sticky tape. Alternatively, the children can bring in an adult tee-shirt to which decoration can be added by printing, appliqué, etc.**

- **Hats – younger children can start with a wide strip of card that fits around the head, that can then have appropriate symbols and decorations made from a range of coloured paper and other materials. Older children can design and make their own hat from scratch, and solve problems of fit along the way, as well as making the final decoration appropriate to the festival. Christmas party hats and Easter bonnets can be made in design and technology lessons.**

- **Food – all festivals involve food and children can sample and make traditional seasonal delights. They can also decorate plates and table mats on which to serve the food.**

- **Decorations – encourage children to design their own and steer clear of handing out templates of robins, plum puddings, etc. at Christmas time. It is easy to succumb to mass production of sticky paper on card mobiles in order to rapidly fill the classroom and give the children a bagful to take home. Be realistic – can the school really afford such extravagance with resources, will most parents hang them up, and wouldn't just a couple of well-made and individually designed products be better?**

- Greetings cards. These can again fall prey to the mass-production mania at Christmas time, so ensure that your class have designed their own and that you studiously ignore those beautifully neat ones made by younger children who have obviously had little input apart from sticking on the pre-cut decorations and signing their name. Think carefully about what your class can actually achieve and pitch the activity to their level of capability. This can be a good opportunity to talk about the aesthetics of making a quality product and the need to practise techniques or trying several arrangements before gluing. Cards can, and should, be made for other festivals – Hannukah, Divali, Eid, Chinese New Year, etc. These encourage children to identify the most important features of the festival and its culture and to use these elements to create a product for a specific audience (most probably their family).

Music-makers

Every known civilisation, tribe and human group had or has music, rhythm and dance. The only universal tools are the lever and the spear. The only technological skill common to all human groups alive today is interweaving and knot-tying. (Pinker, 2002 pp435ff).

It has been suggested that language began as song and communities began to develop coherence as music and dance emerged. Every community has folk-lore, metaphor, traditional stories and children's songs. That creative humans should look for ways to make music better is not surprising, especially since music-making is also linked to religion, festivals and celebrations. A wide range of instruments is now available in schools, increasingly coming from a range of cultures and traditions, and often being combined in ways that their creators never envisaged.

Product analysis

Ask children to look closely at a small range of instruments: *how are they made and how and why to they make the sound they do?* This question can be asked of children aged from 5 to 11, the sophistication of the reply is the differentiating factor.

A 5-year-old holding a tambour can say that there is thin plastic stretched across a wooden circle. They can find another instrument (tambourine) that is made in the same way from similar materials. But perhaps there are also tambours and tambourines with skin, rather than plastic. Tambourines have jingles set in the rim. By the age of 11, children should be able to discuss the timbre and tone of the range of tambours and tambourines of different sizes and materials in relation to what is used to strike them (flat hand, knuckles, drum sticks of various kinds). This kind of discussion is not just about music, it is also about design. When children are asked to make their own instruments, the observations they make of ready-made instruments should inform their designing.

Unfortunately, 'musical instruments' made in schools are too frequently not very musical and consist of yoghurt pots containing beans or rice with a tatty piece of sticky-back paper wrapped around them or tissue boxes circled with different-sized elastic bands. Simple percussion instruments *can* be made from tubs, tubes and other recycled materials but there needs to be more emphasis on making a quality product that is fit for the purpose – to make *music*, not just a noise. Looking at existing musical instruments before starting to design is essential, as children need to investigate ways of making sound in order to make design choices.

Investigating, evaluating, designing and making

Rattles and shakers are the simplest to make, and Key Stage I children can experiment with a range of beans, rice, etc. inside different holders (yoghurt pots, drinks bottles, snack tubes, etc.). Link this to science work on sound in Key Stage 2 and conduct fair tests.

Each group could either test each filler in each container or the other way around (rice in everything or everything in take-away tubs). They record the kind of sounds made, discuss possible musical uses for them and create a soundscape or composition.

	Rice	Beans	Paper clips	Plastic cubes
Take-away tub				
Drinks bottle				
Jar				
Cardboard box				
Snack-food tube				

So far, there is science and music – now the design and technology. After these experiences, the children should have sufficient intuitive understanding of timbre and tone for them to be given a picture or poem for which they not only compose the soundscape but design and make the instruments too. Once children have decided on container and filler, then encourage them to think about the aesthetics of the finished product. Some focused practical tasks to experiment with different paints, coverings, glues and decorations will be necessary.

Years 5 and 6 can design and make much more sophisticated instruments, but provide a *design brief* rather than specifying an instrument to be made. For instance:

- **Design an instrument that is played by scraping as well as rattling.**
- **Design and make an instrument that can make two completely different sounds.**
- **Design and make an instrument that can be played in more than two different ways.**
- **Design and make two instruments that have similar sounds but different pitch.**

Case study

Dean is on his final school placement. These are his instructions to his Year 4 class:

This afternoon you are going to work as a group to design and make instruments for a one-man band. When you have finished, one of the group must be able to demonstrate – to be the one-man band and play all the instruments. Each group has a box of resources under their table and you can use any of the card, paper, string and so on, that is on the front desk. Be careful with the sticks – mind other people's eyes. Think first about what parts of the body you can play instruments with. The instruments must really work – no pretending. And remember what we talked about in Music this morning, so choose resources that will make a good clear sound. And try to design instruments that give a good range of sounds – not all high and tinkly and not all bang and crash. OK?

A satisfying project for Key Stage 2 children would be to make their own chime bars from different sized tin cans. With supervision in small groups, the children could use a hammer and large nail to make two holes in the rim of the can (sliding can over a wooden former for safety, an old table leg would do), then push a straw through both holes and thread string through the straw.

Once they have made the basic tin-can chime, then the children work in groups to design and make a frame from which to hang the chimes and each child can decorate their own chime. The cans will need a coat of light-coloured emulsion paint, onto which the children can draw a pattern or picture that can then be painted in with acrylic or household paint (sample pots from DIY stores are cheap). Two layers of varnish protect paint from abrasion in use as well as giving a satisfyingly shiny finish.

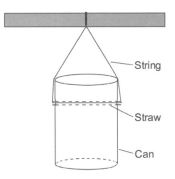

Reflective task

What about PE? Has it been overlooked and forgotten or is there no link between PE and design and technology?

To think about:
The position and movement of the body in and through space and in relation to other people and objects – is it possible to image the rotation of other objects without a secure image of your own body moving up, down, through and around the physical space in your environment? Is it possible to rotate in your mind an imagined object, one that you have just designed and does not yet exist, without the development of such skills in relation to your own body?

The development of physical skills – hand–eye co-ordination, physical strength and manipulation skills, accurate estimation of space, distance, speed and direction.

Working as a member of a team, accepting a role, supporting others in their role, accepting the support of others in your role and accepting that others might choose to support someone else other than you, working together towards a common goal without rivalry.

Developing cross-curricular themes from a design and technology topic

As well as combining subject areas and making explicit links from one area of the curriculum to the other, many schools are thinking in a more holistically cross-curricular way. They are taking a topic, say Houses and Homes, and developing this across all subject areas. The final section of this chapter on cross-curricular thinking demonstrates how this might be done, starting from a design and technology theme or subject. As in all cross-curricular work, it is important that the essential character and way of thinking embodied by each subject area is not lost in the desire for integration.

A group of Year 3 BA(QTS) students were asked to brainstorm ideas for cross-curricular work based on design and technology topics. Three of their concept webs are presented here.

In the first example, starting from an adaptation of the QCA scheme's unit on Slippers, the geography element Where are Shoes Made? could easily be reduced to tokenism, finding that Nike factories are in the Far East, for example. The historical, geographical and social reasons for their location needs to be explored. This would form part of the technological systems and environments underpinning the manufacture of the products.

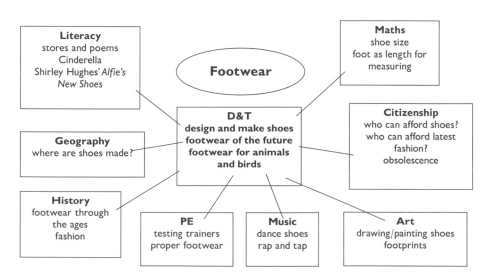

The second thematic project, Plastic bottles, could, it was suggested, begin with a classroom discussion about the number of plastic bottles in the bin after each day's school lunch.

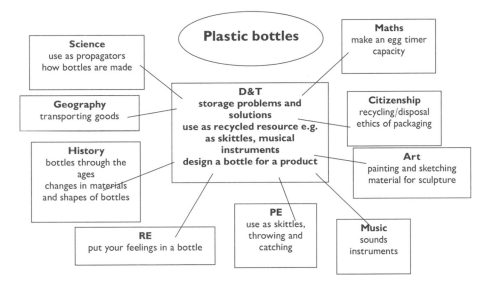

The final cross-curricular example, Carrying Things focuses on bags and baskets. It could begin with a lesson similar to Kelly's first lesson in the Case Study – A Bag for Mother's Day in Chapter 4, in which children examined, tried out and compared a large range of different bags. They could identify purposes and identify reasons for the size, shape, colour of each bag.

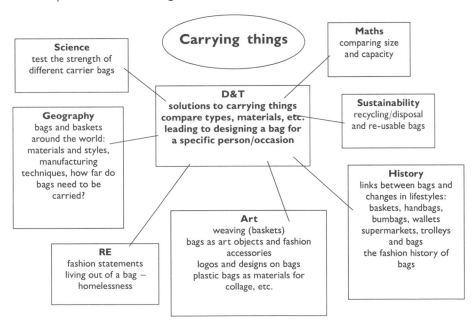

Finally, a cross-curricular scheme that began from an article on the front page of the local paper about the new town plan, which prompted Sarah, teacher of a Year 4 class at Eastgate Primary, to think that a project on the town centre would be a good cross-curricular project, especially since part of the town plan involved the regeneration of their end of town and she had a copy of Hehir and Kean (1992) *Our built environment* in her cupboard. Sarah decided that to impose an adult perspective, based on her reaction to the town plan, would be inappropriate, especially for her lower ability children, so she decided that she would ask the children what they would like to know about their town. Each group were asked to produce a list of six questions in ten minutes. Then Sarah explained that, as she had circulated and listened to their discussions, she had heard questions that fitted into different subjects displayed in a concept map on the interactive white board:

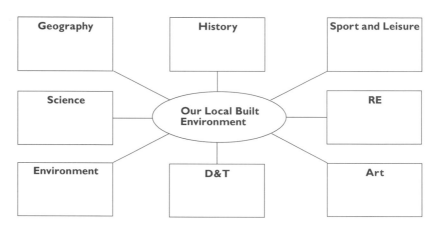

The children's questions were placed in appropriate boxes. As can be seen below, the questions ranged from simple (*How many football pitches are there?*) to sophisticated (*How good are the communications?*). Many of the subject areas overlapped and Sarah allowed the children to decide where each question would go.

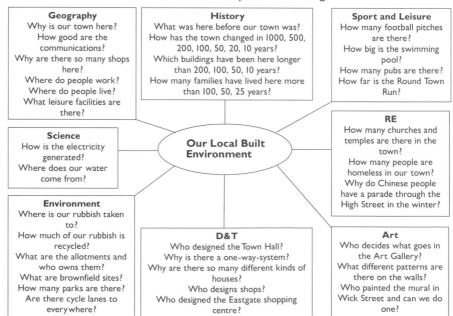

Practical task

If you think of design and technology education as being learning about technological systems and environments, as well designing and making products (see Chapter 1 and the introduction to Chapter 6), there is a design and technology element in many of the questions that the children placed in other subject boxes.

Can you identify which these are and how they relate to technological knowledge and understanding?

Now look for opportunities for children to design and make mock-ups or models.

If they were able to paint a new mural for Wick Street, what might it feature if its subject were to be Technology in our Town? Use paper and pencil to develop your own design in response to this question.

A different model of the curriculum

So far this chapter has explored:

- ways of making links between design and technology and other subjects;
- ways of developing cross-curricular thinking from technology topics through investigating products, systems and environments.

But this remains subject-centred, in the way that British (and predominantly English) education views subjects. In Northern Ireland, for example, technology is linked with science and there is a separate environmental and social area of learning. Australia also has 'areas of learning' rather than 'subjects'. Malaysians study design and technology as part of 'life skills' in the Upper Primary Stage, which includes repairing things that have broken. All national curricula begin from decisions about what is believed to be best for the nation's children to be taught and when (and sometimes, also, how: for example, the UK Literacy Strategy).

Re-inventing education, edited by Vincent Nolan and Gerard Darby (2005), is a 'Thought Experiment' by 21 authors, including the author of this book. In it, the authors address the question of how they believe education should be remodelled and ask such questions as What is 'education'? Who and what is education for? Several articles address the need for fostering creativity. Many writers stress the importance of learning to think or learning to learn.

Reflective task

What areas of design and technology education, as it currently exists in the UK National Curriculum, encourage 'learning to think'?

What about learning to learn?

Is the teaching of these skills embodied in the subject content or the pedagogy?

How does this relate to teaching creatively or for creativity?

Look back at Chapter 2 for some thoughts to get you started.

Crossing curricular boundaries:
a summary of key points

In this chapter you have learnt about the links between design and technology and other areas of the curriculum:

____ *literacy in the broadest sense: language for designing: spoken and written, and the use of fiction and non-fiction texts as research materials, instructions and ideas;*

____ *mathematics (including numeracy): spatial awareness, patterning and a sense of size and scale – as well as measuring;*

____ *science: as an explanation and a starting point for technological discovery;*

____ *information and communication technologies: software, internet, digital cameras, videos and DVDs, 'Chips with everything', and electrical and electronic control technology;*

____ *art: does your design appeal to the inner self; will it stand out from the crowd; or is it merely functional?*

____ *humanities: history, geography and RE provide contexts and clients for your design and technology projects;*

____ *music: investigating, evaluating, designing and making instruments that are worth playing;*

____ *RE: what was your answer to the reflective question?*

We have also examined ways of developing cross-curricular projects that enable the presentation of a holistic learning experience without losing sight of the essential skills and contributions to overall understanding that each subject makes.

References

Association for Science Education (2000) *Science, technology and reading.* Hertfordshire: ASE.

Benson, C and Mantell, J (1999) *Developing language through design and technology.* Wellesbourne: DATA.

Craft, A (1997) *Can you teach creativity?* Nottingham: Education Now.

Edwards, B (2001) *Drawing on the right side of the brain.* London: HarperCollins.

Hann, K (1998) *Science and technology at the Fairground.* London: PCET.

Hehir, L and Kean, J (1992) *Our built environment.* Cheltenham: Stanley Thorne.

Heskett, J (2002) *Toothpicks and logos: designs in everyday life.* Oxford: Oxford University Press.

Johnsey, R, Peacock, G, Sharp, J, and Wright, D (2000) *Primary science: knowledge and understanding.* Exeter: Learning Matters.

Nolan, V and Darby, G (eds) (2005) *Re-inventing education.* Buckinghamshire: Synetics Education initiative.

Penny, S, Young, S, Ford, R and Price, L (2002) *Teaching arts in primary schools*. Exeter: Learning Matters.

Pink, D (2005) *A whole new mind: how to thrive in the new conceptual age*. London: Cyan Books.

Pinker, S (2002) *The blank slate: the modern denial of human nature*. London: BCA.

Rogers, M (2001) Providing evidence of capability in literacy and design and technology in both Year 2 and Year 6 children, in *Conference proceedings*, Third International Primary Design and Technology Conference. Birmingham: CRIPT (Centre for Research into Primary Technology).

Ryle, G (1949) *The concept of mind*. London: Hutchinson.

Stables, K, and Rogers, M (2001) *Enriching literacy through design and technology evaluation project*. London: Goldsmiths College, University of London.

Language links

DATA (1999) *Developing language through design and technology*. Wellesbourne: DATA (Project manager: Clare Benson with Julie Mantell).

Emblem, V and Scmitz, H (1992) *Learning through story*. Warwickshire: Scholastic.

www.naaidt.org.uk/spd/jgershon/SpkList.html for developing speaking and listening skills through design and technology.

Mathematics

DATA (1999) *Developing mathematics through design and technology*. Wellesbourne; DATA (Project manager: Clare Benson).

Science

Burton, N (1993) *Science and technology through traditional tales*. Birmingham Curriculum Support Service.

ICT

Websites with useful design and technology resources and classroom materials are listed in Appendix B.

Suppliers

CoCo3 available from Commotion **www.commotiongroup.co.uk**.

ESIGN AND TECHNOLOGY OR GLOBAL CITIZENS OF THE UTURE

This final chapter will consider the UK National Curriculum in the context of global environmental concerns and of the developments in design and technology education world-wide. Like the ripples of a pond, the chapter will move out from children learning to think about the present needs and wants of others around them to learning to think about the future needs of the whole planet, before focusing once more on the role of government in changing the face of education and the working lives of children and their teachers.

This will be covered through an examination of:

- *designing for others;*
- *multiple perspectives on design and technology education;*
- *designing the future of a changing world.*

Designing for others

In their two-volumed resource pack for cross-curricular work *In the global classroom,* Canadians Graham Pike and David Selby (1998) see global education as bringing together two interrelated strands of thinking, each of which is vital for the 'generation of constructive change on a global scale' – *world-mindedness* and *child-centredness*. The perspective of these two Canadian writers is holistically cross-curricular and demonstrates a deep concern for the future of society and the planet. They stress the importance of education being both world-minded and child-centred. Their 'global classroom' is seen as producing 'practical visionaries' who can identify their preferred futures and take action to realise them, what Toffler (1970) called 'anticipatory democracy'. In terms of design and technology education, this means being able to see the world from different perspectives and understanding issues of sustainability, ecology and the environment. This larger view of the designed world begins with the ability to take the needs and wants of others into account in designing.

Abraham Maslow 'hierarchy of human needs', which he set out in his 1954 paper 'A theory of human motivation' illustrates the difficulties that children from Britain, especially from relatively affluent homes, have of understanding the level of need at which children from other societies might operate. When asked to design a product for a friend or relative, children in Britain will think in terms of the top two levels of Maslow's hierarchy: the need for prestige and self-esteem, the need for self-actualisation or reaching one's potential. Although they can readily imagine recycling plastic containers or oil drums, they find it very challenging to imagine the needs of a refugee from a village in a war zone or an earthquake victim, whose needs are for water, food and shelter (the lowest levels of Maslow's hierarchy). Schools are often partnered with schools in developing countries or support children's charities. Aid organisations can provide information on the kind of technology that is appropriate for different climatic and cultural situations. Asking children to design, say, a water carrier from recycled materials can help to inform them about the real lives of children in a community that the school supports.

Claims were once made that young children were unable to take the perspective of others in a social as well as a spatial sense, based on Piaget's research findings (Piaget and Inhelder, 1956, contested by Hughes, 1975) into young children's spatial awareness and apparent inability to identify the viewpoint of a model mountain from a position other than the one in which they were themselves seated. Anyone who has watched toddlers manipulating older siblings and playing them off against each other knows that this extrapolation from the spatial to the social world does not hold. However, young children do project their own preferences onto others rather than being fully aware that others may have very different viewpoints on life (as do many adults!).

Part of the contribution to children's social and moral development that design and technology can make is learning to see the world from the perspective of another, that of the user or client. Children in Foundation Stage and Year I will find this very difficult and will project their own likes and dislikes onto the user. They will choose to decorate a card for Mother's Day with the colours and materials they like best and tell a questioning adult that these are Mummy's favourites. Even some Year 2 children, when asked to decide who a greeting card will be for and to list all the recipient's favourite things before beginning, will abandon this list and make a card that they themselves would like to receive.

This would suggest that throughout Key Stage I, teachers should give children plenty of practice at thinking about the needs of others, without criticising them for abandoning their plans and good intentions. Encouraging children to talk and discuss their design ideas while they are making their product is essential. Often there is a too formal approach to 'designing' which is relegated to the first few minutes of drawing an idea, followed by too great a level of freedom of interpretation once the making of the artefact begins. Teachers need to circulate and discuss the children's developing ideas in order to refocus them on the design outcome and task criteria.

- **Is the size right?**
- **Is it strong enough?**
- **How will it work?**
- **Will it stand up on its own?**
- **What colour will it be?**

Such questions enable the child to think about the needs of their user or client.

In Key Stage 2, children become increasingly aware of the needs of people beyond home, school and friends or of story characters and fantasy figures. They pay more attention to the news on TV and radio and are aware of human and natural disasters. Children are increasingly aware of such issues as global warming and poverty in Africa. Technology education should confront these issues and provide a perspective on them which, whilst not denying the complexity of the issues, begins to educate children to identify causes and think about possible solutions. There are close links here with geography, RE and PSHE/citizenship education.

Multiple perspectives on design and technology education

Across the UK

The Chinese have a proverb: 'The hills are high and the Emperor is a long way off'. For many teachers and children in the United Kingdom, Westminster is a long way off. Yet most books about teaching and for pupil use are England-centric. Not only should schools in all parts of the UK use their local industrial heritage to inform their design and technology teaching, but should expand children's knowledge of other areas, thus linking design and technology to the geography of all four countries and also to the islands of the UK.

- **The industrial heritage of Scotland, especially shipbuilding, has played a major part in the prosperity of the nation as have Scottish inventors, industrialists and scientists.**

- **How much do English children know about Northern Ireland apart from the Troubles? Why was Belfast strategically important in the Second World War? Apart from Guinness, what else does Ireland export?**

- **The Industrial Revolution would have struggled without Welsh coal and iron. The valleys of South Wales are beautiful places that have witnessed major technological feats in extracting and transporting raw materials from inaccessible places across difficult terrain. Listening to the departures from Cardiff railway station is like hearing a roll-call of industrial history.**

- **And then the islands: the Scilly Isles, the Isle of Wight, the Isle of Man, the Western Isles, the Orkneys, the Shetland Islands, the Channel Islands. All of these islands have contributed and continue to contribute to the technological development and industrial heritage of the UK, yet are frequently omitted from any roll of honour.**

As well as making children aware of the technological developments and industrial heritage of their own locality, teachers need to expand their knowledge of the whole of the UK and role of other parts of the nation, especially those with which they are less familiar.

Case study

The Shetland Islands

The Shetland Islands lie 150 miles north of Scotland, with connections as close to Scandinavia as to the rest of the UK. The largest island is Mainland, and 15 of the 100 or more other islands are also inhabited. The are two main settlements, both on Mainland: Lerwick (population 7,000) and Scalloway (population 1,000). The landscape is one of rolling hills, largely devoid of trees, dotted with stone built crofts, crofting being the traditional way of Shetland life. Deep arms of sea (voes) slice the land into long fingers and off-islands, making travel by sea far easier than by land until recent times. Driving from Burra across Trondra and on to Mainland by bridges has turned the inhabitants of these two off-islands into commuters.

- *What benefits are there in greater mobility, especially for isolated communities?*
- *What is the environmental impact of greater mobility?*
- *How has the building of roads and bridges changed people's lives in your locality?*

Shetland's challenging environment (cool summer and long winter nights) is balanced by its rich natural resources. Fishing is the traditional major industry and there are few voes unused by fish farmers (salmon and mussels). The North Atlantic Fisheries College at Scalloway is a major player in research into the techniques and environmental impact of fish farming. Both the fish stocks and the bird population are highly dependent on the Gulf Stream. In the poor summer of 2005, when the Gulf Stream took a slightly different course, internationally sensitive bird populations plummeted and seagulls became aggressive plunderers in their search for food for their starving chicks.

- *What impact has the Gulf Stream on fishing in other parts of the UK?*
- *How has over-fishing impacted on fish stocks and what steps are being taken to address this?*
- *How has the application of advanced technologies affected the way in which fishermen work?*

The Sullom Voe oil terminal has provided not only jobs but revenue for the benefit of the whole community. Every village has a school and community centre or cafe. Most large villages also have a sports centre and swimming pool. Grants are readily available for small businesses.

- *Oil terminal workers from the south share cars – is this a regular part of life where you live?*
- *What community benefits are there as a result of industrial development in your locality?*
- *The oil industry will eventually collapse due to depletion of oil reserves. What do you think might be the impact of this on the Shetland Islands, based on the impact of pit and mine closures in other parts of the UK?*

The Shetlands are dotted with the remains of brochs and other prehistoric stone-built dwellings that were up to thirty feet high and could contain many rooms. The broch on Mousa is particularly well preserved. It is a technological masterpiece. At ground floor level the double walls have rooms between them and a staircase spirals up between the walls to the top of the broch where a walkway gives a panoramic view of the island, Mainland and beyond. Whoever built this, 2000 years ago, was wealthy and had something to protect, was part of a trading network both local and international that was dependent on sea transport and was able to employ master craftsmen who knew how to handle stone. As well as technological problems involved in the staircase, the inner wall also features a ladder effect of arches above each door, extending the full height of the structure, whose purpose is uncertain but provision of ventilation seems to be most likely.

- *Look at a historical structure (e.g. castle, fort) in your locality –*

- *What technological problems did the builders overcome?*

- *What technological systems (transport, trade, etc.) did the structure support/ depend on?*

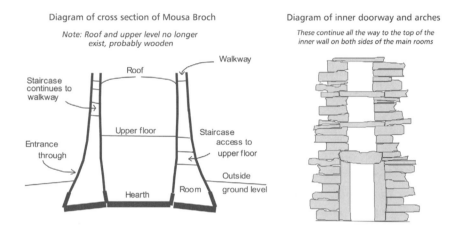

Diagram of cross section of Mousa Broch

Note: Roof and upper level no longer exist, probably wooden

Diagram of inner doorway and arches

These continue all the way to the top of the inner wall on both sides of the main rooms

Walkway

Roof

Staircase continues to walkway

Upper floor

Staircase access to upper floor

Entrance through

Outside ground level

Room

Hearth

Diagrams of Mousa Broch

Respect for All within UK schools

Respect for others is essential for harmony in the classroom and, Howe, Davies and Ritchie (2001) would argue, is part of the contribution of design and technology to children's spiritual development.

The following paragraphs are based on the QCA Respect for All: Guidance for Teachers to be found on **www.qca.org.uk/301.2181.html**.

To develop pupils' respect for the cultural traditions of others (whether represented within the class or school or not), in all lessons, teachers should:

- **use appropriate resources (for example, that portray positive images);**

- **present a broad and balanced view of cultures;**

- **challenge assumptions;**

- understand globalisation;
- create an open climate.

In the specific guidance for design and technology Key Stage 1–3 (**www.qca.org.uk/ 1576.html**) the QCA draw attention to the design and technology mission statement (page 90 of the National Curriculum) as being in itself a vehicle for making 'a significant contribution to pupils' ability to value diversity and challenge racism'. By setting design and make assignments in a range of cultural contexts, children can develop their understanding of their own roots and those of others.

Pupils can:

- **address their own or others' real needs and wants;**
- **bring individuality to design and make assignments;**
- **bring their own culture to their designing and making;**
- **develop their communication skills.**

In focused practical tasks and analysis of products, pupils can:

- **find out about new products and applications (including how societies have been enriched by contact and communication;**
- **learn to use and evaluate products in relation to the indigenous culture to which they belong;**
- **appreciate that all products have cause and effect, and are developed in response to needs and opportunities within a society;**
- **understand different approaches to product development;**
- **consider how technology reflects different cultures and values.**

How might this affect your teaching in design and technology?

MULTILINGUALISM

Many schools, especially in inner city areas, have pupils who speak more than a dozen different mother tongues between them, with English as a second or additional language. These pupils may have been born in the UK of parents also born here who are nevertheless determined that their children grow up able to access their family's cultural roots, or at least be able to speak with grandparents when they visit. Or they may have arrived here as children, perhaps with parents fleeing racial or religious persecution, traumatised by what they have seen, heard, experienced but barely understood. There are also those whose parents are from different language groups, perhaps sharing English as their common family language, but with each parent speaking to the children in their own tongue.

Many bilingual and multilingual children do very well in our educational system. It would seem that the cognitive skills involved in learning more than one language enhance both analysis and synthesis of ideas, both essential skills for designing.

Different languages use different metaphors, imagery and figures of speech, again important skills for imaging design possibilities. The ambiguity inherent in being unsure which language to start speaking in also prepares the mind for the balancing of ambiguity in design situations.

Doyle (2005) points out that drawing is a more universal means of communication than speech or writing – provided that what is being drawn is not culturally specific, of course. Children with little grasp of English can access the design and technology curriculum as readily as the rest of the class, provided they are clear about the learning objectives and the task parameters. They can draw their ideas and then add single word or short caption labels if their English is good enough. Being able to develop ideas in a medium that is not dependent on language learning enables cognitive development to progress without hindrance. Equally, when making products, children with little English have little problem completing the task and performing at their true level of capability.

MULTIRACIALISM

The diversity of heritage of different racial and ethnic groups brings a richness of combinations to bear on possible solutions to design situations. Throughout history, the discovery of one group by another has led to a mixing and mingling of ideas, although not always peaceably. Children need to become aware of the range of solutions to the same human needs and wants around the world. This can be as simple as comparing homes around the world, to examining farming techniques to grow and harvest the same crop. Teachers need to ensure that children understand that design choices in different parts of the world are dependent on natural resources, climate and other external factors as well as the way in which societies are or were structured and the cultural priorities that drive change and determine developments. The effects of colonialism on technological development, both within colonised and colonising cultures needs to be explained. Western nations have inherited a belief in 'progress' that assumes a superiority of those who have 'developed' over the 'developing'. It is important that children understand that the limiters to design opportunities and technological choices do not reside only within people's heads (put crudely: less 'progress' does not imply 'less intelligence' – which is what the Victorians thought!).

MULTICULTURALISM

If asked about cultural affiliation, people may define themselves as members of a racial or religious group, or by broad geographical area (e.g. European), but usually relating to a basic way of life or shared heritage or philosophy. Sharing of ideas across cultures can lead to a new world-view. For example, when Europeans reached the Far East in search of silks and spices, they discovered a whole new way of seeing the world. Only recently, however, has the Chinese philosophy of ying–yang become influential in Western thinking as the influence of the Classical heritage has weakened. Good designers need the 'both/and' thinking of Eastern philosophy more than the 'either/or' dualism of Classical (Greek and Roman) thought, since design problems can frequently have many solutions (see FAQ 3 in Chapter 1). This means that the solutions based on non-European ways of thinking are equally as valid as Western ones. This has been recognised especially in relation to critiques of Western consumerism and children need to become aware that the conservationist viewpoint inherent in many traditional ways of life may have greater viability on a global scale than the 'progress' of continuous production that has fuelled the development of Western culture.

The South African National Curriculum (2005) for technology takes the viewpoint that:

> Today's society is complicated and diverse. Economic and environmental factors and a wide range of attitudes and values needs to be taken into account when developing technological solutions. The development of products and systems in modern times must show sensitivity to these issues.

The curriculum for life sciences goes further:

> In the 1960s, the theory of multiple intelligences forced educationalists to recognise that there were many ways of processing information to make sense of the world ... Now people recognise the wide diversity of knowledge systems through which people make sense of and attach meaning to the world in which they live. Indigenous knowledge systems in the South African context refer to a body of knowledge embedded in African philosophical thinking and social practices that have evolved over thousands of years.

RELIGIOUS DIVERSITY

Schools that have children from a wide range of religious faiths often celebrate everybody's festivals, which gives many opportunities for design and technology activity, especially in the form of cards, gifts and foods. This enables children to take the perspective of others, an essential design skill, especially if it is radically different to their own and their family's. It is easy to assume that 'Christian' is a blanket category for most Europeans without realising the diversity of expression, from Orthodox, Catholic, Anglican, Methodist, Pentecostal, Salvation Army, plus those who believe in Jesus but actively set themselves apart from other groups; for example, Exclusive Brethren, Jehovah's Witnesses, the Church of the Latter Day Saints (Mormons). Religious observance creates strong emotional ties and loyalties and some parents may object strongly to their child bringing home a card wishing them a happy festival day that they do not celebrate. Jehovah's Witnesses do not want their children to participate in any Christian festival activities, for example. Include but do not give offence. If in doubt, ask – accept parental wishes as final, even if the child objects. Never encourage children to design and make things that parents do not want them to do because of deeply held beliefs.

CLOTHING

Be aware that some cultural traditions within religious groups do not wish their girls to roll their sleeves up and show their bare arms, especially in Year 6 as both boys and girls approach puberty. Designing clothes for dolls or cut-out card figures representing different parts of the world or different cultural or religious traditions can enable conversations about clothing choices.

FOOD

Do not do food technology activities in Ramadan, even if there is only one Muslim child in the school. If you are unsure if children can eat specific ingredients or take part in particular food-related activities, ask or send a note home. Jewish children do not mix meat and milk, even in washing-up processes or re-use of utensils. Ask the child to bring in utensils from home and be perfectly matter-of-fact to the others as to why. Jews or Muslims cannot eat or handle pork — that includes Spam and other similar cooked meats. Traditional Catholic families (especially from Southern European countries) do not eat meat on Fridays, so no mince pies on the last Friday of Autumn term (unless they have been made with vegetarian suet). If there are vegetarian or vegan children in the class you must check the ingredients of packet mixes (e.g. dessert whips), sauces, any processed foods, including biscuits and bread brought in for taste analysis..

The New Zealand National Curriculum for technology (1993, p27) has a specific strand called Technology and Society, through which:

> Students will demonstrate progress in awareness and understanding of the relationship between technology and society through their:
>
> - increasing knowledge of and respect for different beliefs and values and their influence on technological development;
>
> - growing recognition of their own values, ethics and the factors that influence them, in relation to technological choices and decisions;
>
> - increasing ability to respond to and accommodate diverse factors and different perspectives in their designs and planning;
>
> - growing ability to take an informed, sensitive role in debate on technological change;
>
> - ability to make informed and imaginative forecasts of possible futures;
>
> - growing confidence that they will be able to take an effective part in the technological shape of the future.

Other national curricula

With a greater emphasis on an international component within ITE courses, it is important that student teachers become aware of different perspectives on design and technology education worldwide. Throughout this book there have been references to the technology curricula of other English-speaking countries.

At the Third International Conference of the Centre for Research into Primary Technology (2003), Clare Benson spoke about international futures of design and technology education. There are, internationally, she said, three levels of engagement:

- **exploratory – countries that are beginning to explore the nature of the subject, its rationale for the subject's inclusion and implementation;**

- **introductory – countries that have introduced design and technology in their national curricula, provide in-service training and curricular support;**

- **developing** – countries where design and technology has been mandatory for some time and have developed their national curricula from that originally introduced.

There are also countries that have, as yet, no plans to introduce a national curriculum for design and technology. This does not mean that no design and technology teaching is taking place. It may be included under their science curriculum and therefore contain little development of either design capability or hand skills. Craft skills (e.g. metal work, textile work) may be offered in secondary schools (sometimes from age 11 but more commonly from age 13 or 14) as vocational training. This may be offered to all children, or only to those for whom it is considered appropriate.

This is true even of some countries with strong industrial economies and the reverse is also true – some countries with a lower GNP nevertheless have a strong belief in technology education. It would be a mistake to equate a strong technological economy with strong technology teaching and learning. It may well be that the needs of the economy are for low-skilled workers in mass-production factory units. In this situation there is little incentive for high levels of design education or even of technological understanding. Conversely, a country may perceive a global niche for their workers as highly skilled, flexible innovators. National curricula are reflections of a country's economic priorities and their perception of their place in the world.

Some countries equate technology with industry and ICT. Canada teaches 'science and technology' rather than 'design and technology', covering mechanisms, structures, engineering, etc. that make links between technology and science. New Zealanders have tried hard to come to terms with the destructiveness of white culture on the highly developed Maori culture that existed before the arrival of white settlers and farmers. Respect for the Maori culture and heritage, along with an understanding of traditional technological heritage, is seen as important to the cultural health and identity of the nation.

Case study

South Africa: a new curriculum for a new nation

With the coming of democracy in 1994, the right of all of South Africa's children to the same high standard of education was established by law. The Technology Association holds conferences and workshops to support teachers in delivering the design and technology curriculum. The subject content and range of activities would be familiar to any visiting UK teacher.

The three learning outcomes in the technology learning area:

technological processes and skills;

technological knowledge and understanding;

the interrelationship between technology, society and the environment.

The third of these South African outcomes has largely slipped from view in the UK National Curriculum, especially in primary schools. This book has argued strongly for its re-establishment. It is a strong feature of the New Zealand National Curriculum for technology (p8):

> The aim of technology education is to enable students to achieve technological literacy through the development of:
>
> ● technological knowledge and understanding;
>
> ● technological capability;
>
> ● understanding and awareness of the relationship between technology and society.

Sustainability, ecology and the environment

Added to the traditional criteria for good design (fit for the purpose and aesthetically pleasing) is the imperative that good design should be sustainable. When analysing products, pupils should be encouraged to consider to what extent the product is needed. Does another, less environmentally damaging product fulfil the need? Is the present product simply a more fashionable variation on one that exists already? These are difficult questions for children, since they are targeted by aggressive advertisement campaigns to put pressure on parents to spend money on particular brands of food, clothing and entertainment. If children can be persuaded to become more discriminating consumers, it would seem that this would be generally agreed to be a good thing.

Sustainability has three aspects:

- **social sustainability: ensuring that other people's quality of life and human rights are not compromised to fulfil our expectations and demands;**

- **environmental sustainability: means ensuring that our actions and lifestyles do not have such a negative impact on the environment that the planet's resources are being used at unsustainable rates;**

- **economic sustainability: means ensuring that there is an economic benefit both to the region from which the purchase came and to the region in which it is marketed.**

Environmental, economic and social issues often overlap; designing and making decisions usually involve a moral choice. They underlie the UK government's Sustainable Development Strategy (to be found at **www.sustainable-development.gov.uk/ publications/uk_strategy/index.htm**).

> The National Curriculum website recognises the inherent complexities within such issues: some people argue that there is no agreed definition of sustainable development and that there may be no need for one. They argue that sustainable development should be viewed as a process of change that is heavily reliant upon local contexts, needs and interests. Sustainable development is then seen as an 'emerging concept', first because it is relatively new and evolves as we learn to grasp its wide

implications for all aspects of our lives, and, second, because its meaning emerges and evolves according to local contexts. **www.nc.uk.net/esd/gql.htm**

Within Key Stage 2, children can begin to be aware of these issues, although it is unlikely to affect their personal choices. However, it is worthwhile sowing the seeds of understanding with regard to issues of sustainability as this will form part of the way in which children view the world. Links with geography, RE and citizen/PSHE are obviously strong:

> *Design and technology promotes education for sustainable development through developing understanding of the principles of sustainable design and production systems, developing skills in creative problem-solving, and exploring values and ethics in relation to the application of design and technology.* **www.nc.uk.net/esd/ teaching/dandt/index.htm**

This is applied directly to Key Stage 2:3c Evaluating processes and products:

> *Requirements: Recognise that the quality of a product depends on how well it is made and how well it meets its intended purpose (for example, how well products meet social, economic and environmental considerations).*

> *Opportunities: Pupils might develop their own set of social, economic and environmental criteria for evaluating and comparing the sustainability of commonly used products and/or their packaging and environments (e.g. fairground rides, parks, play spaces, housing developments, shopping centres).*

The QCA suggest opportunities for enhancing Education for Sustainable Development (ESD) content in selected units of their scheme of work (**www.nc. uk.net/esd/teaching/dandt/schemes_of_work.htm**):

> *Key stage I: Unit ID : Homes: When children are investigating different types of homes in the local environment they could be asked, in addition to practical questions of structure, whether they think the homes or houses would be good to live in and why. Children could consider features that make homes pleasant places, including appreciation of gardens and local surroundings as well as features of the houses themselves.*

> *In addition, children may be able to identify basic features that make houses environmentally sustainable. These might include obvious features such as solar panels, double glazing, types of building materials (e.g. in keeping with the local area; local materials), whether the buildings are old or new or use of other (local) materials such as thatch.*

> *During the model-making activity children could be encouraged to bring and use recycled materials from home such as cardboard boxes or tubes.*

> *Key stage 2: Unit 3A: Packaging: During the design and making phase of the activity children should be specifically directed towards at least one environmental criterion for selecting materials and design, e.g. uses minimum materials, materials are reusable or recyclable. This allows task to be related to previous investigative phase of activity.*

'Managing packaging' is one of the activities within Pike and Selby's (1998) *In the global classroom*, which has a range of suitable activities for developing awareness of the global impact of technological processes and our way of life. A set of packaged items cards, including box of eggs, pre-packaged sandwiches, toothpaste, batteries etc., are to be sorted and placed on a packaging impact graph (pp 98–9).

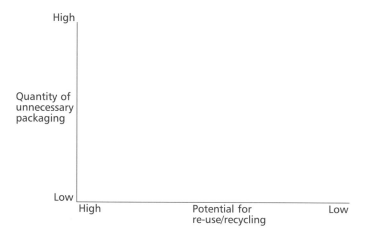

Packaging impact graph

This will promote a discussion, not only of the waste that is generated, but also of such issues as protecting the product (eggs), presentation (sandwiches), hygiene (toothpaste) and safety (batteries). This activity could provide a useful addition to the delivery of the QCA Unit 3A: Packaging.

A similar view is expressed in Howe, Davies and Ritchie (2001) in juxtaposing creativity, citizenship and the curriculum as the subtitle of their book *Primary design and technology for the future: creativity, culture and citizenship*. They too argue for the role of design and technology in education for global citizenship through affirmative action.

One of the biggest changes within technological thinking on a world scale has to be the realisation that environmental issues need to addressed urgently. Further, media coverage of the continued needs of the poorest nations has high-profiled the need to ensure that benefits of technological prowess are shared. In educating children within this framework of global needs, environmental and economic, it is important that children:

- **do not become desensitised through repetition but become aware of the day-to-day challenges that face people in poorer countries (Pike and Selby have an excellent activity for water awareness – the girls in the class have to fetch all the water needed for the class for the whole day, including hand washing, from a tap at the far side of the school site);**

- **are encouraged to see things from the perspective of others (e.g. through designing something for someone else to use);**

- **see themselves as agents of change through the choices that they make, as informed consumers, and in the way in which resources can be recycled or re-used (using recycled or donated resources for design and technology work);**

- are able to evaluate existing products and services and assess their impact on the environment and economic well-being of producers;

- develop their own viewpoint about sustainable technology and the impact of technological processes on the environment and world economy, that can be supported by information gathered from books, websites and electronic media.

The Fairtrade organisation has a website (**www.fairtrade.org.uk/**) that children can access for ideas, recipes and information; it applies ICT skills to investigating and disassembling familiar products within design and technology, to answer questions such as:

- **Where are bananas/coffee/cotton grown with most money going to growers?**
- **How can homes be heated with least impact on the environment?**
- **What happens to our waste and how much is recyclable?**
- **Where is wood/paper produced from sustainable forestry?**

As well as providing factual answers to such questions, the act of setting them alerts children to the issues. For example, **www.fairtrade.org.uk/resources.recipes. htm** keys straight into issues that concern all children: food.

Designing the future of a changing world

In Hope (2005) it is argued that:

> By the nature of its subject matter, design and technology is a continually and fast-changing field, requiring a paradigm of teaching and learning which fits its recipients for a future of rapid and possibly radical change ...

> It is surely a contradiction to hold a backward-looking, conventional view of a subject that involves children planning their own future actions within each activity or project ... The most certain thing about the future is change, rapid and continuous. The most important resource in the face of rapid technological and economic change is the capacity of companies and individuals for creativity, innovation, flexibility and adaptability. These are generic capabilities which design and technology education should foster and develop in our pupils.

What role can be found for 'Industrial Man' (as Toffler, 1970, p361 calls him, see Chapter 2 above), in a conceptual age, post-industrial economy, post-modernist culture? And what kind of design and technology education would fit and prepare Toffler's Johnny, 'living in the hurricane's eye of change' (p371)? Design for sustainability would most certainly need to be on Johnny's curriculum.

Pike and Selby (1998) see education as involving consideration of the interactions between:

- **alternative futures;**
- **possible futures;**

- **probable futures;**

- **preferred futures.**

They present this as a diagram (1998, vol I, p218):

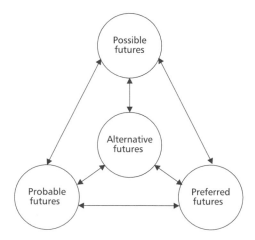

Pike and Selby's four futures

This view of future-orientated education has parallels in the process of designing. Pike and Selby use the term *zone of potentiality* to describe *knowledge of what is possible rather than knowledge of certainties*. This seems to be a very similar skill to that embedded within design capability.

Very similar views are expressed by Kimbell and Perry in *Design and technology in a knowledge economy*: *Designers continually model their concept of the future to enable them to experience it vicariously and thereby make informed judgements about it before committing themselves to it* (2001 p6).

The essential cognitive skill of designing is imagining that which does not yet exist, which, on however humble a scale, is modelling the future. As a cognitive capacity, this future modelling is essentially the same whether a child is evaluating the look of their Easter basket and deciding which colour ribbon to choose (will it look better blue or red or yellow?) or whether a manager of an industrial plant is deciding the possible future impact of a new process. The pros and cons must be weighed up, alternative futures must be considered. To equip future managers, workers and consumers with such analytical, reflective and evaluative capabilities, children need to be given the opportunity to make design choices and evaluate the results.

Pink, in *A whole new mind* (2005) conjectures that Design is the first of the six senses that will become essential as advanced Western economies move into what he calls the Conceptual Age:

> It's no longer sufficient to create a product, a service, an experience, or a lifestyle that's merely functional. Today it's economically crucial and personally rewarding to create something that is also beautiful, whimsical or emotionally engaging. (p65)

He views this need to rethink as being based on:

- **abundance: Americans have so much choice that sales depend on a design that hits the emotional spot;**
- **Asia: people over there, just as qualified as those over here, will do the same job for far less pay;**
- **automation: machines can do all the routine jobs anyway.**

Design and technology education has a role to play in education for the future of the community, in encouraging children to solve problems that relate to the needs and wants of users or clients. In considering issues such as the siting of a new supermarket, children begin to develop a sense of social responsibility whilst exploring the technological as well as the environmental impact. Such a project enables children to role play community involvement. Real community involvement might come through designing and making items for sale for a charity event (e.g. biscuits for Comic Relief) or through designing a garden plot for elderly or handicapped people in the neighbourhood.

Currently, the UK National Curriculum does not have the equivalent of South Africa's 2002 revision of the technology curriculum's 'Technology, Society and the Environment' strand that covers *indigenous technology and culture*, *impacts of technology* and *biases created by technology*. This strand intends to provide pupils with information about technology that will enable them to make informed choices as adult citizens as part of their political rights in a country that is actively developing its democratic ethos.

Howe, Davies and Ritchie, nevertheless, see this as an important part of design and technology education:

> As a society we are faced with increasingly complex decisions about which technologies to adopt, which to discard and which to actively rebel against. Who controls the direction of technological development? Do we as citizens ever have a say, and if so do we have access to the information on which to base an informed decision?... Today's children will need to engage in such technological decision-making with increasing frequency, both as individuals and as members of pressure groups within society as a whole. They need crucially to have available not only the technological information they need, but also the tools in order to evaluate such information ... (2001, p139–40)

Teaching children to 'evaluate familiar products' (Breadth of Study for both Key Stage 1 and 2) is the beginning of this process. The youngest children can consider whether certain people would like specific products or which products do their job the best. By the beginning of Key Stage 2, children become aware of larger issues and can begin to think about pollution, waste management, water conservation, effects on developing economies and global impact of technology. These big issues may have a local impact, of which children, even in Year 3, are very aware. The depletion of fish stocks, for example, that is partly a result of the building of ever bigger boats with sonar locators and huge nets, has had devastating effects on the communities that depend on fishing as a substantial contribution to local employment, economics and community identity.

The 'familiar product' does not have to be sanitised and divorced from its social, political and community context. Children's minds, especially in Year 6, need to be stretched to appreciate the impact of the unfamiliar too. Schools often act as if children's awareness of the world was not heavily influenced by television. Rachel, at age 10, cried her heart out after watching a *Newsround* feature on global warming: 'There won't be a planet to live on by the time I'm 40.' Now aged 24, she is a marine biologist, researching the impact of pollution by fish farms.

By the nature of its subject matter, design and technology, is a continually and fast-changing field, always with an eye to the new and innovative. Every aspect of life is constantly being changed by the impact of new technologies.

Practical task

Consider how many things you own that could not have been bought 5 years ago.

How many things in your house were not available 25 years ago?

What do you believe to be the most important inventions in the past 50 years?

Your answers to the first question probably focused on personal communication and entertainment. Your answer to the second question probably also demonstrates that most household changes in the past 25 years have been in the field of home entertainment and in response to an ever-increasing demand for quality of sound and vision. The labour-saving devices of freezer, microwave, washing machine, dish washer and so on, even the home computer, have been available for more than 25 years, although many homes did not have them.

Your response to the third question probably depends on your knowledge of technological development. The major invention of the past 50 years must be the silicon chip which has transformed the speed at which data of all kinds can be processed and communicated. Integrated circuitry became available in the late 1960s and after a slow start, due to industrial inertia, the speed and reliability, plus the cheapness of manufacture once the initial outlay had been absorbed, meant that the past 40 years have been increasingly 'chips with everything'. Computers have had ticker tape, magnetic tape, hard drives, floppy disks, CD-ROMs and now pen drives to satisfy increasing large memory demands. Telephones have developed from manual switchboards with mechanical switching to optical fibres and satellites. The mobile phone has revolutionised the way people communicate and, as with any new technology, is rapidly changing as changes, additions and improvements become available. The internet is probably the most powerful medium for societal change on a global scale that has ever been invented.

How does this relate to young children cutting, sticking and gluing? Papanek's (1995) *The green imperative* begins with the words: *All design is goal directed play.*

Children need to:

- see themselves as able to make choices and to make changes in their world;
- believe that these choices are valued by adults with whom they spend their day;
- be given time to reflect and come to conclusions about the larger issues that concern them;
- understand that many issues surrounding social and technological choices are complex and that not all the facts or impact of the choices made can be perceived at the outset.

Kimbell and Perry (2001, p14) comment that the flexibility and responsiveness that characterise design thinking are just the skills needed to tackle complex social and environmental problems:

> Design and technology is about change in the made world. It enables us to understand the process of change and to engage in it. It is about the future: about what might be or what should be ... A move away from receiving 'hand-me-down' outcomes and truths to a situation in which we generate our own truths. (2001, pp3, 7)

Design and technology education for the future should:

- meet the present needs of *all* children;
- should encourage children's self-esteem through creating pleasing products and solutions to specific problems;
- must not be prescriptive but recognise the creativity and dynamism of designing;
- be socially responsive;
- educate for reflective consumerism and responsible citizenry;
- address the underlying moral and ethical issues of technology, e.g. the concept of 'progress';
- address the big issues, ethical, social and environmental, whilst trying to solve the specific and particular;
- key into the spiritual dimension of the human psyche, adding to the joy of creation, fun in the process of making, satisfaction in a project completed together.

Design and technology education should foster and develop children's capacity for:

- playfulness, creativity and innovation;
- natural intuition;
- flexibility and adaptability;
- acceptance of multiple solutions, diversity and complexity;
- combining the teleological with the spontaneous;
- accepting and accommodating the ideas and enthusiasms of others;
- negotiating and constructing a jointly created fantasy world.

Reflective task

How does a national curriculum manage creativity and diversity?

Is creativity untameable and is it diametrically opposed to management?

If design is managed will it cease to be creative?

How can a curriculum build for a creative future, when no one knows or can predict what the future might hold?

Does it just require the abandonment of the predetermined one right answer, the kind of lesson plans that say 'At the end of this activity, most children will'…?

If the core capability of design and technology is the ability to combine the flight of imagination with the reality of the problem to be solved, how would you recognise success?

Government reform as an agent of change

The Introduction to this book contains references to two sets of Standards (2002, 2006) for recommendation for Qualified Teacher Status. As indicated in that Introduction, the publication of this book comes at a point in time preceding the introduction of the new 2006 Standards.

Since 1988 there has been continual change in education, from the initial introduction of the National Curriculum as a series of big ring binders, through its revisions, slimming down, introduction of literacy and numeracy hours and the publication of QCA schemes for science and foundation subjects. Design and technology as a school subject was launched in 1991 and needed almost immediate revision since the first document was written in the inaccessible jargon of design specialists. Although the subject emerged from the front-runners in secondary practice, primary teachers were not consulted on the content of the document and it was created by extrapolation downwards and 'best guess'. Despite such teething troubles, Britain became a world leader in design and technology education. Many other nations still do not link *design* with technology or see making things as being part of *technology* education in the way that is the case in the UK, and it is something that must be held on to.

The continual drive to raise standards of achievement (whose appropriateness and attainability remain largely unchallenged) linked to a rigorous inspection regime, has been stifling of genuinely creative teaching. There has been a wealth of guidance to support and clarify the National Curriculum, for example, through the QCA schemes of work, which, at the time of publication, many believed were also statutory. The QCA website offers significant support for delivery of its scheme of work for design and technology, and recently has begun to publish 'beyond the QCA scheme' materials. The problem for such schemes will always be that each subject has been written on a secondary school model of education: discrete subjects delivered in clearly timetabled slots. The *All our futures* report (NACCCE, 1999), QCA Creativity Pack and *Excellence and Enjoyment* (DfES, 2003) are welcomed by teachers as meaning that creativity and innovation within schools is back on the agenda. For design and technology this should not mean that the subject is absorbed into other areas of knowledge and becomes simply 'craft work'. Design and technology has a significant role to play in mapping the way forward. Many of the underlying skills of designing (exploring, experimenting, negotiating, problem-solving) are those identified as central to creative thought.

The launching of web-based resources, whether of government documents or support materials as downloads, has made keeping yourself up to date with new initiatives easier. Fast access to ideas for lessons and schemes of work from a range of sources is readily available. Many websites welcome contributions from teachers (including the QCA), especially for current issues and initiatives for which they are actively searching for examples of good practice. Since design and technology is, unfortunately, poorly represented on many of these sites, the chance of having your contribution accepted is much greater.

Through the impact of continuous government intervention in their working lives, there has been a shift in the professional status of teachers through the introduction of Standards for all levels of teachers' professional development. The staffing demands of recent workforce reform have led some schools to use TAs to teach cross-curricular practical subjects under the umbrella title of 'Creativity' sessions in order to give teachers their planning, preparation and assessment (PPA) time. This, unfortunately, is likely to lower the standards of achievement in design and technology since TAs are less likely to have a secure knowledge and understanding of the nature of design and the conceptual framework of the programme of study for design and technology. All too easily could design and technology sink back into craft activities in which little genuine designing and autonomous creative problem-solving takes place. Teachers must ensure that TAs fully understand the nature of the subject and are not working under the misunderstanding that the *product* is the most important outcome of the lesson and give little thought to developing children's *process* skills.

Although there seems to be no let-up in the 'change and challenge' agenda, there is increasing talk of the autonomy of schools and the rights of pupils as individuals. Perhaps the demise of the 'one size fits all' curriculum (for teachers as well as pupils) is on its way. This should be good for creative subjects and enable teachers to plan exciting, customised projects that fit with their children's needs, interests and enthusiasms. The danger, however, is that with the pressures on teachers' time and the continued emphasis on achievement in literacy and numeracy, planning in subjects such as design and technology can be less than thorough. When the National Curriculum for design and technology was introduced, it was felt strongly that primary teachers would be able to embrace this new subject and incorporate it into their established pattern of working, which at the time was project-based and cross-curricular. Part of the process of the introduction of the National Curriculum was the near eradication of the project-based approach. As primary schools return to cross-curricular working, it is important to ensure that the insights into the teaching of learning to design quality products that have been gained over the past 15 years do not evaporate.

Design, technology and democracy

In *Design and democracy* Ken Baynes (2005) makes the case for the way in which design, rather than being the means by which people make choices about their lives and their futures, has become the hand-maiden of capitalism and part of the production process. This sheds interesting light on some of the models of design process that have been applied from industrial practice to educational settings. The linear model (see Chapter 2) assumes the passing of the product-in-development along a production line of designers, prototypers, developers and analysts before finally going into mass production.

Interestingly, Baynes identifies do-it-yourself as a possible contributor to the consumer's person power. The can-do philosophy that underlies the general public's perception of DIY capability also underlies design and technology education. Is there a link? Baynes suggests that economic forces and resistance to central control of our personal and social lives are more likely to be the driving forces and that consumer's buying power makes a more radical contribution to the direction of market forces and, hence, of design. In order to equip children for participation in the democratic processes of local community and national political action, then, investigating and disassembling familiar products might contribute to sustainable technology as much as, if not more than, focused practical tasks and design and make assignments.

Howe, Davies and Ritchie (2001) commented that the kind of citizenship that is promoted is dominated by the responsibilities of the 'good citizen' and that this does not include the right to protest. It assumes that citizens will function within the political systems, local and national. The kind of creativity envisaged, might, then, be of the same kind. Many design and make assignments have preordained outcomes, or the design choices are artificial. Children do not have a sense of real choice and autonomy within a design brief that expects a genuinely innovative response. With apologies to Anna Craft in misapplying her terminology, perhaps teachers are promoting 'little c' creativity within 'little c' citizenship. Part of the problem might be the sheer quantity of curriculum guidance material generated and/or sponsored by central government. In developing their critical faculties with regard to innovation, as the new 2006 Standards for Qualified Teacher Status recommend, teachers should begin to question the content and ideologies behind the materials.

Certainly there are voices calling for a new way forward with regard to education for the future, from within the ranks of design and technology researchers as well as those from other disciplines. Teachers have, inevitably, their eyes to the future of the children they teach, design is future-orientated and technology never stands still.

Teachers as agent of change

In the eyes of the children in their class, the teacher is a figure of power and authority, an arbiter of taste and arbitrator in dispute, physical, social or moral. The hidden messages that teachers convey to children are formative in a way that teachers themselves scarcely recognise. Telling a child that their idea is really exciting and creative, teaching them how to design and make things, giving them a 'can-do' vision of their own capability helps to equip children for their future, economically, socially and personally. Encouraging children to believe in their own capable creativity promotes their emotional well-being, helps them to become more resilient to the knocks of life, to become problem-solvers and perceptive of opportunities.

Design and technology education:

> prepares pupils to participate in tomorrow's rapidly changing technologies. They learn to think and intervene creatively to improve quality of life. The subject calls for pupils to become creative and autonomous problem-solvers, as individuals and members of a team. They must look for needs, wants and opportunities and respond to them by developing a range of ideas and making products and systems. They combine practical skills with an understanding of aesthetics, social and environmental issues, function and industrial practices. As they do so, they reflect on and evaluate present and past , its uses and effects. Through design and technology, all pupils can become discriminating and informed users of products, and become innovators. (DfEE, 1999, p90)

As a teacher of design and technology, you are part of this process.

Design and technology in the future:
a summary of key points

In this chapter you have begun to consider the wider issues of design and technology education:

_____ *considering the implications of designing for others: focusing on the essential skill of designing for others and of being able to see the world from another person's perspective, leading to:*

_____ *multiple perspectives on design and technology education: both across the UK and within all UK schools, including those in Wales, Scotland, Northern Ireland and the off-shore islands, as well as considering different perspectives on design and technology education worldwide, which leads to:*

_____ *sustainability, ecology and the environment: the viability of human survival on planet Earth depends on human ability to solve these design problems. Children need to be prepared for the challenges that await them.*

Technology never stands still, therefore, neither can design and technology education. The final sections of this chapter considered the political framework in which teachers operate when teaching design and technology in the UK and the role that teachers of design and technology play in the lives of the children they teach.

References

Advisory Group on Citizenship (1998) *Education for citizenship and the teaching of democracy in schools* (Crick Report). London: HMSO.

Baynes, K (2005) *Design and democracy*. Loughborough: Design Education Research Group, Loughborough University/DATA.

Department of Education (South Africa) (2002) Revised National Curriculum Statement Grades R-7 (Schools) Policy: Technology. Pretoria: Department of Education.

DfEE (2003) *Excellence and Enjoyment: a strategy for primary schools*. London: Department for Education and Employment.

DfEE (1999) *The National Curriculum*. London: Department for Education and Employment.

Doyle, M (2005) Refounding education on evolutionary psychology, in Nolan, V and Darby, G (eds) *Re-inventing Education*. Buckinghamshire: Synectics Education Initiative.

Hope, G (2002) Questioning the design and technology paradigm, in *Conference proceedings*, DATA International Design and Technology Research Conference 2002), Coventry.

Hope, G (2005) Technology education for the future, in Nolan, V and Darby, G (eds) *Re-inventing education*. Buckinghamshire: Synectics Education Initiative.

Howe, A, Davies, D and Ritchie, R (2001) *Primary design and technology for the future: creativity, culture and citizenship*. London: David Fulton Publishers.

Hughes, M (1975) Egocentrism in pre-school children, unpublished PhD thesis quoted in Donaldson, M., (1978) *Children's minds*. Glasgow: Fontana/Collins.

Kimbell, R and Perry, D (2001) *Design and technology in a knowledge economy*. London: The Engineering Council

Maslow, AH (1954) Motivation and personality (2nd edition). New York: Harper & Row Publishers Inc.

NACCCE (National Advisory Committee on Creative and Cultural Education) (1999) *All our futures: creativity, culture and education*. Sudbury, Suffolk: Department for Education and Employment.

Papanek, V (1995) *The green imperative: ecology and ethics in design and architecture*. London: Thames & Hudson.

Piaget, J and Inhelder, B (1956) *The child's conception of space*. London: Routledge & Kegan Paul.

Pike, G and Selby, D (1998) *In the global classroom*, vols 1 and 2. Toronto: Pippin.

Pink, D (2005) *A whole new mind: how to thrive in the new conceptual age*. London: Cyan Books.

Toffler, A (1970) *Future shock*. London: The Bodley Head.

The New Zealand National Curriculum can be accessed via **www.minedu.govt. nz/web/downloadable/dl3614_vl/tech-nzc.pdf.**

The new Standards for Classroom Teachers are to be introduced in September 2007. This Appendix has, therefore, perforce been written with the February 2006 draft of the Standards for Classroom Teachers in view. It is understood that the framework of the Standards for Classroom Teachers has been agreed and that changes that will occur across the consultation period will relate to specific content.

This Appendix links the content of the new Standards for Classroom Teachers to the relevant sections within this book. However, given the timing of publication and in order to provide guidance for teacher educators, teachers and students who will be qualifying before September 2007, generic titles have been used to indicate the contents of the Standards. It was felt also to be unwise to employ the numbering system of the new Standards for individual standards, since some of these may also change across the consultation period.

Q1 Professional characteristics, qualities and responsibilities

These are generic professional values that should characterise all teachers, whatever subject they teach. These are considered in relation to teaching design and technology in the following chapters:

High expectations of pupils	Chapter 3: pp35–8
Establish respectful, trusting and constructive relationship with pupils	Chapter 9: pp186–90
Support policies and practice of the workplace	Chapter 5
Understand their contribution to pupils' attainment	Chapter 6: pp112–24
Understand and respect parents' and carers' role and contribution	Chapter 4: pp61–9
Communicate effectively with pupils	Chapter 5
Commitment to continued professional development	Chapter 3: p40
Adopt open, positive and constructively critical approach to innovation	Chapter 9

Q2 Professional knowledge and understanding

Much of the content of this book has been aimed at assisting the development of your knowledge and understanding of the teaching of design and technology. You will find information that will help you towards achieving these Standards within design and technology in the following chapters:

Secure, up-to-date subject knowledge	See below
Knowledge of statutory, non-statutory curricula for the subject	Chapter 2
Knowledge of current initiates for the subject	Chapter 3
Assessment requirements	Chapter 6
Know and employ range of teaching strategies	Chapter 5
Use understanding of influences on learners to inform teaching	Chapters 4 and 9
Health and safety	Chapter 5
Use of literacy, numeracy and ICT skills in teaching the subject	Chapter 8
Recognise and provide for equality, inclusion and diversity	Chapters 5 and 9

As well as understanding the structure of the National Curriculum for design and technology for Key Stages I and 2, this should include subject-specific content:

Knowledge, skills and understanding

Developing, planning and communicating ideas	Chapters 3 and 4
Working with tools, materials and components to make quality products	Chapter 7
Evaluating processes and products	Chapter 6
Knowledge and understanding of materials and components	Chapter 7

Breadth of study

Investigating familiar products	Chapters 2, 4 and 8
Focused practical tasks	Chapters 2, 5 and 7
Design and make assignments	Chapters 2, 5,7 and 8

Q3 Teaching, learning and assessing

These are generic professional capabilities that should form part of your everyday practice in all subjects. You will find information that will help you towards achieving these Standards within Design & Technology in the following chapters:

Working collaboratively with colleagues	Chapter 5
Establish safe working environment	Chapter 5
Managing learners' behaviour	Chapter 5
Planning lessons and sequences of lessons	Chapter 5
Use a range of teaching strategies	Chapter 5
Evaluate own teaching	Chapter 5
Identify opportunities to develop pupils' literacy skills	Chapter 8
Identify opportunities to develop pupils' numeracy skills	Chapter 8
Identify opportunities to develop pupils' ICT skills	Chapter 8
Assessment for learning: feedback to pupils, parents and colleagues	Chapter 6
Assessment for learning: informing planning	Chapter 6
Encourage pupils' self-evaluation of learning	Chapter 6

DATA (2005) *Guidance for Foundation and Primary Phases Initial Teacher Training and Continuing Professional Development in Design and Technology* (available through the Design and Technology Association www.data.org.uk) provides detailed guidance on achieving the 2002 Standards, and this booklet will continue to be relevant to inform practitioners working within the new Standards when these come into force.

The brief of the working party (Carolyn Chalkey, Maggie Rogers, Owain Evans and the author of this book) was to apply the 2002 standards Qualifying to Teach to the teaching of design and technology and to provide guidance for student teachers, mentors, ITE educators and teachers. The working party identified three levels of competence in teaching design and technology in the primary classroom, according to the level of professional development and/or teaching input during Initial Teacher Education. These were called tiers rather than levels, to avoid confusion with the use of the word 'level' in National Curriculum documents. Tier I contains the competences necessary to teach design and technology satisfactorily. Tier 2 builds on tier I, and applies to those choosing to become design and technology specialists. Tier 3 is for subject leaders. The new Standards for Classroom Teachers mean that a revision of this booklet will be necessary, but in the interim:

- **tier I could be used as guidance for achievement of the new Qualified Teacher Standards;**

- **tier 2 could be used as guidance for achievement of the new Qualified Teacher Standards for those who have chosen design and technology as a subject specialism as well as for achievement for all teachers of the new Induction Standards;**

- **tier 3 could be used as guidance for achievement of either Senior Teacher Standards or Excellent Teacher Standards, where design and technology was a teacher's area of responsibility within the school.**

National Curriculum and government documents

www.nc.uk.net/nc/contents/DT-home.htm
www.ncaction.org.uk/subjects/design/index.htm
Virtual Teacher Centre: **vtc.ngfl.gov.uk/**
For creativity: **www.ncaction.org.uk/creativity/**
QCA: **www.qca.org.uk/7902.html**
Schemes of work **www.standards.dfes/gov.uk/schemes/designtech/**

National design and technology organisations

DATA (The Design and Technology Association) **www.data.org.uk/**
NAAIDT (National Association of Advisors in Design and Technology) **www.naaidt.org.uk/**
The Nuffield Foundation **www.primarydandt.org./home/index.asp**

Useful sites to support teaching design and technology

www.dtonline.org/
www.sln.org.uk/d&t/Primary/index.htm (Staffordshire LEA's very useful design and technology site)
www.dialsolutions.com/nyorks/apps/siteview/ (another useful site, from North Yorkshire LEA)

LINKS WITH INDUSTRY
www.technology.org.uk/menuf.htm

GENERAL RESOURCES SITES WITH GOOD SECTIONS ON DESIGN AND TECHNOLOGY
www.primaryresources.co.uk
www.teacherxpress.com/

Research

www.data.org.uk/data/primary/research.php (DATA's Primary Design and Technology Research web page)
www.ed.uce.ac.uk/cript/ CRIPT (Centre for Research Into Primary Technology)
www.iteaconnect.org/D4c.html (provides portal to Technology for all Americans, the International Journal of Technology and PATT (Pupils' Attitudes Towards Technology) Conferences
www.jiscmail.ac.uk/lists/idater-on-line.html (for research papers of International Design and Technology Education Research)

Other design and technology websites can be found through

www.technology.org.uk/linksf.htm

Year 1 Summer term 1st half

The Needs of Seeds

Aims To work in groups to generate and evaluate design ideas, to design products that are fit for purpose

Objectives To take into account needs of seeds and small plants in designing containers, watering devices and protection from predators

Links to previous and future learning Foundation Stage KUW; Science: Growing things; Geography: weather

Lesson details Not necessarily weekly – depends on speed of growth of seeds

	Objectives	Outline	Health and safety	Organisation of activities	Differentiation	Key vocabulary	Resources
Lesson 1: Sowing seeds	To design and make a suitable container for growing and sprouting seeds and use this for its intended purpose	Introduction: show seeds collected from bean and sunflower plants in Autumn term and remind of plant life cycle. Children to choose/ design suitable containers for seed sowing and sprouting taking account of needs of seeds (esp. water); record through annotated drawing	Seeds not to be put into mouths; washing hands after handling soil; craft knife for adult use only	2 adults required. Whole class introduction, followed by group work. Need to plan other activities for groups waiting their turn for seed sowing	Mixed ability groups, ensure integration of SEN children; re-enforce understanding of science concepts with SEN children; extension vocabulary and concepts for G&T	Air, water, soil, warmth, container, support, sprouting, names of seeds used Extension vocabulary: propagator	Propagator; seeds saved from autumn term, bean sprouts. Recycled containers, including plastic take-away trays and soft drinks bottles; seeds for sowing in soil and sprouting (including marigolds); damp cloth; kitchen rolls, foil, paper sticks, sticky labels, craft knife for adult
Lesson 2: Healthy snack – sprouted seeds; timing dependent on growth of sprouts – probably one week	To design and make a healthy snack based on sprouted seeds	Introduction to stress health and safety as well as introduce task. Children to combine their sprouted seeds with other salad vegetables and choice of bread to make healthy snack; happy eating!	Use sterilising spray on tables prior to use; wash hands prior to handling food. Wash all bought salad veg. Demonstrate correct use of buttering knife	Whole class working in groups, extra adult support needed – one adult per group	Mixed ability groups, ensure integration of SEN children	Sprouted, grown, roots, shoots, names of beans, grains and seeds used; healthy, tasty, crunchy, etc.	Sprouted seeds from Lesson 1, plus: range of pre-sliced bread, margarine, pre-sliced salad veg; paper plates, plastic knives; napkins, wet wipes, paper towels, damp cloths, steriliser, plastic table covers

Lesson 3: Care over long weekend/holiday – this will depend on term dates, so unlikely to be week following Lesson 2; small group working will need to be spread across whole day	To design a self-watering system to enable plants to survive over long weekend/half term	Whole class discussion to review needs of seeds and plants (link science): problem – how will seeds survive over holiday? Children to design and make watering system; test system on test platform in water tray; record by photographs	Stress sensible working and co-operation; water to be poured only under adult supervision and in water tray	In groups in shared area outside classroom with TA and parent helper; children working individually but encourage co-operation and sharing ideas	Mixed ability groups, TA to support SEN children as needed; parent helper to supervise water tray testing; extension vocabulary and concepts for G&T	Waterproof, stable, flow, damp, moist, soggy, overflow, Extension vocabulary: saturated	Recycled materials, modelling clay, sticky tape, wire ties; card, paper sticks, short canes for supports; water tray, jugs and funnels, upturned tray for test platform, plastic sheeting for floor; aprons for children
Lesson 4: Protection of plants; timing – when plants are ready to go outside in garden area	To design means of protecting plants from predators – slugs and snails, insects, birds and small mammals	Introduction – book on garden pests – will these eat our plants? Children to identify hazards to the plants from predators and design plant protection; record by list in book with drawings	Commercial slug or bug killer not to be used! Research alternative methods of pest control, e.g. companion plants (garlic and marigolds); care with garden canes	In classroom, working in groups	Mixed ability groups, ensure integration of SEN children, extension vocabulary and concepts for G&T	Predator, protection, pest, slug, snail, insect Extension vocabulary: mammal	Recycled plastic trays, gardeners' tips ingredients; garlic cloves and marigolds to plant between other plants; string, CDs, aluminium foil and foil pie dishes, canes; netting, stones
Lesson 5: Scarecrows	To work in groups to construct a full-size scarecrow from garden canes and sheet and recycled materials	Introduction – link with literacy story about scarecrow; children to design and build own full-size scarecrow; lead into drama – children being their scarecrow	Garden canes: adults to make basic framework ahead of lesson – and transfer to final site once completed; need one adult per group	Outdoors in garden area; one adult per group; take photos of work in progress	Mixed ability groups, ensure integration of SEN children, extension vocabulary and concepts for G&T	Scarecrow; protect, shiny, reflect, reflective, stable. Extension vocabulary: effective	Garden canes – 5 per scarecrow (4 for stable base) held together with wire ties; plastic sheeting/sacks, bubble wrap, shiny materials, cooking foil, foil dishes, CD ROMs, string, packing tape

Assessment: Assess quality of design thinking in Lesson 3

Title: Year I Summer term, Ist half, Lesson 5: Scarecrows

Aims: To integrate understandings from science, D&T and literacy.

Objectives: To work in groups to generate and evaluate design ideas, to design a product that is fit for purpose of protecting plants from birds.

Learning outcomes: To work in groups to construct a full-size scarecrow from garden canes and sheet and recycled materials.

Implications from prior learning: Science and D&T work on growing things. Scarecrow story in literacy a.m. today. TA to re-read story to Green Group during quiet reading before this lesson. Check whole class understanding of plant protection (relate to last week).

Resources: One adult per group – self, TA, student on Ist placement, dinner lady and parent helper.
Garden canes – 5 per scarecrow (4 for stable base) held together with wire ties – prepared ready next to garden area – student to do this.
Plastic sheeting/ sacks, bubble wrap, shiny materials, cooking foil, foil trays, pie cups, CD ROMs etc.; packing tape. All in box – one per group – student to prepare during ICT before lunch.

Organisation of activities: Outdoors in garden area; in groups with one adult per group.
Self to take photos of work in progress (for student's portfolio).

Health and safety: Garden canes: adults to make basic framework ahead of lesson – and transfer to final site once completed; need one adult per group.

Differentiation: Mixed ability groups, ensure integration of SEN children, extension vocabulary and concepts for G&T.

Key questions and vocabulary: Scarecrow; protect, shiny, reflect, reflective, stable.
Extension vocabulary: effective.

Lesson outline:
Introduction – reminder of literacy story about scarecrow; explain activity: working in groups with adults to make a scarecrow. Framework already in place. Show samples of materials – question reasons for choice of these – purpose of scarecrow.
In groups, with adults – stress H&S – garden canes and eyes, no trampling on plants, stay on grass.
In garden area – in groups, design and build full-size scarecrow; think about – secure attachment of parts – effect of rain and wind; flapping and shiny objects will deter birds – could attach CDs, etc. with string; how to make hands, head, hat?
Return to cloakroom to remove coats and outdoor shoes, on with plimsolls, wash hands, line up ready to go into hall.
Straight into drama – children being their scarecrow. Student with camera. TA takes adult helpers to staff room for tea.
Plenary for this lesson back in classroom after drama lesson. At home time, exit via garden area to see scarecrows – stress that visitors to scarecrows must ensure they stay on grass and do not walk on plants.

Assessment methods: Informal – success of each group's structure – stability, effectiveness to be assessed later! This lesson will lead straight on into drama lesson, so part of assessment is in ability to transfer learning.

Evaluation of teaching and learning: A good cross-curricular afternoon, bringing together children's learning across science, D&T and literacy. Parent helper made shiny hands first so the children could see the ends of the canes – sensible – will suggest this to all in future. Having large box for each group's materials worked well. Moving straight into drama was good idea – children had developed a character for their scarecrow and became him. Need this level of adult support – need another good student next year.

Implications for future planning: Would do this as integrated afternoon again. Cross-curricular thinking made strong learning possible. Will need to give time for visiting scarecrows – see TA about taking groups out to paint them – check number of easels – perhaps student will like to do this. Maths vocabulary – wide, tall, etc. could be linked.

Year 5/6 Summer term, 2nd half — Portable Homes

Aims To work in groups to develop design specification, evaluate results of practical experiences and produce product fit for purpose

Objectives To develop understanding of structures, taking account of stability and ease of assembly and disassembly

Links to previous and future learning: D&T: Year I Term 3: Where I Live; History: Plains Indians; Geography: Nomads (Lapps, Mongols, Inuits, etc.)

Lesson Details

	Objectives	Outline	Health and safety	Organisation of activities	Differentiation	Key vocabulary	Resources
Lesson I: Shelters	To work in groups to build stable shelter from rolled newspaper, large enough for one child to sit under	Introduction: use 'Aliens have landed' PowerPoint – need shelter; in groups, make shelter large enough for one child to sit in; oral feedback at end; record by drawing and take photo	Sensible working and co-operation; warning about plastic sack over heads	Outdoors on playground/in hall if wet, working in groups. Take photos of work in progress	Mixed ability groups, ensure integration of SEN children	Shelter, struts, force, tension, stable, collapse	One plastic sack per group, containing 2 newspapers, and I roll masking tape, one sheet of flip chart paper, pens and pencils; digital camera to record event; paper, pencils, clipboards
Lesson 2: Structures	To work in groups to explore stable structures, using construction kits and consumable resources	Round robin with range of construction kits; transfer to using consumables	Sensible working and co-operation	In classroom, working in groups	Mixed ability groups, ensure integration of SEN children	Structure, construction, struts, force, tension, stable, collapse	Construction kits, lolly sticks, toffee apple sticks, tissue paper, glue, sticky tape, pipe cleaners
Lesson 3: Design development	To work in groups to develop a design specification for a portable shelter made from garden canes and fabric sheeting	Whole class discussion to review learning in previous lessons, group brainstorming to produce design for portable shelter, presentation to rest of class for evaluation, changes in light of feedback	Sensible working and co-operation	In classroom, working in groups	Mixed ability groups, TA to support SEN children as needed	Shelter, construction, structure, struts, force, tension, stable, collapse	Flip chart paper, one set of materials for Lessons 4–6 available to show, to enable realistic designing

Lesson	Objective	Activity	Safety	Location	Organisation	Vocabulary	Resources
Lesson 4: Building mock-up of portable shelter	To work in groups to build a trial, small-scale version of design developed in Lesson 3 in preparation for Lesson 5	Introduction of task – must build design as finally drawn last week. Can annotate design as they build, need final working diagram by end of lesson	Using paper sticks – beware eyes, etc.	In classroom, working in groups	Mixed ability groups, ensure integration of SEN children	Mock-up, temporary fixings, small scale, shelter, construction, struts, force, tension, stable, collapse	Design specifications from Lesson 3; paper sticks/dowel, string, fabric, Blu-tack®, sticky tape. Paper for final design
Lesson 5: Building full-sized portable shelter	To work in groups to construct a full-size shelter from garden canes and sheet fabric that can be easily constructed, taken apart and rebuilt	Using design specification and previous experience from building mock-up, groups will construct a full-size shelter for whole group to sit inside; feedback of evaluations	Garden canes, etc. be aware of stabbing, poking hazards – teach and demonstrate safe handling of canes	Outdoors on field/in hall if wet. Take photos of work in progress	Mixed ability groups, ensure integration of SEN children	Full size, large scale, shelter, construction, structure, struts, force, tension, stable, collapse	Design specifications from Lesson 4; garden canes, string, re-usable cable ties, sheeting/old blankets/curtains
Lesson 6: Construction of shelters and picnic. Evaluation discussion	To work in groups to construct a full-size shelter from garden canes and sheet fabric that can be easily constructed, taken apart and rebuilt	Using evaluation of previous construction experiences, groups will construct a full-size shelter, large enough for whole group to sit inside; on completion – whole class evaluative discussion sitting in front of shelters with drink and biscuits	Garden canes, etc. – be aware of stabbing, poking hazards – teach and demonstrate safe handling of canes	Outdoors on field/in hall if wet. Take video of work in progress and final shelter to view video and have final evaluation discussion outside of timetables D&T time	Mixed ability groups, ensure integration of SEN children	Full size, large scale, shelter, construction, structure, struts, force, tension, stable, collapse	Garden canes, string, re-usable cable ties, sheeting/old blankets/curtains. Drink and biscuits

Assessment: Use group portfolio to keep record of process and products – photographs Lessons 1, 4, 5 and 6; design development and evaluations Lessons 3–5; video recording of final assembly, picnic and disassembly in Lesson 6

Title: Year 5/6 Summer Term, 2nd half, Lesson I: Portable Shelters
Aims: To work in groups to develop design specification, evaluate results of practical experiences and produce product fit for purpose.
Objectives: To develop understanding of structures, taking account of stability and ease of assembly and disassembly.
Learning outcomes: To work in groups to build stable shelter from rolled newspaper, large enough for one child to sit under.
Implications from prior learning: Introduction to nomadic way of life – history/ geography.
Resources: Two newspapers, I plastic sack and I roll masking tape per group, digital camera.
Organisation of activities: Outdoors on playground/in hall if wet, working in groups. Each group supplied with plastic sack containing other resources: 2 newspapers, I roll of masking tape, I sheet of flip chart paper, pens and pencils. Take photos of work in progress.
Health and safety: Sensible working and co-operation, beware slipping on sheets of newspaper on floor, care when moving around to avoid ruining other groups' work; no plastic sacks over heads.
Differentiation: Mixed ability groups, ensure integration of SEN children.
Key questions and vocabulary: Shelter, struts, force, tension, stable, collapse.
Lesson outline: Introduction in classroom if dry, in hall if wet: Show 'Aliens have landed' PowerPoint – the aliens need shelter; discuss in groups what they might find around lighthouse. Explain task – in groups, make shelter large enough for one child to sit in. Line up to move outside/spread out across hall in groups. Show resource bags and explain contents – flip chart paper for initial brainstorming, newspaper and masking tape for construction, plastic sack to make waterproof. 45 minutes. Self to take photos to record process. On completion, children to draw their shelter and take photos. Return to classroom for oral feedback and to write evaluations. Allow time to visit and say goodbye to shelters before they have to be disassembled.
Assessment methods: Begin group portfolio to keep record of process and products, store this week's work in document wallet – unlikely to be time in this lesson to store properly.
Evaluation of teaching and learning: Groups worked well together. Would consider using hall next time, even if dry – moving from classroom to outside to work was too exciting for some and the lesson lost some momentum. Two groups did not want to brainstorm onto paper and needed strong direction to do so. One still didn't and ran out of paper because of lack of planning. Try it and see doesn't work too well with limited resources and 5 people all having different ideas! Good work by Luke in Saturn Group – good leadership shown. Amy in Mars got upset – poor group working skills still. Generally, good negotiating and discussion, compromises worked out. Drawings were good – would use this at end again – meant that they were occupied as they finished. Impromptu decision to stand them all in large circle at end and tour round all shelters was good idea – able to evaluate others and compare with own.
Implications for future planning: Would do this again, with slight changes (esp. venue). Need to think about groupings – friendship groups still tended to be ability groups – and single sex. Good start to project. Next week, need to recap and introduce vocabulary – this didn't really get used this week – children used own words to describe.